Durkheim on Politics and the State

Durkheim on Politics and the State

Edited with an introduction by
Anthony Giddens

Translated by W. D. Halls

Stanford University Press
Stanford, California
1986

Stanford University Press
Stanford, California
© 1986 Polity Press
Originating publisher: Polity Press, Cambridge,
    in association with Basil Blackwell, Oxford
First Published in the U.S.A. by
    Stanford University Press, 1986
Printed in Great Britain
ISBN 0-8047-1337-5
LC 85-63767

Contents

Preface and Acknowledgements

This book marks a further step towards the consolidation of something like a standard edition of Durkheim's writings in English. New translations of *The Rules of Sociological Method* (London: Macmillan 1982) and *The Division of Labour in Society* (London: Macmillan 1984) have been published in recent years. They have each been translated by Dr W. D. Halls, as has the collection entitled *Durkheim and the Law*, edited by Steven Lukes and Andrew Scull (Oxford: Martin Robertson 1983). The present book is intended as a parallel volume to *Durkheim and the Law*. It makes available, for the first time as an integrated collection, the main body of writings in which Durkheim sets out his understanding of the nature of the State and political life. After some deliberation, I have decided to include in this work a certain segment of Durkheim's article on 'Deux lois de l'évolution pénale', even though this overlaps in some part with the Lukes and Scull collection. The arguments developed in the article are not widely known in the English-speaking world, and are of basic importance to Durkheim's account of State power. With the exception of several pages translated by the editor, plus sections translated by Cornelia Brookfield, all of the material included in the book has been freshly translated by Dr Halls. Thanks are due to Routledge and Kegan Paul and to Cambridge University Press for translation permissions.

Anthony Giddens

Introduction[1]

Anthony Giddens

THEMES IN DURKHEIM'S POLITICAL WRITINGS

Durkheim is not ordinarily thought of as an author who has made significant contributions to political sociology. He was only marginally involved in practical political activity, and did not in his lifetime publish any major works concerned primarily with political analysis. Nonetheless, it would be quite wrong to suppose that he did not develop a systematic outlook on questions of the nature of politics, government and the State. Although it has in some part to be constructed from a diversity of sources — including, in particular, lecture notes which did not appear in published form until well after his death — such an outlook is certainly there in his writings. In this brief overview of his political ideas, I shall seek to indicate the outlines of this standpoint, as well as offering a critical appraisal of it.

The conception of the 'political', Durkheim pointed out, is one which has only come into being with the development of the modern form of society, since it presupposes a differentiation between government and the governed which does not exist in more primitive societal types. A 'political society' for Durkheim, however, is not to be defined purely in terms of the existence of constituted authority in a grouping. A family, for example, is not a political society, even though it may possess an individual or group in authority, such as a patriarch or a council of elders. An additional criterion is necessary. This is not to be found in the characteristic of the fixed territorial area; unlike Weber, Durkheim rejected this as of major importance. Rather it is to be discerned in the degree of complexity in social organization: a political society is one which manifests a clear-cut division of authority, but which is composed of a plurality of kinship groups, or of larger secondary groups. A political society does not necessarily possess a State: a 'State', in Durkheim's terminology, refers to an administrative staff or officialdom which is formally entrusted with the function of government.[2]

To understand how these concepts were arrived at, and how they relate to the development of Durkheim's writings, we have to turn first of all to *The Division of Labour in Society*. Durkheim's earliest major study, in many respects it established a foundation for the rest of his work — even though he modified some of the ideas it contains and elaborated others in much greater detail subsequently. *The Division of Labour* identifies and contrasts two types of society, the 'mechanical' and the 'organic'. The former corresponds to small-scale, unified communities associated with a low level of social and occupational differentiation. The latter refers mainly to the large-scale, industrialized form of society characteristic of modern times. In circumstances of mechanical solidarity, individuals are dominated by the *conscience collective* — the set of collective beliefs and values upon which the continuity of social life depends. But this situation becomes altered during the course of social development.

In societies cohered by mechanical solidarity, there is no State. States only come into being with the progressive displacement of the mechanical type of social system by the organic one. In *The Division of Labour*, a rather simple evolutionary theory is offered as the basis for specifying the connections between social and political development. The State is seen as expanding in tandem with the advance of organic solidarity. According to the thesis of *The Division of Labour*, the development of society towards increasing internal differentiation produces the progressive emancipation of individual thought and action from subordination to the *conscience collective*. *Prima facie* this might appear to be paradoxical, when juxtaposed to the increasing role of the State. On the one hand, the growth in the division of labour is associated with expanding individual freedoms; yet on the other it is held to involve the widening power of the State to subject individuals to its authority. In *The Division of Labour*, Durkheim sought to demonstrate that such a relationship is not at all paradoxical. In the modern form of society, in which organic solidarity is supreme, the State is a prime (although not the only) institution concerned with the implementation and furtherance of individual rights.

According to this early standpoint, the capability of the societal collectivity to mobilize coercive sanctions against its members declines progressively with the transfer from mechanical to organic solidarity. Increasing social differentiation is connected with a burgeoning of State authority, but this authority depends less and less upon the invoking of coercive sanctions. Thus *The Division of Labour* proclaims:

> Similarity between individuals gives rise to juridical rules which, with the threat of repressive measures, impose uniform beliefs and practices upon all. . . . The division of labour produces juridical rules which determine the nature and the relations of divided functions, but whose violation calls forth only restrictive measures without any expiatory character.[3]

The problem with such a position — in which the residue of Saint-Simon's views is quite marked — is that it closes off major areas of conceptual space which seem essential to the analysis of class division in modern societies. For Durkheim, as for Saint-Simon, class and class conflict tend to appear as no more than expressions of the strains involved in completing the transition from traditional to modern forms of social order. It becomes difficult, and perhaps impossible, to relate private property to mechanisms of class domination or generic features of industrial capitalism. The term 'capitalism' rarely appears in Durkheim's writings, something which is obviously not fortuitous. In respect of class division, and its linkages to political power, Marx and Weber surely still have a great deal more to teach us than does Durkheim.

Later Durkheim came to see that 'kinds of society should not be confused with different types of states'[4] and that the coercive powers possessed by the State apparatus can vary in some degree independently of the level of the development of the division of labour. In 'Deux lois de l'évolution pénale',[5] written at the turn of the century, he presented a systematic analysis of the implications of this position. The coercive sanctions which have existed in different types of society can be classified along two partially independent dimensions: the 'quantitative' and the 'qualitative'. The first refers to the intensity of punishment for deviation from a norm or a law, the second to the modality of punishment (death versus imprisonment, for example). The intensity of sanctions varies in relation, not only to the level of development of the division of labour, but also in relation to the centralization of political power. We can thus establish a 'law of quantitative variation' which holds that, 'The intensity of punishment is greater to the degree that a society belongs to a less advanced type, and that the central power is of a more absolute character'.[6]

According to Durkheim, there is not an intrinsic connection between how far 'all of the directive functions of society [are] in the same hands', and the degree of absolute power wielded by government. What determines the existence, or otherwise, of absolutism is not, as Spencer held, the number of functions exercised by the State, but how far there are other sources of institutional power which can act as a counterweight to that possessed by the State.[7] It follows — and Durkheim made this one of the cornerstones of his exposition of the nature of democratic government — that the extension of the directive influence of the State, which is a 'normal' characteristic of contemporary societies, does not in itself lead to a growth in State oppression. Conversely, it does not follow that, where the State only has a relatively limited range of operations, it cannot be absolute in character: indeed, this is often the case. It is not the degree of absolutism of State power but the range of activities engaged in by the State which varies directly with the division of labour:

The development of collective life in general in the same way as the dimensions of the nervous system of the individual differ according to the importance of organic connections. The directive functions of society are thus only rudimentary when other social functions are of the same nature; and the relation between the two hence remains the same. . . . Nothing is simpler than the government of certain primitive kingdoms; nothing is more absolute.[8]

The 'law of quantitative variation' refers only to the intensity of punitive sanctions. It can be complemented by a 'law of qualitative variation', concerning modalities of punishment: this 'law' states that there is a direct relationship between the level of societal development and the use of deprivation of liberty as a mode of punishment. Imprisonment for criminal activity is almost unknown in primitive societies; and it is only amongst the peoples of Western Europe (since the latter part of the eighteenth century) that it has become the primary type of sanction. This can be explained in the following way. Imprisonment is absent from the penal system of the less developed societies because responsibility is collective. When a crime is committed, the demand for reparation falls not upon the culpable individual, but upon the whole clan group. But with the development of more complex forms of society, and the increasing emergence of organic solidarity, responsibility becomes individualized, and the concept of punishment of the individual through imprisonment makes its appearance.

The most important point in this analysis is that, while maintaining the basic view of *The Division of Labour*, it faces squarely the previously neglected problem of political power, and more specifically the problem of coercive power, in society. The theme that the tyranny of the *conscience collective*, through the growth of organic solidarity, is gradually dissolved in favour of a cooperative order, is affirmed. The 'normal' tendency of the advancing complexity of society is to produce both a decline in the intensity of coercive sanctions, and to 'individualize' punishment through imprisonment. What gives rise to the heavy dominance, in the less developed forms of society, of repressive sanctions, is the fact that crime is interpreted as an offence against the collectivity, and therefore as a religious transgression. It is crime against strongly held collective values, against 'transcendent beings'; 'the same act which, when it concerns an equal, is simply disapproved of, becomes blasphemous when it relates to someone who is superior to us; the horror which it stimulates can only be assuaged by violent repression.' This 'religious' quality is appropriated by the absolutist State, and is what enables it to legitimate the use of coercive power: offences against the State are treated as 'sacrilege', and hence, to be violently repressed.[9]

If the political structure of society is not, at least in any simple manner, 'determined' by the level of complexity of the division of labour, then the status of democratic mechanisms in the modern social order is, in an important sense, problematic. What are the conditions which provide for the implementation of a democratic political order? Durkheim's answer to this question effects a neat tie with his overall discussion of the division of labour.[10] The State becomes absolutist to the degree to which secondary groupings, which intervene between the State and the individual, are not strongly developed: in modern society, these groupings are the occupational associations stimulated by the differentiation of the division of labour. The family, Durkheim argued, is of declining significance in this respect, and must cede place to *corps intermédiaires* or occupational associations. He rejected the traditional theory of democracy, according to which the mass of the population 'participate' in the exercise of government. For Durkheim, this is a situation which is only possible in a society which, according to his own definition, is not a 'political society'. Such a conception of democracy cannot be sustained.

> We must therefore not say that democracy is the political form of a society governing itself, in which the government is spread throughout the milieu of the nation; such a definition is a contradiction in terms. It would be almost as if we thought that democracy is a political society without a state. In fact, the state is nothing if it is not an organ distinct from the rest of society. If the state is everywhere, it is nowhere. The state comes into existence by a process of concentration that detaches a certain group of individuals from the collective mass. . . . If we agree to reserve the name democracy for political societies, it must not be applied to tribes without definite form, which thus far have no claim to being a state and are not political societies.[11]

Government, by definition, must be exercised by a minority of individuals. 'Democracy', therefore, must concern the relationship between the differentiated political society, or the State, and the other institutional structures of society — more specifically, according to Durkheim, how far there is an interplay of communication between State and society. Where the citizens are regularly informed of the activities of the State, and the latter in turn is aware of the sentiments and wishes of all sectors of the population, then a democratic order exists. A democratic system thus presupposes a balance between two opposed tendencies: on the one hand, that in which the State directly reflects the 'general will', and on the other, in which the absolutist State, 'closed in upon itself', is cut off from the people. Each of these conditions tends to inhibit the effective occurrence of social change. The first, in Durkheim's view, produces a situation in which only superficial change can take place. In the second case, although it might appear as though the political power wielded by the State would allow the possibility of bringing about radical social transformation, such is not in fact the case. Such States 'are indeed all-powerful against the individual and this is what the term "absolute" means, as applied to them. But against the social condition itself, against the structure of society they are relatively powerless.'[12] In a democratic order, however, the pace of change can be advanced, because the conduct of social life assumes a more 'conscious' and 'controllable' character. Democratic government makes it possible for many aspects of social organization previously dominated by unthinking custom or habit to become open to effective intervention on the part of the State. In a democratic order, the State does not simply express the sentiments held in a diffuse fashion among the population, but is often the origin of new ideas: it leads society as well as being led by it. The extension of the activities of the State, whereby it penetrates into many spheres of society formerly controlled by custom or tradition — in the administration of justice, in economic life, in science and the arts — is therefore certainly not to be identified as necessarily leading to the autocratic domination of State over society. On the contrary, it is just this phenomenon which permits the active interplay between the 'government consciousness' and the views and feelings of the mass. A democracy, therefore, has two primary characteristics: the existence of close, and two-way, communication between government and governed; and the increasing extension of the contacts and ties of the State with other sectors of the society. But these characteristics do not imply that the State 'merges' with society. Rather, they presuppose the existence of a differentiated political agency: this is what saves a society from being the 'victim of traditional routine'.[13]

The occupational associations play a vital role in both of these respects. Since they are the intermediaries between the State and the individual, they are a principal medium whereby the expanding range of activities of the State is channelled to the rest of society, and they also thereby facilitate communication between State and the less organized levels of the society. It is thus the occupational associations which are of primary importance in checking two divergent possibilities whereby democracy can be undermined: the emergence of an autocratic State, separated from the people, and the 'absorption' of the State by society. This is the reason why it is desirable that the occupational associations should intervene in the electoral process between electorate and government:

> These secondary groups are essential if the state is not to oppress the individual: they are also necessary if the state is to be sufficiently free of the individual. . . . They liberate the two confronting forces, whilst linking them at the same time.[14]

Even if it is partly latent, in this analysis there is a theory of bureaucracy. A bureaucratic State, in which officialdom possesses the real power — and thereby, through adherence to bureaucratic routine, effectively promotes the maintenance of the status quo — is more likely to arise where the State is weak than where it is strong. In an absolutist State, although the officialdom may be used as the instrument of the domination of a ruler or an oligarchy, it is not the officials who dominate. But where the State tends to become 'absorbed', this situation of apparent 'democracy' actually conceals a bureaucratic domination. In modern societies, where the hold of traditional customs and beliefs has been largely dissolved, there are many avenues for the display of critical spirit, and changes of opinion and mood among the mass of the population are frequent. Where government simply 'reflects' this, the outcome is a constant vacillation in the political sphere and because of this dearth of active leadership, power devolves upon the officialdom: 'Only the administrative machine has kept its stability and goes on operating with the same automatic regularity.'[15]

A democratic society therefore, according to Durkheim, is a society which is 'conscious of itself'. On analogy with an organism, one can say, as Durkheim frequently did, that the State is the 'brain' — the conscious, directive centre — which operates, via the intermediary organs, within the complex nervous system of a differentiated society. Thus a democratic order enjoys the same relative superiority over other societies as the self-conscious being does over an animal whose behaviour is unreflective or instinctive. Durkheim placed considerable emphasis upon the 'cognitive' as opposed to the 'active' significance of the State. In particular, the State makes articulate and furthers the moral aims and sentiments embodied in the diffuse *conscience collective*.[16] This is important for understanding Durkheim's conception of moral authority as it exists in modern societies. The State within a democratic polity is the main agency which actively implements the values of moral individualism; it is the institutional form which replaces that of the church in traditional types of society. But only when it tends towards absolutism does the moral authority of the State approach that characteristic of earlier societal types, in which the individual, 'absorbed, as he was, into the mass of society . . . meekly gave way to its pressures and subordinated his own lot to the destinies of collective existence without any sense of sacrifice'.[17] The specific role of the democratic State is not to subordinate the individual to itself, but in fact to provide for individuals' self-realization. This is not something which can occur when the operations of the State are kept to a minimum. The self-realization of the individual can only take place through membership of a society in which the State guarantees and advances the rights embodied in moral individualism.

For Durkheim, discipline, in the sense of the control of egoism, is an essential characteristic of all moral authority — whether of the State or of other agencies. But, according to his analysis, the view which equates discipline inherently with the limitation of human self-realization is fallacious. All forms of life-organization, both biological and social, are controlled by defined, regular principles; by this very fact the mere existence of any type of society presupposes the regulation of behaviour according to moral rules. Certainly the moral authority characteristic of traditional forms of society, or of autocratic States, is inherently repressive, denying any great range of possibilities of self-development to the individual. But the moral regulation of modern societies and States is the very condition of the individual's self-realization and freedom. Durkheim's theory of moral authority is thus far from being the rationale for authoritarianism which it is sometimes portrayed to be.[18] Those who present Durkheim's view in this way tend to suppose that there are close parallels between Durkheim's position and that of Hobbes about the relationship between the individual and society. According to this idea, Durkheim's theory of moral authority rests upon the premise that human beings 'naturally' are refractory, and so must be rigidly restrained by society.[19] In fact, however, Durkheim criticized Hobbes on precisely this point. Hobbes's error was to stand outside of history, by positing a 'state of nature' and thereby to assume that there is a 'break in continuity between the individual and society': this results in the notion that 'man is thus naturally refractory to the common life; he can only resign himself to it when forced.'[20]

'Our very egoism' is thus, according to Durkheim, 'in large part a product of society'. Moral individualism involves values which stress the dignity and worth of the human individual *in abstracto*: individuals apply these to themselves as well as to others and hence become more sensitive both to the feelings and needs of others and to their own. 'Their griefs, like our own, are more readily intolerable to us. Our sympathy for them is not, accordingly, a mere extension of what we feel for ourselves. But both are effects of one cause and constituted by the same moral state.'[21] The characteristic problems facing the constitution of moral authority in the modern age derive from this confrontation of egoism and moral individualism, from the fact that 'it is wholly improbable that there will ever be an era in which man is required to resist himself to a lesser degree, an era in which he can live a life that is easier and less full of tension,' and that 'all evidence compels us to expect our effort in the struggle between the two beings within us to increase with the growth of civilisation.'[22] These are problems of a pluralistic society, in which the despotism of the moral authority of traditional types of social order has been broken. The moral authority characteristic of traditional societies, founded upon a poverty of individuality and repressive discipline, is wholly inappropriate in modern, highly differentiated society.

THE POLITICAL BACKCLOTH OF DURKHEIM'S THOUGHT

Some have claimed that Durkheim's writings were strongly conditioned by what he saw as necessary political reforms following the shattering effects of the German victory in the Franco-Prussian War of 1870—1.[23] But this says too much, and too little. Too much, because Durkheim's work also has to be seen as embedded in the traditions of French positivist philosophy which stretch back to Comte, Saint-Simon, and beyond; too little because — by this very token — the social and political background to Durkheim's thought embodies important elements which were the legacy of the Revolution in the eighteenth century, of which the events of 1870—1 were in part a direct outcome.[24] If the Revolution successfully disposed of the *Ancien Régime*, it also prepared the ground for certain generic social and political problems which were to haunt France for more than a century afterwards. Rather than introducing the liberal, bourgeois society which was proclaimed in its slogans, the Revolution opened up social cleavages of a chronic nature. If it was a 'successful' revolution, it was not successful enough, and produced that cycle of revolution and restoration which has dominated French history to the present day. The 1789 Revolution did not create a 'bourgeois society', if this is to be taken to mean one which conjoined political democracy and the hegemony of a capitalist class. Throughout the nineteenth century, heavily conservative elements, centred particularly in the Church, *rentiers* and peasantry, retained a deep-seated influence in government and society. The writings of Saint-Simon and Comte, in their somewhat variant ways, incorporated and gave expression to this precarious balance of liberal and conservative influences. Both perceived this as a transitory situation, and both looked forward to a new and more stable order in the future. Their divergent conceptions of this future order are among the main issues which Durkheim sought to resolve in his sociology. Is the emergent form of society to be one in which there is a single 'class' of *industriels*, where equality of opportunity will prevail, and in which government is reduced to the 'administration of things', not of persons? Or is it to be the hierocratic, corporate State of Comte's *Positive Polity*?

As in the writings of Max Weber, the problem, not of 'order' in a generic sense,[25] but of the form of authority appropriate to a modern industrial State, is the leading theme in Durkheim's work. But whereas in Germany a different combination of political and economic circumstances helped to establish a tradition of *Nationalökonomie* which led liberal scholars of Weber's generation to an overwhelming concern with 'capitalism',[26] in France the problem was posed within the context of the long-standing confrontation between the 'individualism' embodied in the ideals of the Revolution, and the moral claims of the Catholic hierocracy. Thus the Third Republic certainly came into being amid an atmosphere of crisis — and of class conflict, as manifest in the Paris Commune and its repression — but, so it seemed to Durkheim and his liberal contemporaries, the disasters of 1870—1 also provided the possibility of completing the process of social and political change which had been initiated in the Revolution almost a century earlier. The exigencies involved can be interpreted in terms of the progressive implementing of organic solidarity. The most important substantive conclusion which Durkheim reached in *The Division of Labour* is that organic solidarity presupposes moral individualism. In other words, that 'it is wrong to contrast a society which comes from a community of beliefs (mechanical solidarity) to one which has a cooperative basis (organic solidarity), according only to the first a moral character, and seeing in the latter simply an economic grouping.'[27] The immediate source of this moral individualism, as Durkheim made clear in his contribution to the public discussion of the Dreyfus affair,[28] is in the ideals generated by the 1789 Revolution. Moral individualism is by no means the same as the pursuit of self-interest, as is posited in classical economic theory and utilitarian philosophy. The social order which is coming into being demands the realization or concrete implementation of the ideals of the French Revolution.

This theory provided a resolution of the issues separating Saint-Simon's and Comte's otherwise closely comparable views.[29] The emergent social order is certainly to be one founded in the complex division of labour entailed by modern industry — as specified by Saint-Simon. Comte was mistaken in supposing that the condition of unity in traditional societies, the existence of a strongly formed *conscience collective*, is necessary to the modern type of society.[30] But it is not to be a society in which authority will be confined to the 'administration of things', as Saint-Simon envisaged.[31] On the contrary, the division of labour in industry must be infused with moral controls, and these must be under the general moral guidance of the State.

Durkheim's assessment of the underlying factors in the Dreyfus affair focused these issues with some clarity. The immediate stimulus to his discussion of the questions raised by the Dreyfus controversy was the publication of an article by Brunetière, the Catholic apologist, who accused the *dreyfusards* of fostering moral anarchy by rejecting traditional values in favour of egoistic rationalism.[32] Durkheim replied by asserting the existence of a radical distinction between 'egoism' and 'rationalist individualism'. It is true that no society can be built upon the pursuit of self-interest; but the latter is not at all the same thing as 'individualism'. Individualism must not be identified with 'the utilitarian egoism of Spencer and of the economists'.[33] Indeed, Durkheim continued, there would be no need to attack individualism if it possessed no other representatives, for utilitarian theory is in the process of dying a natural death. Individualism is in fact quite distinct from this: it is not merely a 'philosophical construction', but is a living part of the social organization of contemporary society. It is 'that which the Declaration of the Rights of Man sought, more or less successfully, to give a formula to; that which is currently taught in our schools, and which has become the basis of our moral catechism'.[34] This is, in an important respect, the very opposite of egoism. It involves, not the promotion of self-interest but of the welfare of others: it is the morality of cooperation. Individualism, or the 'cult of the individual', is founded upon sentiments of sympathy for human suffering, a desire for equality and for justice.

There can be no retreat to the traditional deism of the church, or to the patterns of hierocratic control associated with it. Individualism nonetheless preserves a 'religious' character, as do all moral rules. This 'cult of the individual' is the only moral form possible in an industrial society having a highly differentiated division of labour:

> To the degree that societies become larger, and embody broader territorial areas, traditions and practices must necessarily exist in a state of plasticity and ambiguity which no longer offers as much resistance to individual differences; thus traditions and practices are able to adapt themselves to a diversity of situations and to changed circumstances. Individual differences, being much less confined, develop more freely, and multiply; that is to say, everyone pursues, to a greater degree, his own bent [*son propre sens*]. At the same time, because of the more advanced developments of the division of labour, each person finds himself turned towards a different point on the horizon, reflects a different aspect of the world and, consequently, the content of individual minds differs from one man to another. Thus we move little by little towards a situation, which has now almost been reached, where the members of the same social group will share nothing in common save their quality of humanness [*leur qualité d'homme*], the constitutive characteristics of the human person in general. This idea of the human person, somewhat modified according to differences in national temperament, is thus the only one which is maintained, immovable and impersonal, above the flux of particular opinions. . . . Let us therefore use our freedoms in order to discover what must be done and in order to do it. Let us use them to soften the functioning of the social machine, still so harsh to individuals, so

as to put at their disposal all possible means for the free development of their faculties in order finally to progress towards making a reality of the famous precept: to each according to his works![35]

As Richter has pointed out,[36] Durkheim's political liberalism and his sociological defence of republicanism played a major role in the promotion of his academic career, and in facilitating the rise of sociology as a recognized discipline in the French academic system. The opprobrium which was directed at sociology — especially from Thomist critics[37] — bears witness to the degree to which the new discipline (especially in its Durkheimian form) came to be regarded as the hand-maiden of an ascendant republicanism. The struggle for the secularization of education, of course, was an element of primary significance as a background to this. Durkheim was first appointed to the Sorbonne in 1902 as a professor of education, and in his courses on pedagogy he set out a systematic theoretical exposition of the factors which necessitated the transformation of the educational system.[38] But while it was true that the ideological complementarity between Durkheim's sociology and victorious republicanism accounts for much of the considerable influence which he and the *Année sociologique* school exerted in French intellectual circles, it would be a mistake to see this as deriving too directly from political patronage. Durkheim never affiliated himself directly to any political party, although he maintained a close contact with his fellow *normalien* Jaurès, and both influenced and was influenced by some of the leading trends in Radical Socialism.[40]

To trace Durkheim's intellectual indebtedness to socialism is to reveal some of the most important sources of his thought. Mauss has stated that Durkheim originally conceived the subject-matter of *The Division of Labour* in terms of an analysis of the relationship between individualism and socialism.[41] 'Socialism' here does not refer, however, to the traditions of revolutionary thought which are so richly represented in French political life from the concluding decades of the eighteenth century onwards. If Durkheim's attitudes towards other branches of socialism were less than wholly unambiguous, his views on revolutionary socialism were clear-cut and unchanging. Major social change is not brought about by political revolution. According to Durkheim, the history of France in the first two thirds of the nineteenth century bears witness to this. 'It is among the most revolutionary peoples', he wrote, 'that bureaucratic routine is often most powerful'; in such societies, 'superficial change disguises the most monotonous uniformity.'[42] Thus, rather than being the harbingers of an entirely new social order,[43] the class struggles which manifested themselves in 1848 and 1870—1 bear witness to the fact that the underlying social changes (of which even the 1789 Revolution was more of a symptom than a cause) had not yet been accommodated within the general framework of modern French society. *The Division of Labour* established the theoretical grounding of this position, showing that class conflict derives from the fact that the transitional phase between mechanical and organic solidarity has not been completed. In reviewing Labriola's *Essais sur la conception matérialiste de l'histoire* in 1879, Durkheim made this position fully explicit. The 'sad class conflict of which we are the witnesses today' is not the cause of the malaise which the contemporary European societies are experiencing; on the contrary, it is secondary and derived. The transition from the traditional to the newly emergent type of social order is a protracted process, which does not begin at any definite date and which is evolutionary rather than revolutionary in character. The elimination of class conflict, therefore, does not necessitate an 'upheaval and radical reorganisation of the social order', but instead demands the consolidation and absorption of the basic social and economic transformations which have already taken place.[44]

Although Durkheim seems to have been acquainted with Marx's writings at a very early stage in his intellectual career, according to his own testimony[45] he was not substantially influenced by Marx either in formulating his general conception of sociology and sociological method or in arriving at the theory of social development set out in *The Division of Labour*. In France prior to the turn of the twentieth century, Marxism was not, of course, the major political and intellectual force which it was in the last two decades of the nineteenth century in Germany. The thought of Max and Alfred Weber, Sombart, Tönnies, and the other younger members of the *Verein für Sozialpolitik* was in substantial part shaped through a confrontation with Marxism.[46] Whatever the naivety and oversimplification of Marx's ideas which became current in Germany, both Marx's self-professed followers and the leading critics of Marxism there possessed an understanding of Marx vastly more advanced than that which became diffused into French intellectual circles from the 1880s onwards. The Guesdist variety of Marxism, which held sway up until the middle of the 1890s, when translations of more sophisticated Marxist writings (such as those by Labriola) became available, was raucous and shallow. Hence, by the time Marxism made a substantial penetration into French intellectual consciousness, Durkheim had already worked out most of the essential components of his sociology.

His lectures on socialism, given at Bordeaux in 1895–6 were, however, partly stimulated by the spread of Marxism at this period;[47] some of his own students, indeed, became converted to Marxism at the time.[48] But Durkheim was by this stage equipped to meet with and to assimilate the challenge of Marxism in his own terms. His *Socialism* lecture-course sets out, in the face of the revolutionary Left, the same basic position which, at the height of the Dreyfus affair, was made against the reactionaries of the Right. And at the same time he affirms the key role of sociology in the analysis and resolution of the 'contemporary crisis'. Moreover, in these lectures Durkheim made explicit the continuity between the intellectual problems tackled by Saint-Simon and those which face the modern age. The writings of Saint-Simon, and of his followers, comprised — in a confused form — three sets of ideas. First, the conception of a scientific sociology; second, the notion of a religious revival; and third, a body of socialist doctrine. It is not by chance, Durkheim asserted, that the three sets of ideas have again come to the fore, since 'there are striking analogies between the period we have just been studying and the one in which we now live.'[49] These ideas appear at first sight to be quite distinct and even opposed to each other. In fact, each derives from the same circumstance — the 'condition of moral disorder' which prevailed before 1848, and which had been reactivated after 1870.[50] Each expresses, in a partial fashion, aspects of this 'disorder'. The religious movement arises from a felt need to control egoism and hence to recreate a strong moral authority. It is inadequate, because it seeks to re-establish forms of ecclesiastical domination which are only appropriate to an earlier type of society. Socialism recognizes that the old order has been superseded and that consequently traditional institutions must cede place to new forms of social organization. But it looks to purely economic transformations in order to remedy a situation of crisis which is primarily moral in character. The impetus towards sociology stems from the desire to understand and to explain the origins of the changes which are taking place. It, too, is limited because, as a scientific study, it necessarily proceeds only cautiously and slowly, while the demands of the day stimulate a desire for instant and all-embracing solutions. Nevertheless, it is clear that, in Durkheim's thinking, sociology claims a definite primacy over the other two. For while each of the others gives only a distorted picture of the modern crisis,[51] sociology is able to reveal its true nature. Sociological analysis cannot in and of itself be a substitute for the other two sets of ideas. Each has something to offer which no science can provide. But only sociology can show what those necessary elements are:

> Our conclusion therefore is that if you wish to allow these practical theories (which have not advanced much since the beginning of the century) to go forward a step, you must force yourself habitually to take account of their different tendencies and discover their unity. That is what Saint-Simon attempted. His undertaking must be renewed and in the same direction. His history can serve to show us the way.[52]

Saint-Simon's thought contained an essential weakness. He looked to 'industry' — that is, economic change — to supply the main remedy for the modern crisis. This emphasis was in turn transferred to subsequent branches of socialism, including that created by Marx. Marxist socialism, in common with all other forms, is a product of the social and economic changes set into motion in the late eighteenth and early nineteenth centuries in

Western Europe. It is certainly a more 'scientific' type of socialism than other more idealistic strains in socialist thought — 'it has thus rendered social science more services perhaps than it received from it'[53] — but, however valid certain of its propositions and insights, its programme still rests upon a combination of purely economic measures. The principal thesis of *Capital* is that the 'anarchy of the market', characteristic of capitalism, will, under socialism, be replaced by a system in which production will be centrally regulated. In short, in Marxist socialism, the productive capacity of society is to be regulated centrally. But while this might allow the overcoming of the 'forced' division of labour [*la division du travail contrainte*], it would do nothing to reduce the moral hiatus which derives from the anomic conditions of modern industry. On the contrary, it would deepen it, since it would further elevate the importance of the 'economic' at the expense of the 'moral'.[54]

Although this is not made explicit in *Socialism*, there can be no doubt that the theory of the division of labour is basic to the differentiation between 'communism' and 'socialism' as this is formulated by Durkheim.[55] Communist ideas, which have sprung up at many diverse periods of history, advance the notion that private property is the essential source of all social evils. Therefore the accumulation of material wealth must be subject to severe restrictions. According to communist theory, the political sphere must be strictly separated from the potentially corrupting influence of economic production. Socialism, on the other hand, which has only come into being with the social and economic transformations of the late eighteenth century, is founded upon the view that the progress of human welfare depends upon the expansion of industry. The main principle involved in socialism is exactly contrary to that proposed in communist theory; socialism advocates the fusion of the political and economic. Socialism claims not simply that production should be controlled by the state but that the role of the State should be defined in economic terms — that is, that the 'administration of things' should replace the 'administration of people'. Whereas therefore the aim of communism is the regulation of consumption, that of socialism is the regulation of production.[56] Communism, in Durkheim's understanding of the term, is a form of political protest and theory which corresponds to societies having a low division of labour. Everyone works in a like fashion, as a separate producer, and there is not a large measure of economic interdependence; consequently, the conception of the regulation of production cannot emerge. In the ideal society envisaged by communism,

> There is no common rule which determines relationships among the different workers, or the manner in which all these diverse activities should cooperate for collective goals. As each one does the same thing — or almost the same — there is no cooperation to regulate.[57]

The appearance of socialism, on the other hand, is only possible with the development of a differentiated division of labour, since it presupposes the idea of a (coordinated) economy of interdependent producers.

Durkheim's proposals for the revival of occupational associations within the general framework of the State have definite affinities with the solidarism of the Radical Socialists, and more broadly with the traditions of corporatism which intertwine with socialism in the history of French political theory.[58] But it would be mistaken to suppose that he developed these ideas in close and direct relation to the political interests of the solidarists, although his views did exert some considerable degree of influence over a number of major contemporary figures associated with the movement. The solidarists advocated a programme of State intervention in economic affairs which was roughly comparable to that proposed by the *Kathedersozialisten* in Germany. Durkheim made the acquaintance of the writings of the 'older generation' of the *Kathedersozialisten* at an early stage in his career, whilst studying in Germany in 1885–6. He was especially impressed with what he perceived in the writings of Schmoller, Wagner and others as an attempt to break away from utilitarianism in political and social theory. They showed that, in utilitarian theory, 'the collective interest is only a form of personal interest' and 'altruism is merely a concealed egoism'.[59] Neither society nor the State can be understood except as moral agencies: no society exists where economic relationships are not controlled by the regulative force of custom and law. Thus measures involving State intervention in economic life must be clothed in a moral and legal framework.

The 'paradox', which Rousseau 'wrestled with in vain',[60] of the fact that the State must rest upon common moral sentiments and yet play an active part in promoting genuine social change, can be resolved if the occupational associations are given an intermediary role in the electoral system. Durkheim thus proposed that the regionally based electoral system should be abandoned, arguing that regional differences in culture and interests were becoming increasingly eradicated by the advance of industrialization. The main differences which continue to exist stem from the diversification of the division of labour, and these are not bound to regional variations:

> nowadays, the links that bind each one of us to a particular spot in an area where we live are extremely weak and can be broken with the greatest ease. . . . Professional life, on the other hand, takes on increasing importance, as labour goes on splitting up into divisions. There is therefore reason to believe that it is this professional life that is destined to form the basis of our political structure. The idea is already gaining ground that the professional association is the true electoral unit, and because the links attaching us to one another derive from our calling rather than from any regional bonds of loyalty, it is natural that the political structure should reflect the way in which we ourselves form into groups of our own accord.[61]

Durkheim's portrayal of the moral character of the State, and his version of democratic republicanism, gave minimal importance to the external relationships of the modern nation-state. Although Durkheim rejected Spencer's contention that industrial society necessarily tends to be pacific in character, he emphasized that there is an intrinsic compatibility between the republican State and the progress of international harmony. The ideals of moral individualism, at their most abstract level, refer not to the citizens of any particular nation, but to mankind in general. Consequently, it is probable that the future will see an evolution towards the decline of national differences, and that the expansion of the division of labour in the international context will eventually lead to the formation of a supra-national community. At the time of the writing of *The Division of Labour*, Durkheim thought he discerned a definite movement towards the creation of a European community, quoting Sorel in order to substantiate this judgement.[62] This optimistic perspective, of course, contrasted sharply with the subsequent deterioration of the relationships between the major powers culminating in the First World War. Together with most other intellectuals of his generation, Durkheim experienced the outbreak of the war with a profound sense of tragedy and shock. But he did not abandon the notion that it 'is the tendency of patriotism to become, as it were, a fragment of world patriotism'.[63] This is made clear in the various patriotic pamphlets which Durkheim wrote during the war.[64] These have often been dismissed as mere exercises in propaganda, but in fact they stand in close relationship to his theory of the State. The main point in the most important of Durkheim's wartime publications, '*L'Allemagne au-dessus de tout*', is that German militarism rests upon a 'pathological' form of mentality which is a kind of 'collective anomie'. This phenomenon results from 'a certain manner of conceiving the state, its nature and its role',[65] which Durkheim found to be expressed in a clearly defined way in the thought of Treitschke. Treitschke, according to Durkheim, was not an original thinker, but a writer whose works represent the ideas and sentiments of the collectivity, and thus contain 'all the principles which German diplomacy and the German state has daily put into practice'.[66]

For Treitschke the State is the highest value, can accept no limits to its power, and must ultimately pursue its aims by warfare. Constant struggle between nation-states is an inevitable characteristic of the modern world. According to his conception, the power of the State is the criterion in terms of which all other values are to be judged; but the State itself is not a moral entity. This is a 'pathological' form of national patriotism, in Durkheim's analysis, because it treats the State purely as a system of power, which recognizes no intrinsic limits to its rule. But, as in the case of the individual, the State cannot exist as an amoral being which acknowledges no constraints upon the expansion of its ambitions. Treitschke's conception of the State is based upon a false view of the relationship between State and society. According to him, 'there is a difference in nature . . . between the individual and the state.'[67] This is a standpoint which perpetuates the Hegelian notion of the State as existing on a different plane from that of life in civil society, and which readily serves to legitimize an autocratic tyranny. To admit the sovereignty of the State, internally and in external relations, Durkheim concluded, does not at all entail acceptance of such a view. The sovereignty of the State is 'relative', both to the internal moral structure of civil society — 'a multitude of moral forces which, although not possessing a rigorous juridical form and organisation, are none the less real and efficacious' — and to the morals of international relations, 'the attitudes of foreign peoples'.[68] Although German imperialism must be defeated militarily, it is by its very nature an unstable phenomenon, and is incompatible with the moralization of international relations which characterizes the modern world. 'There is no state which is not incorporated into the broader *milieu* formed by the totality of other states, that is to say, which is not part of the great human community. . . .'[69]

Examination of Durkheim's writings on the growth of moral individualism, on socialism, and on the State, in the context of the social and political issues which he saw as confronting the Third Republic, shows how mistaken it is to regard him as being primarily 'conservative' in his intellectual standpoint.[70] The proponents on this view[71] have recognized Durkheim's liberalism in politics, but have sought to show that the most important intellectual parameters of his sociology were derived from those traditions of French social philosophy (especially the so-called 'counter-reaction' to the French Revolution) which emphasized cohesion rather than conflict, order rather than change and constraint rather than freedom. Conservatism here means, in Coser's words, 'an inclination to maintain the existing order of things or to re-enforce an order which seems threatened'.[72] As a description of Durkheim's concerns, however, this is quite one-sided. Not the defence of the 'order' against change, but the objective of achieving change is what Durkheim sought to promote. The point is that France in the first two thirds of the nineteenth century, while manifesting various periods of apparently rapid political 'change', in fact remained basically stable: the socio-economic transformations necessary to further the transition to a modern industrial order had not been realized.

THE CRITICAL EVALUATION OF DURKHEIM'S
POLITICAL THOUGHT

In the preceding discussion I have stressed the central role of Durkheim's political thought in his sociology as a whole. Any attempt at a critical assessment of his political ideas must thus be placed within a broader evaluation of his writings in sociology and social philosophy. The 'orthodox' interpretation of Durkheim readily delivers him up to a number of apparently conclusive criticisms, such as that he emphasized the importance of cohesion or consensus in society to the almost total exclusion of conflict; that he failed to develop a theory of institutions, because he concentrated above all upon the relationship between society and the individual, neglecting intermediate structures; that he displayed a lack of concern with the role of political power, since he was overwhelmingly interested in the nature of moral ideals, and that 'he did not duly appreciate the import of social innovation and social change because he was preoccupied with social order and equilibrium . . .'[73] While each of the accusations contains an element of truth, none of them can be sustained in the sweeping fashion in which they are frequently made. Those who interpret Durkheim's work as being essentially concerned with a conservative 'inclination to maintain the existing order of things'[74] have inevitably tended to present a misleading picture of Durkheim's position on each of these dimensions.

Both in political temper and in sociological conviction, Durkheim was an opponent of revolutionary thought. Evolution, not revolution, provided the framework for his conception of social change. He frequently emphasized that significant change only takes place through the cumulation of long-term processes of social development. His refusal to see in class conflict the mechanism which would generate a radical social transformation separated him conclusively from Marxism. But to say this is not to hold that he neglected the phenomenon of social conflict, or of class conflict, or that he sought to accommodate them to his theoretical position by denying the reality of the aspirations of the working class. His constantly echoed assertion that 'the social problem' (i.e. the problem of class conflict) cannot be solved through purely economic measures, because of the 'instability' of human appetites, has to be read against his equally emphatic stress upon the basic changes in the economic order which have to be made to complete the institutionalization of moral individualism. The reality behind the occurrence of class conflict is the new desire for self-realization and equality of opportunity of those in the lower socio-economic strata. This cannot be repressed but demands ultimately the abolition of all economic and social barriers to 'external equality', to 'everything that can even indirectly shackle the free unfolding of the social force that each carries in himself'.[75]

Since the publication of *Leçons de sociologie*, (which first appeared in French in 1950) it has become impossible to maintain that Durkheim gave no attention to intermediate institutions in society. *Leçons de sociologie* makes it particularly clear, however, that a profound transformation of the institutional organization of traditional forms of society is a necessary concomitant of the transition from mechanical to organic solidarity. The relationship between the State and the corporation is seen to be fundamental to the modern social order. It is in these terms that Durkheim sought to tackle the question of political power. Although it can hardly be granted that he dealt satisfactorily with the nature and sources of political power, it is quite clearly not the case that he merely ignored the issues posed by it. Finally, not only is it fallacious to hold that 'he did not duly appreciate the import of social innovation and social change', but it is not possible to understand the main themes in his work without locating it within the scheme of social development set out in *The Division of Labour*. In one of his earliest works, a dissertation on Montesquieu, Durkheim established his position on this point. Montesquieu, he showed, 'fails to see that every society embodies conflicting factors, simply because it has gradually emerged from a past form and is tending towards a future one'.[76]

Durkheim frequently asserted that sociology should, at some point, find its justification in practice: that a sociology which had no relevance to practical problems would be a worthless endeavour. It is one of the major tasks of sociology to determine the nascent directions of change which a society at any given time is experiencing, and to show which trends 'should' be fostered as the coming pattern of the future. The closure between the 'is' and the 'ought' Durkheim sought to achieve in terms of his distinction between the 'normal' and 'pathological', conceived on analogy with health and disease in the organism. The theory set out in *The Division of Labour* is founded upon this conception. The work was conceived by Durkheim to show that the ideals of moral individualism correspond to the 'social needs' engendered by the growth of mechanical solidarity — that these ideals are 'normal' to the modern type of society, and hence are to be protected and promoted. No aspect of Durkheim's writings has been more universally rejected than his notion of normality and pathology, and rightly so: even if it were possible to determine 'scientifically' whether or not a given moral norm were a 'necessary' element in the functioning of a particular society, it is altogether another thing to hold this *ipso facto* to be 'desirable'. The questions at issue here are not to be resolved by any sort of appeal to the criteria of health and disease in biology: medicine, in this respect, is a technology to be applied in pursuit of given values. In spite of — or perhaps because of — the fact that the conception of normality was integral to Durkheim's work, he never fully clarified his position in this respect. In his most systematic formulation of the principle, in *The Rules of Sociological Method*, he definitely attempted to establish scientific criteria for the verification of ethical ideals, rejecting the view that 'science can teach us nothing about what we ought to desire'.[77] But, in replying later to critics of these views, he appeared to retract his earlier formulation, indicating that ethics and sociology are concerned with two 'different spheres', and claiming that 'we ask simply that ethical constructions should be preceded by a science of morality which is more methodical than the ordinary speculations of so-called theoretical ethics.'[78]

Durkheim's ambiguity on this matter is reflected in his failure to deal in an explicit manner with the relationship between sociological analysis and political intervention in the interests of securing practical social change. As Marx realized, this demands a dialectical conception of the role of sociological knowledge as a means of knowing the world and at the same time as a mode of changing it. Durkheim wanted to relate sociology to practical concerns. But he also sought to defend a conception of the 'neutral' character of sociological analysis as a 'natural science of society'. Although this was no doubt reinforced by his personal characteristics and his disdain for the squabbles of party politics, his general aloofness from politics was certainly supported by this position. The result was that, in practice, the relation of sociology to the achievement of real social change remained obscure. Durkheim attempted to escape from this difficulty by placing stress upon the 'partial' character of sociological knowledge: the emphasis that the advance of sociology is slow and painstaking, because it must conform to the rigorous criteria of scientific validation. Since the needs of life in an everyday social and political context require immediate decisions and policies, the relevance of the 'scientific' knowledge of the sociologist has definite limitations. But his own writing, often dealing with the broadest issues of social organization and social change, belies this sort of modest prescription — as, indeed, does the more abstract analysis of the 'therapeutic' role of sociology in diagnosing what is normal and what is pathological at given stages of societal evolution.

In Durkheim's writings this uneasy tension between theory and practice finds expression in a constant tendency to shift from the analytical to the optative. Durkheim's discussions of extant reality frequently slide into a portrayal of what he expects to be the case in the future, because of what is supposedly entailed by the 'normal' conditions of functioning of a society or social institution. Thus the development and strengthening of the occupational associations is due to occur because this is demanded by the 'normal' operation of the division of labour. This analysis is not based upon an empirical demonstration that there is a discernible trend towards the emergence of such corporations; it derives from the attempt to implement the notion that the functionally necessary supplies the criterion of what is desirable — in this case, that 'the absence of all corporative institution creates . . . a void whose importance it is difficult to exaggerate.' As with all of Durkheim's attempts to diagnose 'normality', this barely avoids degenerating into crude teleology: the 'evil', the 'malady *totius substantiae*', of the anomic division of labour, calls into being the 'remedy' of the development of the corporations.[79]

The shortcomings of Durkheim's writings in these very general respects are undoubtedly related to inadequacies in his conceptual treatment of the State and political power.[80] While it is not the case that he ignored the problem of power, or more specifically the role of force, in society, it is true that he established the basic framework of his thought, in *The Division of Labour*, before he developed a systematic analysis of the State and politics. His subsequent exposition of the partial 'independence' of State power only effected a restricted modification of the theory of the division of labour. While this enabled him to deal more adequately with the existence of coercive power, it dealt only inadequately with the conditions which generate the development of an absolute State. The analyses given in *Leçons de sociologie* and 'Deux lois de l'évolution pénale' leave this as a residual factor. Durkheim nowhere undertook to show what determines the degree to which the State is able to 'separate itself' from society. He continually underlined the point that every form of State, weak or strong, is rooted in civil society, and nourished from it; but he failed to analyse in any detail at all the nature of these connections.

In this, Durkheim certainly remained a prisoner of the main intellectual sources in which his thought is steeped. The concept of the State which he employed indicates as much, and while he used it to attempt to break away from Comte's treatment of the State, his own conceptual formulation actually here resembles that of Comte.[81] The State is defined as the 'organ of social thought', the 'ego' of the *conscience collective*. Durkheim specifically rejected the notion that the State is primarily an executive agency. The main task of the State is to be 'a special organ whose responsibility is to work out certain representations which hold good for the collectivity'; the 'true meaning' of the State 'consists not in exterior action, in making changes, but in deliberation . . .'[82] His treatment of democracy, of course, is intimately tied in with this conceptualiztion. In analysing the role of the occupational associations, he saw them as 'balancing' the power of the State. The view that an integral element in democratic government is the sharing of power, as he made fully explicit, is to him not a viable one. He rejected not only the classical conception of 'direct democracy' but also what has today come to be called the 'theory of democratic elitism'. A minority must govern, in any developed society, and it makes little odds how this minority comes to power. The activities of an aristocracy might often conform more closely to the will of the people than that of an elected elite. The difference between a system in which 'the governing minority are established once and for all', and one which 'the minority that carries the day may be beaten tomorrow and replaced by another' is only 'slight'.[83] Democracy, for Durkheim, thus becomes a matter of the interplay of sentiments and ideas between government and mass. His discussion of democratic government contains no developed examination of the functioning of political parties, or of parliament, or of the franchise, and indeed these considerations are regarded as of rather minor significance.

The weaknesses inherent in this viewpoint are nowhere more clearly exposed than in Durkheim's discussion of the German State in *'L'Allemagne au-dessus de tout'*. As has been indicated previously, the weight of Durkheim's theoretical perspective directed his thinking towards asserting the basic compatibility, in the modern world, between national ideals, patriotism, and the growth of a pan-national community. Characteristically, his response to the growth of German militarism — since the latter fell outside the expectations generated by his standpoint — was to treat it as a 'pathological' phenomenon. This pathology is explained by Durkheim as a 'moral disorder' manifest in the grandiosity of national ambition such as is revealed in the ideological writings of Treitschke. The effect of Durkheim's analysis, however, is to consider power itself only from the moral aspect, in terms of the immoderate emphasis which Treitschke places upon the supremacy of the State. German militarism surely can only be properly interpreted in terms of the structural properties of the nineteenth-century German State — of the leading part played by Prussian military strength in securing the political unification of the country, and the continued domination of the land-owning elite in government. These made Germany into a 'power-state' as Max Weber well understood and it is of course more than happenstance that Weber's conceptualization of the State, which eschews any possibility of defining the State in moral terms, places primacy upon just those aspects which Durkheim underplayed — the successful claim to monopoly of the legitimate deployment of force and the existence of fixed territorial boundaries.[84]

Although Parsons has claimed that, according to his own definition of these terms, Durkheim's political sociology marks him out as being closer to 'communism' rather than 'socialism',[85] it is surely evident that the reverse is true. Communism, for Durkheim, expresses the constantly reappearing, but ultimately futile, hope that human egoism can be eradicated. It is thus essentially both a-historical and unrealizable. Socialism, on the other hand, according to him, is an expression of the consciousness that radical changes have and are occurring in contemporary societies, and that these changes have brought about a condition of crisis which presses for resolution. This consciousness is filtered by the social circumstances of which it is an expression. That is to say, it reflects a condition of society in which economic relationships have come to dominate social life; hence it assumes that the remedy for the modern crisis must be purely economic. The flaw in all socialist doctrines is that they fail to see that the resolution of the crisis must entail moral reorganization, whereby the primacy of the 'economic' over the 'social' will be readjusted in favour of the latter.[86] But they are correct in holding that regulation of the capitalist market is necessary. Although Durkheim repudiated the possibility of reorganizing capitalism by revolutionary means, it is a main part of his ideas that the forced division of labour, the exploitative relationship of capital and wage-labour, must be eliminated. This is to be accomplished by the disappearance of the inheritance of property:

Now inheritance as an institution results in men being born rich or poor; that is to say, there are two main classes of society, linked by all sorts of intermediate classes: the one which in order to live has to make its services acceptable to the other at whatever the cost; the other class which can do without these services, because it can call upon certain resources . . . as long as such sharp class differences exist in society, fairly effective palliatives may lessen the injustices of contracts; but in principle, the system operates in conditions which do not allow of justice.[87]

The abolition of inherited property is a process which is to take place through the action of the State. Although Durkheim was not entirely unambiguous on this point, it seems that he did not envisage the abolition of private property as such,[88] but rather that differentials in possession of property should be entirely determined by differences in the service which individuals render to society. Functional importance in the division of labour is to govern property rights. This is a 'work of justice' which has to be accomplished if the morality of individualism is to have regulative force in modern society. The advance of moral individualism is incompatible with a social order in which class situation determines from birth an individual's position in the occupational structure. Thus there is an intrinsic connection between the elimination of the 'forced' division of labour and the amelioration of the 'anomic' division of labour. What is required in order to reduce anomie is not simply the imposition of regulation upon the existing market system: this would only lead to an intensification of class conflict. 'It is not sufficient that there be rules . . . for sometimes the rules themselves are the cause of evil.' The morality of organic solidarity demands major economic changes, which create a system in which there is a free or 'spontaneous' ordering of individuals in the division of labour, such that no 'obstacle, of whatever nature, prevents them from occupying the place in the social framework which is compatible with their faculties.'[89]

1

The Concept of the State

An essential element that enters into the notion of any political group is the opposition between governing and governed, between authority and those subject to it. It is quite possible that in the beginning of social evolution this gap may not have existed; such an hypothesis is all the more likely since we do find societies in which the distance between the two is only faintly perceptible. But in any case, the societies where it is seen cannot be mistaken for those where it does not occur. The former differ from the latter in kind and require different terms of description: we should keep the word 'political' for the first category. For if this expression has any one meaning, it is, above all, organization, at any rate rudimentary; it is established authority (whether stable or intermittent, weak or strong), to whose action individuals are subject, whatever it be.

But an authority of this type is not found solely in political societies. The family has a head whose powers are sometimes limited by those of a family council. The patriarchal family of the Romans has often been compared to a State in miniature. Although, as we shall soon see, this expression is not justified, we could not quarrel with it if the sole distinguishing feature of the political society were a governmental structure. So we must look for some further characteristic.

This lies possibly in the especially close ties that bind any political society to its soil. There is said to be an enduring relationship between any nation and a given territory. 'The State', says Bluntschli, 'must have its domain; the nation demands a country.' But the family, at least in many countries, is no less bound to the soil — that is, to some charted area. The family, too, has its domain from which it is inseparable, since that domain is inalienable. We have seen that the patrimony of landed estate was sometimes the very kernel of the family; it is this patrimony that made its unity and continuity and it was about this focus that domestic life revolved. Nowhere, in any political society, has political territory had a status to compare with this in importance. We may add, however, that where cardinal importance attaches to national territory, it is of comparatively recent date. To begin with, it seems rather arbitrary to deny any political character to the great nomad societies whose structure was sometimes very elaborate. Again, in the past it was the number of citizens and not the territory that was considered to be the primary element of the State. To annex a State was not to annex the country but its inhabitants and to incorporate them within the annexing State. On the other hand, we may see the victors preparing to settle down in the country vanquished, without thereby losing their own cohesion or their political identity. During the whole early period of our history, the capital, that is, the territorial centre of gravity of the society, had an extreme mobility. It is not a great while since the peoples became so identified with the territories they inhabit, that is, with what we should call the geographical expression of those peoples. Today, France is not only a mass of people consisting in the main of individuals speaking a certain language and who observe certain laws and so on, but essentially a certain defined part of Europe. If indeed all the Alsatians had opted for French nationality in 1870, we might have with justice still considered France as mutilated or diminished, by the sole fact that she had abandoned a delimited part of her soil to a foreign power. But this identification of the society with its territory has only come about in those societies that are the most advanced. To be sure, it is due to many causes, to the higher social value that the soil has gained, perhaps also to the relatively greater importance that the geographical bond has assumed since other social ties of a more moral kind have lost their force. The society of which we are members is in our minds all the more a well-defined territory, since it is no longer in its essence a religion, a corpus of traditions peculiar to it or the cult of a particular dynasty.

Leaving territory aside, should we not find a feature of a political society in the numerical importance of the population? It is true we should not ordinarily give this name to social groups comprising a very small number of individuals. Even so, a dividing line of this kind would be extremely fluctuating: for at what precise moment does a concentration of people become of a size to be classified as a political group? According to Rousseau, it would be at the ten thousand figure, but Bluntschli rates this as too low. The estimates of both are equally arbitrary. A French *département* sometimes has more inhabitants than many of the city-states of Greece and Italy. Any one of these, however, constitutes a State, whilst a *département* has no claim to such a term.

Nevertheless, we touch here on a distinctive feature. To be sure, we cannot say that a political society differs from family groups or from professional groups on the score that it has greater numbers, for the numerical strength of families may in some instances be considerable while the numerical strength of a State may be very small. But it remains true that there is no political society which does not comprise numerous different families or professional groups or both at once. If it were confined to a domestic society or family, it would be identical with it and hence be a domestic society. But the moment it is made up of a certain number of domestic societies, the resulting aggregate is something other than each of its elements. It is something new, which has to be described by a different word. Likewise, the political society cannot be identified with any professional group or with any caste, if caste there be; but is always an aggregate of various professions or various castes, as it is of different families. More often, when we get a society made up of a collection of secondary groups varying in kind, without itself being a secondary group in relation to a far bigger society, then it constitutes a social entity of a specific kind. We should then define the political society as one formed by the coming together of a rather large number of secondary social groups, subject to the same one authority which is not itself subject to any other superior authority duly constituted.

Thus, and it should be noted, political societies are in part distinguished by the existence of secondary groups. Montesquieu was conscious of this in his day, in speaking of the social form that seemed to him the most highly organized, that is, the monarchy. He said that it involved 'intermediary, subordinate and dependent powers.'[2] We can see the whole importance of these secondary groups we have been discussing so far. They are not only necessary for directing the particular interests, domestic or professional, that they include and that are their own *raison d'être*; they also form the primary condition for any higher organization. Far from being in opposition to the social group endowed with sovereign powers and called more specifically the State, the State presupposes their existence: it exists only where they exist. No secondary groups, no political authority — at least, no authority that this term can apply to without being inappropriate. Later on, we shall see the source of this solidarity that unites the two kinds of grouping. For the moment, it is enough to record the fact.

It is true that this definition runs counter to a theory long accepted as established: this is the theory to which Sumner, Maine and Fustel de Coulanges have given their name. According to these authorities, the elementary society, from which the more composite societies are held to have sprung, is considered to be an extensive family group made up of all the individuals linked by ties of blood or ties of adoption and placed under the direction of the oldest male ascendant, the patriarch. This is the patriarchal theory. If this were a fact, we should find a constituted authority in the very beginning, analogous at all points with the authority we find in the more complex State; it would therefore be truly political, when in reality the society of which it is the keystone is single and uncompounded, and not made up of any smaller societies. The supreme authority of cities, of kingdoms, of nations, constituted later on, would have no original and specific character whatever; it would derive from the patriarchal authority and be formed on its model. The society called political would be only families on a greater scale.

But this patriarchal theory is no longer tenable today; it is a hypothesis which rests on no fact whatever of direct observation, and which is disproved by a host of known facts. The patriarchal family as described by Sumner, Maine and Fustel de Coulanges has never been under observation. A group made up of consanguines, living in a state of autonomy under the control of a more or less powerful head, has never been known. All the family groups that we do know which show even a vestige of organization and which recognize some definite authority, form part of greater societies. We define the clan as being at the same time a political and family subdivision of a wider social aggregate. But, it will be asked, how about the beginning? We may legitimately suppose that in the beginning there existed simple forms of society which did not comprise any society of a still simpler form; both logic and the comparative study compel us to make a hypothesis which is confirmed by certain facts. On the other hand, nothing entitles us to think that such societies were subject to an authority of any kind. And one fact that should make us reject this hypothesis as altogether unlikely is that the more the clans of a tribe are independent one of another and the more each one tends towards autonomy, the more we look in vain for anything resembling an authority or any kind of governmental power. They are masses that are almost entirely amorphous or without structure, all the members of which are on the same level. Therefore the organization of partial groups, of clans, families and so on . . . did not precede the organization of the total aggregate which came about from their combination. We should not, however, go on to conclude that, conversely, the organization of the groups, etc. sprang from the organization of the aggregate. The truth is that they are interdependent, as we said just now, and that they condition each other mutually. The parts were not organized in the first instance to form a whole which was subsequently designed on their pattern, but the whole and the parts were organized at the same time. What also follows from the foregoing is that political societies imply the existence of an authority:

since this authority can only emerge where the societies comprise within themselves a number of elementary societies, the political societies are of necessity polycellular or polysegmental. This is not to say that there have never been societies consisting of one segment alone, but they form a different species and are not political.

It remains true, however, that one and the same society may be political in some respects, and only constitute a partial and secondary group in others. This is what occurs in all federal States. Each individual State is autonomous to a certain degree: this degree is more limited than if there were not a federation with a regular structure, but the degree, although diminished by this federation, is not reduced to nil. Each member constitutes a political society, a State in the true meaning of the term, to the extent to which it is answerable only to itself and is not dependent on the central authority of the federation. On the other hand, to the extent to which it is subordinate to some organ superior to itself, it is an ordinary secondary group, a partial one and analogous to a district, a province, a clan or a caste. It ceases to be a whole and no longer emerges except as a part. Thus our definition does not establish an absolute line of demarcation between political societies and others; but that is because there is not and could not be such a line. On the contrary, the sequence of things is continuous. The major political societies are formed by the gradual aggregation of the minor. There are periods of transition when these minor societies, still keeping something of their original nature, begin to develop into something different and take on new characteristics, and when consequently, their status is ambiguous. The main thing is not to record a break in continuity where none exists, but to be aware of the specific features which distinguish political societies and which (according to their degree of 'more or less') determine whether these societies are really more, or less, entitled to this term.

Now that we know the distinguishing marks of a political society, let us see what the morals are that relate to it. From the very definition just made, it follows that the essential rules of these morals are those determining the relation of individuals to this sovereign authority, to whose control they are subject. Since we need a word to indicate the particular group of officials entrusted with representing this authority, we are agreed to keep for this purpose the word 'State'. It is true that very often we apply the word 'State' not to the instrument of government but to the political society as a whole, or to the people governed and its government taken as one, and we ourselves often use the term in this sense. It is in this way that we speak of the European States or that we call France a State. But since it is as well to have separate terms for existent things as different as the society and one of its organs, we apply the term 'State' more especially to the agents of the sovereign authority, and 'political society' to the complex group of which the State is the highest organ. This being granted, the principal duties under civic morals are obviously those the citizen has towards the State and, conversely, those the State owes to the individual. To understand what these duties are, we must first of all determine the nature and function of the State.

It is true it may seem that we have already answered the first question and that the nature of the State has been defined at the same time as the political society. Is not the State the supreme authority to which the political society as a whole is subordinate? But in fact this term 'authority' is pretty vague and needs definition. Where does the group of officials vested with this authority begin and end, and who constitutes, properly speaking, the State? The question is all the more called for, since current speech creates much confusion on the subject. Every day, we hear that public services are State services; the Law, the army, the Church — where there is a national Church — are held to form part of the State. But we must not confuse with the State itself the secondary organs in the immediate field of its control, which in relation to it are only executive. At very least, the groups or special groups (for the State is complex) to which these secondary groups (called more specifically administrative) are subordinate, must be distinguished from the State. The characteristic feature of the special groups is that they alone are entitled to think and to act instead of representing the society. The representations, like the solutions that are worked out in this special *milieu*, are inherently and of necessity collective. It is true, there are many representations and many collective decisions beyond those that take shape in this way. In every society there are or have been myths and dogmas, whenever the political society and the Church are one and the same, as well as historical and moral traditions: these make the representations common to all members of the society but are not in the special province of any one particular organ. There exist too at all times social currents wholly unconnected with the State, that draw the collectivity in this or that direction. Frequently it is a case of the State coming under their pressure, rather than itself giving the impulse to them. In this way a whole psychic life is diffused throughout the society. But it is a different one that has a fixed existence in the organ of government. It is here that this other psychic life develops and when in time it begins to have its effect on the rest of the society, it is only in a minor way and by repercussions. When a bill is carried in Parliament, when the government takes a decision within the limits of its competence, both actions, it is true, depend on the general state of social opinion, and on the society. Parliament and the government are in touch with the masses of the nation and the various impressions released by this contact have their effect in deciding them to take this course rather than that. But even if there be this one factor in their decision lying outside themselves, it is nonetheless true that it is they (Parliament and government) who make this decision and above all it expresses the particular *milieu* where it has its origin. It often happens, too, that there may even be discord between this *milieu* and the nation as a whole, and that decisions taken by the government or parliamentary vote may be valid for the whole community and yet do not square with the state of social opinion. So we may say that there is a collective psychic life, but this life is not diffused throughout the entire social body: although collective, it is localized in a specific organ. And this localization does not come about simply through concentration on a given point of a life having its origins outside this point. It is in part at this very point that it has its beginning. When the State takes thought and makes a decision, we must not say that it is the society that thinks and decides through the State, but that the State thinks and decides for it. It is not simply an instrument for canalizing and concentrating. It is, in a certain sense, the organizing centre of the secondary groups themselves.

Let us see how the State can be defined. It is a group of officials *sui generis*, within which representations and acts of volition involving the collectivity are worked out, although they are not the product of collectivity. It is not accurate to say that the State embodies the collective consciousness, for that goes beyond the State at every point. In the main, that consciousness is diffused: there is at all times a vast number of social sentiments and social states of mind (*états*) of all kinds, of which the State hears only a faint echo. The State is the centre only of a particular kind of consciousness, of one that is limited but higher, clearer and with a more vivid sense of itself. There is nothing so obscure and so indefinite as these collective representations that are spread throughout all societies — myths, religious or moral legends, and so on. . . . We do not know whence they come nor whither they are tending; we have never had them under examination. The representations that derive from the State are always more conscious of themselves, of their causes and their aims. These have been concerted in a way that is less obscured. The collective agency which plans them realizes better what it is about. There too, it is true, there is often a good deal of obscurity. The State, like the individual, is often mistaken as to the motives underlying its decisions, but whether its decisions be ill motivated or not, the main thing is that they should be motivated to some extent. There is always or at least usually a semblance of deliberation, an understanding of the circumstances as a whole that make the decision necessary, and it is precisely this inner organ of the State that is called upon to conduct these debates. Hence, we have these councils, these regulations, these assemblies, these debates that make it impossible for these kinds of representation to evolve except at a slow pace. To sum up, we can therefore say that the State is a special organ whose responsibility it is to work out certain representations which hold good for the collectivity. These representations are distinguished from the other collective representations by their higher degree of consciousness and reflection.

We may perhaps feel some surprise at finding excluded from this definition all idea of action or execution or achievement of plans outside the State. It is not generally held that this part of the State (at all events the part more precisely called the government), has the executive power? This view, however, is altogether out of place: the State does not execute anything. The council of ministers or the sovereign do not themselves take action any more than Parliament: they give the orders for action to be taken. They coordinate ideas and sentiments, from these they frame decisions and transmit these decisions to other agencies that carry them out: but that is the limit of their office. In this respect there is no difference between Parliament (or the deliberate assemblies of all kinds surrounding the sovereign or head of State) and the government in the exact meaning of the term, the power known as executive. This power is called executive because it is closest to the executive agencies, but it is not to be identified with them. The whole life of the State, in its true meaning, consists not in exterior action, in making changes, but in deliberation, that is, in representations. It is others, the administrative bodies of all kinds, who are in charge of carrying out the changes. The difference between them and the State is clear: this difference is parallel to that between the muscular system and the central nervous system. Strictly speaking, the State is the very organ of social thought. As things are, this thought is directed towards an aim that is practical, not speculative. The State, as a rule at least, does not think for the sake of thought or to build up doctrinal systems, but to guide collective conduct. Nonetheless, its principal function is to think.

But what is the direction of this thought? Or, in other words, what end does the State normally pursue and therefore should it pursue, in the social conditions of the present day? This is the question that still remains, and only when it has been solved can we understand what the citizen's duty is to the State and the State's to the citizen. Two conflicting solutions are usually given to this problem.

First, there is that known as individualistic, as expounded and defended by Spencer and the classical economists on the one hand and by Kant, Rousseau and the spiritualistic school on the other. The purpose of society, it is held, is the individual and for the sole reason that he is all that there is that is real in society. Since it is only an aggregate of individuals, it can have no other aim than the development of individuals. Indeed, by the very fact of the association, society makes human activity more productive in the realm of science, the arts and industry. Thanks to this greater yield, the individual finds more abundant nourishment, material and moral as well as for the intellect and so he thrives and develops. But the State is not of itself a producer. It adds nothing and can add nothing to this wealth of all kinds that the society stores up and that the individual benefits from. What then is the part it should play? The answer is, to ward off certain ill effects of the association. The individual in himself has from birth certain rights, by the sole fact that he exists. He is, says Spencer, a living being, therefore he has the right to live, the right not to be obstructed by any other individual in the regular functioning of his organism. He is, says Kant, a moral personality, by virtue of which he is endowed with a particular character that calls for respect, whether in his civil status or in that status known as natural. These inborn rights, in whatever way one may understand or explain them, are in some respects shaped by the association. Any person, in his dealings with me, by the very fact that we are in social intercourse, may either threaten my existence or obstruct the regular activity of my vital forces, or, to use the language of Kant, he may be lacking in the respect due to me or transgress in me the rights of the moral individual that I am. Therefore some agency must be assigned to the precise task of watching over the maintenance of these individual rights. For if the society can and should add something to what I hold by natural endowment (and held before ever society had any hand in founding such rights in my behalf), it must first of all prevent their being impinged upon: otherwise it has no further *raison d'être*. That is a minimum, to which the society need not confine itself, but below which it must not allow one to fall, even if it were to offer us some luxury in place of it, which could have no value if the necessity were lacking in whole or in part. Likewise, many thinkers, of divergent schools, have held that the prerogative of the State should be limited to administering a wholly negative justice. Its role was to be reduced more and more to preventing unlawful trespass of one individual on another and to maintain intact on behalf of each one the sphere to which he has a right solely because he is what he is. It is true they know well enough that in fact the functions of the State in the past were far more numerous. But they attribute this number of prerogatives to those conditions in which societies exist that have not reached a sufficiently high stage of civilization. In these the state of war is sometimes chronic, and always recurring. War, of course, leads to a disregard of individual rights. It demands severe discipline and this discipline in turn presupposes a strongly entrenched authority. It is from this source there comes the sovereign power over individuals that is so often lodged in the State. The State, on the strength of this authority, has intervened in fields which by their nature should remain alien to it. It controls religious beliefs, industry and so on by regulation. But this unwarranted spread of its influence can only be justified wherever war plays an important part in the life of a people. The more it retreats, the less often it occurs, the more possible and imperative it becomes to disarm the State. War has not yet entirely disappeared and there are still threats of international rivalry: so the State, even today, still has to preserve a measure of its former prerogatives. But here, in war, we have only something of an anomalous survival, and gradually the last traces of it are bound to be wiped out.

At the point we have reached, there is no need to refute this theory in detail. First, obviously, it does not agree with the facts. As we read on in history, we see the functions of the State multiplying as they increase in importance. This development of the functions is made materially perceptible by the parallel development of the organ itself. What a far cry from the instrument of government in a society such as our own to what it was in Rome or in a Red Indian tribe. In the one, a score of ministries with all their interlocking, side by side with huge assemblies whose very structure is infinitely complex, and over all, the head of State with his own particular administrative departments. In the other, a prince or a few magistrates, some counsellors aided by secretaries. The social brain, like the human brain, has grown in the course of evolution. And yet war during this time, except for some passing setbacks, has become more and more intermittent and less common. We should therefore consider as radically abnormal this theory of a progressive development of the State and the unbroken expansion of its functions, say, in the administration of justice; and given the continuity and regular course of this expansion throughout history, such a hypothesis is untenable. We should need supreme confidence in the force of our own dialectic to condemn as unhealthy such constant and general changes in the name of a particular system. There is not one State whose budget is not visibly becoming inflated. The economists see in this the deplorable result of a clear case of faulty reasoning and they moan over the prevailing blindness. It would perhaps be a better idea to consider a tendency so universally inevitable as regular and normal: always excepting, of course, certain passing excesses and abuses, which no one would deny.

Apart from this doctrine, it remains to say that the State has other aims and offices to fulfil than watching over individual rights. But here we are likely to be faced by a solution quite contrary to the one we have just been examining — one I might perhaps call the mystic solution. It is this that we find more systematically set out in the social theories of Hegel than elsewhere, at any rate in some respects. Seen from this point, it is argued that every society has an aim superior to individual aims and unrelated to them. It is held that the part of the State is to pursue the carrying out of this truly social aim, whilst the individual should be an instrument for putting into effect plans he has not made and that do not concern him. It is to the glory of the society, for its greatness and for its riches he has to labour: he has to find recompense for his pains in the sole fact that as a member of the society he has some sort of share in the benefits he has helped to win. He does receive some of the rays of this glory; a reflection of this splendour does spread to him and that is enough to hold his interest in the aims that lie beyond his reach. This argument deserves to hold our attention all the more because its interest is not solely speculative or historic; the existing confusion in ideas gives it strength and it is about to enjoy a kind of revival. Our own country, which has hitherto been deaf to this argument, now seems ready to welcome it. Since the old individual aims I have just set forth no longer suffice, there are those who throw themselves in despair back on the opposite faith and, renouncing the cult of the individual which was enough for our fathers, they try to revive the cult of the city-state in a new guise.

THE STATE[3]

Few words are employed with their meaning so ill-defined. Sometimes by 'the State' is meant political society in its entirety, sometimes only a part of that society. Even when the term is understood in the latter connotation, the limits determining the scope of its meaning vary in each case. It is commonly said that the Church, the army, the education system, and in short all the public services form part of the State. Yet then one mixes up two types of organization that are entirely different, namely the various administrations — judicial, military and educational — and the State proper. The bodies of engineers, teachers and judges are one element; the governmental councils, the deliberative assemblies, the ministries, the Council of Ministers, with their directly dependent bodies — these are something else. The State is properly the sum total of social entities that alone are qualified to speak and act in the name of society. When Parliament has passed a law, or the government has taken a decision within those councils over which it wields authority, the whole collectivity by this very fact is bound by them. As for the administrative bodies, these are secondary organs, subordinated to State action, but which do not constitute the State. Their function is to implement the decisions decreed by the State. In this way can be explained how the State and the body politic have become synonymous terms. It is indeed because, from the moment when political societies have reached a certain level of complexity, they can no longer act collectively save through the intervention of the State.

The utility of this kind of organism lies in the fact that it introduces an element of reflective thought into social life, and such thinking plays all the greater a role in it the more developed the State. Certainly the State does not create collective life, any more than the brain creates the life of the body and is the prime cause of the solidarity that unites the various functions within it. There can exist, and there do exist, political societies without a State. What effects their cohesion are the opinions and beliefs scattered among each individual consciousness, and which in an obscure fashion move them. Yet in that case such a mass of people is like a permanent crowd, and we know that the behaviour of crowds is characterized by being wholly unthinking. Various pressures surge up within it, and the most violent is the one that leads to action, even if it may be the most unreasonable. This is because among such crowds there exists no centre where all such blind tendencies to action may converge. It is such a centre that can call them to a halt, and resist their passing to action before they have been scrutinized, in order that intelligent commitment may be given to [their implementation] once the investigation has been completed.

This is precisely the role fulfilled by the State. When the State exists, the various motivations that can impel the anonymous crowd of individuals in divergent directions are no longer adequate to determine the collective consciousness, for this process of determination is the action of the State proper. But the reasons that conflicting parties put forward in favour of their opinions must be laid before the organs of government, which alone are qualified to decide. The different opinions at work within society are brought face to face [in opposition] with one another, and subjected to a comparative appraisal. Then either a choice is made, if one opinion should apparently prevail over the others, or else some fresh solution emerges from the confrontation. This is because the State is located at the central point where all will come together; because it can better take into account the complexity of situations and all the elements in them; because it is capable of perceiving matters that all the parties that seek to further them overlook; it is because it is [capable of] framing for us forms of behaviour preferable to all those that are being urged upon it in this way.

Thus the State is above all an organ of reflection. . . . It is intelligence substituted for an obscure instinct. From this springs the nature of the constitutions that [shape it]. All constitutions have as their purpose the stopping of action that is over-hasty and erroneous, so as to allow for discussion. This is why around the sovereign who represents the State we see progressively forming councils of ever increasing complexity, which formulate plans for action ... and where these must be submitted to prior discussion before assurance regarding them is given to the highest authority, which takes the final decision upon the action to be taken. This is why the councils are as far as possible constituted in such a way as to ensure that all the profusion of sentiments which divide the country can come together in them and be expressed and, consequently, be compared. It is on this condition that the parties. ... [break in text]

What now is the aim of the State? That consciousness that the State takes from society: on what is it, and should it, be employed?

Historically the action of the State can be very varied: one aspect is external, the other internal. The former is made up of manifestations of violence and aggression; the latter is essentially peaceful and moral.

The farther one goes back into the past, the more the former aspect appears to be preponderant. Then the principal task of the State was to increase the material power of a society, either by adding to its territory or by incorporating within it an ever-increasing number of citizens. The sovereign was above all the man whose gaze was turned outwards, and whose whole effort was directed to rolling back the frontiers or destroying neighbouring countries. A prince, whatever else he may be, is above all the military leader; the army is supremely the instrument of his activity and the organ of conquest. The causes that give rise to this manner of interpreting the duties of the State are not reducible merely to the economic difficulties with which lower societies struggle. Above all they relate to the conception that we form at the time of the State. It is represented as being reified. ...

It does not exist for the men whose actions it coordinates; it is there for its own sake. It is not the means whereby greater happiness or greater justice is intended to be realized; but it appears as the objective of all the efforts of individuals. From then on the aim in both private and public life is to make it as serious, as strong and as tranquil as possible.

But . . . although the State is charged with a military function it is . . . the organ of social justice. Through it is organized the moral life of the country. To the extent that there are written rights, law exists only in so far as it is desired and has been deliberated upon by the State. Now it is easily demonstrated that as progress takes place the more it can be seen that the internal functions of the State evolve much later than the external ones. . . . Whereas formerly military activity was almost unceasing, today a state of war has become the exception. On the contrary, it is judicial activity that has become almost continuous. The assemblies, the councils where laws are elaborated, never, so to speak, adjourn. In all ages we have seen the size of the legal codes grow progressively bulkier, which demonstrates that law has penetrated into spheres of social life from which it was formerly absent — and penetrates ever more deeply, subjecting to its activity all kinds of relationships that were once exempt from it. Thus we have seen develop progressively domestic, contractual, commercial and industrial law. This signifies [State intervention] in family life, and in contractual and economic relationships. And each one of these particular codes continues in the same manner to spread its influence ever more widely.

Furthermore, as history progresses we see that social relationships become increasingly more just, as at the same time the organs of the State develop. In order to demonstrate that the State has grown, becoming stronger uninterruptedly from the very beginnings of moral evolution, it is sufficient to compare the complex political organizations that are characteristic of the most civilized societies, their deliberative assemblies, the multiplicity of ministries, the councils that assist the ministries, the countless administrative bodies that are subject to them — compare all these with the rudimentary form that the State assumed in associative or primitive societies. Here there were a few magistrates, there a body of public officials and representatives that continued to grow. At the same time the place accorded to the . . . of justice becomes ever more important. Indeed the

progress of justice is measured by the degree of respect accorded
to the rights of the individual, because to be just is to grant to
everyone what he has the right to demand. Today it has become a
commonplace of history to state that the rights of the individual
are continually multiplying, assuming an increasingly social
character. Whereas originally the human person had no value,
today it is the supremely sacred thing. Any attack upon it brings
about the same result as did attacks directed against those
divinities favourable to believers in primitive religions. These
advances in justice and in the State are therefore possible because
the State is the civil organ of justice, but through . . . this
characteristic. . . . [break in text]

But how is it possible for it to play such a role? It suffices . . . to
represent to oneself what is the main source of injustice. It
springs from inequality; it therefore supposes that there exist in
society forces that are material or moral — no matter which —
that, because of their superiority, are capable of submitting
themselves to one another, having gone beyond the individual
rights that fall within their sphere of action: castes, classes,
corporations, coteries of all kinds, and all economic entities. In
our country the family can in certain respects be, and has often
been, a source of repression for the individual. To keep a rein on
all these inequalities, and on all the injustices that of necessity
ensue from them, there must thus be, rising above all these
secondary groupings, all these special forces in society, an equal
[sovereign] force of a higher order than all others and consequently
capable of containing them and curbing their excesses. That force
is the one possessed by the State. On the other hand, because of
its central function the State is [therefore] — more than any other
collective body — [fitted to] take account of the general needs of
life lived in common and prevent these being subordinated to
individual interests. Such are the most [real] causes of the great
moral role that it has played in history. This does not mean that it
can be sufficient for everything. It likewise needs to be contained
by the set of secondary forces that are subject to it. Otherwise,
like any other organ that has no check upon it, it develops out of
all proportion, becoming tyrannical and imposing itself unduly.
Nevertheless, in complex societies it is the necessary instrument

through which equality, and consequently justice, is attained.

Seen from this viewpoint many of the contradictions that are occasionally paraded before the public consciousness, and which disturb it, vanish. Thus occasionally the State has been [presented] as the antagonist of the individual, as if the rights of the one could only develop at the expense of the rights of the other, whereas they progress in parallel. The stronger, the more active the State becomes, the more the individual increases his liberty. It is the State that sets him free. Thus nothing is more harmful than to awaken in the child, and foster in the man, these feelings of mistrust and jealousy towards the State, as if it were the work of an individual, whereas it is the individual's natural protector, and indeed his only possible one.

From all these facts it emerges that the activity of the State has increasingly . . . a duty to be directed towards the law. It should concentrate on the law, [ensuring] that law that is aggressive and expansive should become peaceful, moral and scientific. Undoubtedly its military functions necessarily still remain; they are indispensable to ensure the existence of each individual, and consequently the moral existence of the country. They are no less than instinct subordinated to higher forces that surpass it. The State must therefore increasingly strive, not to base its glory on the conquest of new territories, which is always unjust, but to bring about the reign of greater justice in the society that it personifies. This is [a fact] of the greatest importance that cannot be impressed in too paternal a fashion upon the child. The prejudice must go that views public life as being constituted so that it is entirely directed towards and against what is foreign. On the contrary, for action outside one's country there is material rich enough . . . that must be organized for . . . ever more lofty functions. We must become aware of all there is to be accomplished in this domain, and see that we cannot exert too great an effort in order to realize the individual progress that is necessary.

ARISTOCRACY, DEMOCRACY AND MONARCHY[4]

The respective duties of State and citizen vary according to the particular form taken by a State. These forms are not the same in what is known as an aristocracy, a democracy or a monarchy. It is therefore of importance to know what these different forms represent and what the origin and basis are of the one that is becoming fairly general in European societies. It is only on these terms that we can understand the origin and basis of our civic duties of the present day.

Ever since the time of Aristotle, States have been classified according to the number of those who have a part in the government. 'When the people taken as a whole have sovereign power', says Montesquieu, 'it is a democracy. When the sovereign power is in the hands of a section of the people, it is called an aristocracy.'[5] The monarchic government is one in which a single individual governs. For Montesquieu, however, it is only a true monarchy if the king governs according to fixed and established laws. When, on the other hand, 'a single individual, without law or statutes, drives all before him by his will and his caprices,'[6] the monarchy takes the name of despotism. Thus, apart from this matter of there being a constitution or not in existence, it is by the number of those governing that Montesquieu defines the form of a State.

It is true that later on in his book, when he examines the sentiment that is the mainspring of each of these kinds of government, such as honour, valour or fear, he shows that he had a sense of the qualitative differences seen in these varying types of State. For him, however, these qualitative differences are only the result of the purely quantitative differences which we referred to in the first instance and he derives the qualitative from the quantitative. The nature of the sentiment that has to act as driving force for the collective activity is determined by the very number of those governing and so are all the details of organization.

But this way of defining various political forms is as common as it is superficial. To begin with, what are we to understand by 'the number of those governing'? Where does it begin and where end, this governmental organ whose varied forms are to determine the form of the State? Does this mean the aggregate of all those who are appointed to conduct the affairs in general of the country? But all these powers are never or almost never, concentrated in the hands of a single individual. Even though a ruler be absolute, he is always surrounded by advisers and ministers who share these functions for control by rule. Seen from this angle, there are only differences of degree between a monarchy and an aristocracy. A sovereign has always about him a host of officials and dignitaries often as powerful as himself or even more so. Should we consider for our purposes only the highest level of the government organ, the level where the supreme powers are concentrated? I mean those powers which — to use the old term of political theory — appertain to the sovereign. Is it the head of State alone whom we have in mind? In that case, we should have to keep distinct the State with a single head, the State with a council of individuals and the State where everyone takes a hand. By this reckoning, seventeenth-century France, for example, and a centralized republic like our own present-day France or the United States, would all come under the same heading and would all alike be classed as monarchies. In all these instances there is a single individual at the summit of the monarchy with its officials, and it is his title alone that varies according to the society.

On the other hand, what are we to understand by the words 'to govern'? To govern, it is true, means to exercise a positive control over the course of public affairs. In this respect, a democracy may not be distinguishable from an aristocracy. Indeed, very often, it is the will of the majority that shapes the law, without the views of the minority having the slightest influence. A majority can be as oppressive as a caste. It may even very well happen that the minority is not represented at all in the government councils. Remember, too, that in any case, women, children and adolescents — all those who are prevented from voting for one reason or another — are kept off the electoral lists. The result is that the lists in fact comprise only the minority of the nation. And since those elected represent only the majority in these constituencies, they represent in fact a minority of the minority. In France, out of a population of 38 million, there were in 1893 only 10 million electors; out of these 10 million, 7 million alone made use of their voting rights, and the deputies elected by these 7 million represented only 4,592,000 votes. Taking the whole electorate, 5,930,000 voters were not represented, that is to say, a greater number of voters than those who had returned the deputies elected. Thus, if we confine ourselves to numbers, we have to admit that there has never been a democracy. At the very most we might say — to show where it differs from an aristocracy — that under an aristocratic system the governing minority are established once and for all, whereas in a democracy, the minority that carries the day may be beaten tomorrow and replaced by another. The difference, then, between them is only slight.

Apart from this rather dialectic treatment, there is one historical fact that throws some light on how inadequate these ordinary definitions are.

These definitions would indeed have us approximate types of States that lie, so to speak, at the opposite extremes of evolution. In fact we give the name democracy to those societies where everyone has a share in directing communal life and the word exactly suits the most inferior forms of political society known to us. This description applies to the structure that the English call tribal. A tribe is made up of a certain number of clans. Each clan is ruled by the group itself; when there is a chieftain, his powers are without much force, and the confederation is ruled by a council of representatives. In some respects it is the same system as our own. This resemblance has given weight to the argument that democracy is essentially archaic as a form of society and that an attempt to establish it in present-day societies would be throwing civilization back to its primitive beginnings and reversing the course of history. It is these lines of thought that are sometimes used to draw a parallel between socialist planning and the economic life of communism in the ancient world, in order to demonstrate its alleged futility. We must recognize that in both cases the conclusion would be justified if the postulate were right, that is, if the two forms of social structure here assumed to be the same, were in very fact identical. True, there is no form of government to which the same criticism might not apply, at least, if we confine ourselves to the foregoing definitions. Monarchy is hardly less archaic than democracy. Very often clans or federated tribes were brought together under the hand of an absolute ruler. The monarchy in Athens and in Rome came before the republic, in time. All these ambiguities are merely a proof that the various types of State should be defined in some other way.

To find an appropriate definition, let us look back to what has been said of the nature of the State in general. The State, we said, is the organ of social thought. That does not mean that all social thought springs from the State. But there are two kinds. One comes from the collective mass of society and is diffused throughout that mass; it is made up of those sentiments, ideals, beliefs that the society has worked out collectively and with time, and that are strewn in the consciousness of each one. The other is worked out in the special organ called the State or government. The two are closely related. The vaguely diffused sentiments that float about the whole expanse of society affect the decisions made by the State, and conversely, those decisions made by the State, the ideas expounded in the Chamber, the speeches made there and the measures agreed upon by the ministries, all have an echo in the whole of the society and modify the ideas strewn there. Granted that this action and reaction are a reality, there are even so two very different forms of collective psychic life. The one is diffused, the other has a structure and is centralized. The one, because of this diffusion, stays in the half-light of the sub-conscious. We cannot with certainty account for all these collective preconceptions we are subject to from childhood, all these currents of public opinion that form here and there and sway us this way and that. There is nothing deliberately thought out in all this activity. There is something spontaneous, automatic, something unconsidered, about this whole form of life. Deliberation and reflection, on the other hand, are features of all that goes on in the organ of government. This is truly an organ of reflection: although still in a rudimentary stage, it has a future of progressive development. There all is organized and, above all, organized increasingly to prevent changes being made without due consideration. The debates in the assemblies — a process analogous to thought in the individual — have the precise object of keeping minds very clear and forcing them to become aware of the motives that sway them this way or that and to account for what they are doing. There is something childish in the reproaches directed at deliberative assemblies as institutions. They are the sole instruments that the collectivity has to prevent any action that is unconsidered or automatic or blind. Therefore there exists the same contrast between the psychic life diffused throughout society and the parallel life concentrated and worked out especially in governmental organs, as exists between the diffused psychic life of the individual and his clear consciousness. Within every one of us, then, there is at all times a host of ideas, tendencies and habits that act upon us without our knowing exactly how or wherefore. To us they are hardly perceptible and we are unable to make out their differences properly. They lie in the subconscious. They do, however, affect our conduct and there are even individuals who are moved solely by these motives. But in the part of us that is reflective there is something more. The ego that it is, the conscious personality that it represents, does not allow itself to follow in the wake of all the obscure currents that may form in the depths of our being. We react against these currents; we wish to act with full knowledge of the facts, and it is for this reason that we reflect and deliberate. Thus, in the centre of our consciousness, there is an inner circle upon which we attempt to concentrate light. We are more clearly aware of what is going on there, at least of what is going on in the underlying regions. This central and relatively clear consciousness stands to the nameless and indistinct representations that form the substratum of our mind, as does the scattered collective consciousness of the society to the consciousness lying in the government. Once we have grasped what the special features of this consciousness are and that it is not merely a reflexion of the obscure collective consciousness, the difference between the various forms taken by the State is easily recognized.

And so we perceive that this government consciousness may be concentrated in the organs that have rather limited scope, or again, may be spread through the society as a whole. Where the government organ is jealously guarded from the eyes of the many, all that happens within it remains unknown. The dense mass of society receives the effect of its actions without taking part, even at a distance, in its discussions and without perceiving the motives that decide those who govern on the measures they decree. As a result, what we have called the government consciousness remains strictly localized in these particular spheres, that are never very extensive. But it sometimes happens that these, as it were, watertight bulkheads that separate this particular *milieu* from the rest of the society are less impervious. It does occur that a great deal of the action taken in this *milieu* is done in the full light of day and that the debates there may be so conducted as to be heard by all. Then, everyone is able to realize the problems set and the circumstances of the setting and the at least apparent reasons that determine the decisions made. In this case, the ideas, sentiments, decisions, worked out within the governmental organs do not remain locked away there; this whole psychic life, so long as it frees itself, has a chain of reactions throughout the country. Every one is thus able to share in this consciousness *sui generis* and asks himself the questions those governing ask themselves; every one ponders them, or is able to. Then, by a natural reversal, all the scattered reflections that ensue in this way, react on the governmental thought which was their source. From the moment that the people set themselves the same questions as the State, the State, in solving them, can no longer disregard what the people are thinking. It must be taken into account. Hence the need for a measure of consultation, regular or periodic. It is not because the custom of such consultations had become established that governmental life was communicated the more to the citizens, taken as a whole. It is because such communication had previously become established of itself that these consultations became imperative. And the fact that has given rise to such communication is that the State has ceased more and more to be what it was over a long era; that is, a kind of mysterious being to whom the ordinary man dared not lift his eyes and whom he even, more often than not, represented to himself as a religious symbol. The representatives of the State bore the stamp of a sacred character and, as such, were set apart from the commonalty. But by the gradual flow of ideas the State has little by little lost this kind of transcendence that isolated it within itself. It drew nearer to men and men came to meet it. Communications became closer and thus, by degrees, this circuit — just described — was set up. The governmental power, instead of remaining withdrawn within itself, penetrated down into the deep layers of the society, there received a new turn of elaboration and returned to its point of departure. All that happens in the *milieux* called political is observed and checked by every one, and the result of this observing and checking and of the reflections they provoke, reacts on the government *milieu*. By these signs we recognize one of the distinctive features of what is usually called democracy.

We must therefore not say that democracy is the political form of a society governing itself, in which the government is spread throughout the *milieu* of the nation. Such a definition is a contradiction in terms. It would be almost as if we said that democracy is a political society without a State. In fact, the State is nothing if it is not an organ distinct from the rest of society. If the State is everywhere, it is nowhere. The State comes into existence by a process of concentration that detaches a certain group of individuals from the collective mass. In that group the social thought is subjected to elaboration of a special kind and reaches a very high degree of clarity. Where there is no such concentration and where the social thought remains entirely diffused, it also remains obscure and the distinctive feature of the political society will be lacking. Nevertheless, communications between this especial organ and the other social organs may be either close or less close, either continuous or intermittent. Certainly in this respect there can only be differences of degree. There is no State with such absolute power that those governing will sever all contact with the mass of its subjects. Still, the differences of degree may be of significance, and they increase in the exterior sense with the existence or non-existence of certain institutions intended to establish the contact, or according to the institutions' being either more or less rudimentary or more or less developed in character. It is these institutions that enable the people to follow the working of government (national assembly — parliament, official journals, education intended to equip the citizen to one day carry out his duties — and so on) and also to communicate the result of their reflections (organs for rights of franchise or electoral machinery) to the organs of government, directly or indirectly. But what we have to decline at all costs is to admit a concept which (by eliminating the State entirely) opens a wide door to criticism. In this sense, democracy is just what we see when societies were first taking shape. If every one is to govern, it means in fact that there is no government. It is collective sentiments, diffused, vague and obscure as they may be, that sway the people. No clear thought of any kind governs the life of peoples. Societies of this description are like individuals whose actions are prompted by routine alone and by preconception. This means they could not be put forward as representing a definite stage in progress: rather, they are a starting point. If we agree to reserve the name 'democracy' for political societies, it must not be applied to tribes without definite form, which so far have no claim to being a State and are not political societies. The difference, then, is quite wide, in spite of apparent likeness. It is true that in both cases — and this gives the likeness — the whole society takes part in public life but they do this in very different ways. The difference lies in the fact that in one case there is a State and in the other there is none.

This primary feature, however, is not enough. There is another, inseparable from it. In societies where it is narrowly localized, the government consciousness has, too, only a limited number of objects within its range. This part of public consciousness that is clear is entirely enclosed within a little group of individuals and it is in itself also only of small compass. There are all sorts of customs, traditions and rules which work automatically without the State itself being aware of it and which therefore are beyond its action. In a society such as the monarchy of the seventeenth century the number of things on which government deliberations have any bearing is very small. The whole question of religion was outside its province and along with religion, every kind of collective prejudice and bias: any absolute power would soon have come to grief if it had attempted to destroy them. Nowadays, on the other hand, we do not admit there is anything in public organization lying beyond the arm of the State. In principle, we lay down that everything may for ever remain open to question, that everything may be examined, and that in so far as decisions have to be taken, we are not tied to the past. The State has really a far greater sphere of influence nowadays than in other times, because the sphere of the clear consciousness has widened. All those obscure sentiments which are diffuse by nature, the many habits acquired, resist any change precisely because they are obscure. What cannot be seen is not easily modified. All these states of mind shift, steal away, cannot be grasped, precisely because they are in the shadows. On the other hand, the more the light penetrates the depths of social life, the more can changes be introduced. This is why those of cultivated mind, who are conscious of themselves, can change more easily and more profoundly than those of uncultivated mind. Then there is another feature of democratic societies. They are more malleable and more flexible, and this advantage they owe to the government consciousness, that in widening has come to hold more and more objects. By the same token, resistance is far more sharply defined in societies that have been unorganized from the start, or pseudo-democracies. They have wholly yielded to the yoke of tradition. Switzerland, and the Scandinavian countries, too, are a good example of this resistance.

To sum up, there is not, strictly speaking, any inherent difference between the various forms of government; but they all lie intermediate between two contrasting schemes. At one extreme, the government consciousness is as isolated as possible from the rest of the society and has a minimum range.

A difficulty comes perhaps in distinguishing between the two kinds of society, aristocratic and monarchic. The closer communication becomes between the government consciousness and the rest of society, and the more this consciousness expands and the more things it takes in, the more democratic the character of the society will be. The concept of democracy is best seen in the extension of this consciousness to its maximum and it is this process that determines the communication.

STATE AND SOCIETY IN RUSSIA: REVIEW OF P. MILIOUKOV,
ESSAIS SUR L'HISTOIRE DE LA CIVILISATION RUSSE (PARIS, 1901)[7]

What is peculiar about the social organization of Russia is that it is entirely the creation of the State. Among the Western peoples of Europe, the State, on the other hand, has resulted from the spontaneous development of society. Political organization has been formed gradually under the influence of the economic, demographic and moral conditions prevailing in a country. The historical process has developed upwards, from the bottom to the top. In Russia it has occurred in the reverse order. The State was organized there before society, and it is the State that has organized society. It was the political structure that determined the social structure.

The base of the construction was constituted by the peasant class. By itself the rural population of Russia formed a kind of enormous mass, homogeneous, amorphous and lacking consistency. It was distributed over a certain number of territories, but the bonds that united the inhabitants to the prince that owned the territory were all personal, temporary, and almost of a contractual nature. Every subject could leave his master if he so wished, going off to place himself under the protection of a neighbouring prince. The population was therefore not fixed in any way. In the midst of 'this fluid element' the first solid nucleus that was formed was the Muscovite State. It was the first stable, well-defined grouping. It was this State that tried to fix, incorporate and organize the inconsistent matter upon which its action was exerted.

It was needs of an external and military nature that gave rise to it and developed it. To combat the Tartar Oulous on the one hand, and the Lithuanians on the other, the Muscovite princes 'became military organizers in the style of the Turkish conquerors'. This first seed, once planted, grew of its own accord. Conquests engendered conquests. For this to occur it was necessary to enlarge the army and improve its techniques, the activity of government being almost exclusively employed to this end.

However, in order to satisfy these needs it was indispensable not to leave the Russian population in the inchoate, anarchical condition in which it was, for a great army cannot exist if the State's financial resources are not regularly assured it. Thus the Tsars were led to organize the country. But this organization only arose to meet military and fiscal needs, and consequently bears the imprint of the causes that determined it.

Thus it was in order to regulate the collection of taxes that the State consolidated the *mir*. This commune grouping was charged collectively, and from then on had an interest in exerting pressure upon its members so as to prevent their leaving and going off to establish themselves elsewhere, for the departure of one member increased the burden for others. In this way the population lost its primitive mobility. More generally, the administrative districts were exclusively fiscal districts. Again, in the same way social classes were formed. The nobility was not constituted spontaneously. It was the State that created it by granting those subjects that owed a duty of military service certain privileges (the right to ownership of their lands and of the peasants that occupied them).

Thus the Russian State is not a product of society, but on the contrary is external to it. It is from the outside that the State has always sought to act upon that society. The analogy will be noticed between this situation and that in the Chinese State, to which we drew attention last year.[8] But then a question is posed: what has been the extent and the real penetration of the action exerted in Russia upon society by the State? Has it made an impact upon the mental make-up of the populations, or has it merely succeeded in modifying the external patterns of life without reaching down into that life itself? To this question the interesting work we are analysing gives no answer. However, from many indications it appears that the State's effect is superficial and rootless. Because the political organization does not express the moral constitution of the country it has hardly been able to affect it profoundly. In all likelihood there has been a mere superposition, as in China. Thus there exists a species of State of a certain generality that is characterized by the kind of externality in which it is placed in relation to the underlying social life.

POLITICAL GEOGRAPHY: REVIEW OF FRIEDRICH RATZEL,
POLITISCHE GEOGRAPHIE (MUNICH AND LEIPZIG, 1897)[9]

The object of this important work is to constitute political geography as a science and more particularly even, as a social science.

Ratzel is even not far off the mark in seeing it as the most fundamental of all the social sciences. Already in his *Staat und sein Boden*, analysed here [in the *Année sociologique*] last year, he had attempted to establish that the geographical factor had a preponderant influence over the whole of social evolution, and his entire argument is reproduced in the first part of the present work. We shall not go over it in detail, particularly since the general considerations on which it rests are somewhat too simplistic in their sociology. According to the author, the members of a society are allegedly so many autonomous units in themselves, capable of being self-sufficient. Thus no other permanent links exists between them save that which attaches them to the common soil on which they live. Consequently the soil is the predominant *vinculum sociale* (*Das stoffliche Zusammenhängende am Staat ist nur der Boden*), and it assumes this character even more when the individualization of the parts is more prominent. But neither psychology nor sociology allow us any longer to attribute such a degree of autonomy to the individual. The human personality, at whatever moment in history we observe it, has nothing absolute about it. Each individual consciousness is directly attached to all others by bonds that lack any territorial origin, and yet are utterly primordial.

Nevertheless, for political geography to become a science it is not at all necessary for territory to play such a key role in the genesis of social facts. What would be much more important would be to determine, with the utmost possible exactness, the object of this science and the methods that render it possible. It is to be regretted that Ratzel did not expressly deal with this question. It is true that he states the task of political geography as to study the relationships of the State with the earth. But the expression is very vague and fails to delimit clearly a field of research. For in what do these relationships consist? By what signs can we recognize them? However, from the work as a whole the reader gleans a notion of geography that, we believe, can be formulated as follows.

There is no political society that does not occupy an area of the earth whose size and form have been determined: this is the territory of the State (*Staatsgebiet*). This domain is not simply a thing or set of things exterior to the State, and which it owns: it is an integrating element in collective life, so much so that each State can be characterized by its territorial form. But these various forms are perpetually in evolution. They extend and contract; their contours are modified, just as is their internal arrangement, at different moments in history. To seek out the laws of this evolution, the conditions on which depend the various elements of the territorial factor and the functions they fulfil in society — this must be the object of political geography. Conceived of in this way, the research system designated by this term ceases to be what it has too often been, a simple descriptive inventory of political or administrative divisions, and becomes a veritable explanatory science. Its object is everything in public life that is capable of being expressed in territorial terms. But it proposes not merely to expound the facts, defined in this way, as they are, once they have been fixed, but it undertakes to account for them, namely, to link the variations that occur in them to the causes that explain them.

Such an explanation can naturally only be attempted by means of broad comparisons, including the most varied forms of human groupings, from the most rudimentary and most primitive to the most recent and most advanced, for there are none that cannot be instructive. Here, as in the other life sciences, it is very often the embryo types that on occasion shed the most light. Thus political geography will not be limited to a consideration of the most civilized states in their perfected form: it will go back to the lowest types of political establishments. By comparing those societies that are best constituted it will succeed in determining the laws of their geographical evolution. And in fact it is on comparison of this kind that the deductions of Ratzel rely. He refers back to the geography of ancient peoples or the most savage tribes as well as to that of the great European States.

This evolution consists of a double process. The one relates to the State that rolls back or contracts the limits of the territory over which it is sovereign, depending on whether it is progressing of falling into decay. The other relates to the effect of transforming that territory so as to harmonize it with that collective life of which it is the substratum. The relationships of the State with the earth are in fact of two kinds: the State's action reaches out, to a greater or a lesser extent, over a portion of the globe, and, on the other hand, it holds fast to that portion of the globe through links that are close, or less so. Two States of the same size can be dependent in differing degrees upon their geographical base, according to whether their activity is superficial or, on the contrary, is deeply involved in the nature of the soil. An agricultural people, for example, is more strongly attached to it than is a purely commercial or military nation. The fortresses that stand at the frontier, the roads, canals and constructions of all kinds are so many links that attach the State to its territory. The more a society leaves its mark upon the soil, the more of itself it also puts into it, and the less easily, in consequence, can it disengage itself. The first process is therefore one extension (*Ausbreitung*) the second a process of consolidation (*Befestigung*), or implantation. They are so different that they differ in their organs. The first process has as its essential agent the State itself, the political power; the second has the mass of society. Doubtless the moment comes when the State itself cooperates in this implantation. But the first artisans of this transformation are individuals who spread themselves slowly and silently over the territory, cultivating it and shaping it in every possible way. The action of the State comes only afterwards.

This distinction is fundamental to the doctrine of Ratzel, and recurs in the most diverse forms. It is at the root of the clear-cut antithesis that he establishes between nomadic and settled peoples. Nomadism is in fact the condition of societies where the territorial bond is the least active, since nomads change their territory with extreme ease. And since at the same time they need vast spaces over which to move, the two processes are here in inverse.

relationship to each other. The same contrast is to be found between agricultural civilization and military civilization, with commercial civilization in the middle. However, no matter how different these two processes may be, they never occur separately from each other, nor in an absolutely pure state. On the contrary, they are continually overlapping. As soon as the State has grown, it feels the need to assimilate its conquests and consolidate them. As soon as this work of consolidation has begun, a tendency to expand even farther makes itself felt again. Moreover, the two movements continue in parallel throughout history. The most civilized societies are the most extensive that exist, and at the same time they penetrate more deeply down into their territory than do all others.

Having described this evolution in its general aspect in the first three parts of the book, Ratzel reviews in succession the principal geographical factors, with the aim of determining what role they play in it.

I The situation (die Lage)

The situation of a country is the totality of relationships that the place where the country is situated sustains with other places on the earth. To a certain extent this naturally varies according to the spatial area (*der Raum*), for what changes perceptibly the size of a society changes also its situation, since it does not maintain the same relationships with other regions. However, these two geographical elements must be distinguished from each other. The proof is that France, for example, has seen the dimensions of its territory vary extremely considerably during the course of its existence, and in many different ways, although it has always remained in the same situation between the North Sea, the Atlantic, the Alps and the Mediterranean.

In certain respects even spatial size depends upon the situation. Depending on whether a society is well, or less well situated, it is either in a better or a worse position to seize neighbouring areas. The advantage that it derives from its favourable situation means that the surrounding territories are naturally drawn into its sphere of action. On the other hand it is in the northern hemisphere that are to be found the largest stretches of land. Thus the northern States, by the very nature of things, have at their disposal spaces that are vaster than those of the southern peoples. Already from this can be seen the great importance of situation, for States develop more easily the more dry land they have available. Furthermore, the less water there is, the less the land surfaces are divided from one another, and consequently the more closely peoples are in contact with one another. And the closeness of this contact is a social factor of the first order. Situation still plays an essential role by the very fact that it determines the climates, and climate affects the organization of societies. Finally, on the situation depend the distances that separate the various parts of the land, and the effect of one region upon another varies according to whether they are more or less distant from one another. In this way the central situation of Asia, placed between Europe, Africa and America, facilitated the spread of Asian civilization over the rest of the world and thus contributed to making this continent the cradle of humanity.

But what is still more important are the very different effects brought about by the situation, depending on whether it is central or peripheral. Countries situated on the periphery of continents are to be found, it follows from this fact, close to the sea. And the proximity of the sea is an advantage of the highest value that makes those spots so located centres of attraction and crystallization. In fact, by means of the sea a people can communicate freely with the most diverse peoples and can fan out in all directions; conversely, it can be a recipient of the most varied kinds of influence and share in every kind of civilization. Thus there is no position that favours so greatly the rapid progress of human culture. On the other hand, a country relegated to inland territories is obliged to fall back upon itself and live in a kind of isolation. Therefore peripheral locations are initially the ones most sought after. It was on the edge of the seas that the first States were founded, and particularly the first ones to flourish. It is there that for preference conquerors establish themselves, and to there also that populations naturally flock. Hence the Mediterranean character of ancient civilization. It was all along the Mediterranean coast that it developed, progressing regularly from east to west. When it ceased to be exclusively Mediterranean, it was toward the shores of ocean that it was carried (Iberian peninsula, Gaul, Great Britain).

II Space

But a State whose centre of gravity is situated on the periphery of a continent in this way can only expand over a limited space. What characterizes the most recent societies is an ambition for space that nothing appears capable of satisfying. Size is increasingly a condition of survival for peoples. Modern civilization could not therefore remain on the periphery. This is why lands in the interior have acquired much more value than in former times. Only there are to be found the spaces necessary for great expansion. This also is what partly makes the situation critical for Europe as compared with other continents. The more dry land there is, the more room there is for great societies, and Europe is more poorly provided with it than America. In Europe States are tightly packed together and are obliged to seek in other parts of the globe the territory they lack.

The importance assumed by this factor derives from a multiplicity of causes. The vaster the dimensions of a society, the greater the diversity of elements it includes, and consequently of the sources on which its collective life is fed. At the same time the different natural forces (plains, waterways, etc.) are naturally of larger dimensions than elsewhere. The strength of resistance of the social organism is increased still further by the very fact that its vital parts, being more situated in the interior, are so to speak less exposed and less liable to external attack. Finally the size of territory even acts upon the spirit of a nation. In every people there is a certain sense of space (*Raumsinn*), a certain way of conceiving it, which is not without its influence upon its history, and which varies according to whether the space effectively occupied is more extensive, or less so. For a small society the world stops a little beyond its frontiers; it has no interest in all that is more distant because its forces cannot reach out so far. On the other hand, the horizon recedes in proportion to the extent of the territory. Men learn better how to represent to themselves vast spaces by the very fact that they already have large spaces at their disposal. Their conception of the universe expands. This enlarged conception is the necessary condition for great undertakings. The privilege of great geniuses lies precisely in going beyond the representation that is made of space by their average contemporaries.

However, this does not mean that small countries henceforth lack all reasons for existence. Not only do they occasionally succeed in maintaining their position beside the most extensive societies, thanks to a combination of exceptionally favourable circumstances, but population complexes only slight in extent have, and will have at all times, a useful function to fulfil. By the very fact of their limited dimensions the social forces concentrated in them, finding themselves more closely and constantly in touch with one another, act and react upon one another with more consistency and energy. The effect of this is rapidly to raise social life to a high level of intensity. This is what brought about the precocious maturity of the Greco-Roman cities. This is still the role that is generally fulfilled by towns in our contemporary societies. They are the result of a concentration that they reinforce. They appear at the spots where several social currents, commercial or otherwise, intersect, and they are the product of this intersection. But at the same time, by enclosing within definite, compact limits the elements from which they are formed, they increase the vitality of the whole. Ratzel is thus led to give a few glimpses of the nature of urban groupings and their functions.

Finally, as the earth acquires its social value only through the population spread over its surface and through the way in which it is adapted to the needs of collective life, particularly in exchange, the author includes in this study of the spatial factor two chapters — one on population density and its distribution, the other on the means of communication.

III Frontiers

Frontiers are represented on maps as mathematical, fixed lines.

But this representation is a mere symbolical abstraction. Far from being something immobile and dead, the frontier is the result of the clash between two impulsions. It arises from the fact that the activity of a people, its natural move to expand, comes up against the contrary activity of a neighbouring people, or the resistance that is proffered to it by an inert environment, unsuitable for social life (the sea, the desert, etc.) Also, because it has for its origin one or more impulsions, it is itself in a state of perpetual mobility. Despite all treaties, a people does not halt once and for all at the precise point assigned to it by diplomats. The inner forces that constitute its life are constantly advancing or retreating, according to whether they are increasing or decreasing, and the real frontier does likewise. For the same reason it does not really consist of a line, but of a zone whose extent can be large, or less so. This is because it corresponds to the fact that the meeting of two bodies, whether they are social or not, gives rise to phenomena at the periphery that are very different from those that occur in inland areas in both. These phenomena require a certain space in which to develop. It is this space that is the true frontier. Thus it is because it is something that is living that it possesses extensiveness, and is continually in the process of being transformed. Even the above does not highlight all the movements that play a role in the genesis of a frontier. As well as this tendency to isolation that impels people in contact with one another to withdraw into themselves, there is also a tendency to mingle together, to become involved with one another, to carry out exchanges. The frontier is a compromise between these two opposing tendencies. Whilst it separates, it serves also as a crossing point. It is even the frontier zone that originally alone existed. It consists of a deserted space that the tribe leaves uninhabited and unexploited around it, and which leaves a void between it and the neighbouring tribes. It is only as the value of territory becomes better appreciated that a society extends to the extreme limit it can reach, namely, to the point where it encounters another society. Thus the frontier zone diminishes in size and, with the need to determine it acting as a spur, one arrives at the abstract concept of a linear frontier.

There are features on the surface of the globe that cause

physical life to stop at certain points on the terrestrial crust without its being able to extend further or at least without being able to extend in a continuous fashion. This is independent of the influences that human groups can exert. Thus physical life was powerless to extend beyond the North Cape, even when men had not yet reached it. The life that develops on one slope of the Alps does not link up with that which develops on the opposite slope. Thus between northern and southern Europe there is a separation that would be as it is even if the continent were not inhabited. The same features can also constitute an obstacle to the expansion of social life and establish a discontinuity between human groupings, just as between the manifestations of physical life. When in this way there is coincidence between political frontiers and these natural limits it may be said of the frontiers that they are also *natural*. The effect of a frontier of this kind is therefore necessarily to create a gap between peoples that is more or less absolute, since its characteristic is to render the earth uninhabitable, no matter where it is located. Thus the perfect natural frontier is to be found only at the extreme limits of the inhabitable earth, since everywhere else the obstacles that militate against the expansion of societies are only relative and provisional. Within these limits there are no natural frontiers that are completely uncrossable, over which peoples cannot succeed in joining up with one another. Hence the author concludes that the social value of natural frontiers is secondary and has been too much exaggerated.

Conceived of in this way, the political frontier is a real social organ. It is a peripheral one. Closely linked to everything that occurs within society, it reflects everything that happens within it. It advances or recedes according to whether the society is growing or diminishing. At spots where social forces bear down with particular intensity, we see it make a dent in the neighbouring frontiers and, on the contrary, grow weaker where life is less strong, etc. It is all these movements that determine the territorial form of the State. Finally, like all organs, it has its functions — protection and exchanges with foreign nations, etc. with whom special arrangements are necessary.

We shall not speak about the other geographical factors that are treated in the rest of this work. The author studies successively, and always from the same standpoint, those features of the earth that serve as a transition between the land and the sea (the coasts, peninsulas, islands, the world of the water, seas, rivers, etc., and finally the mountains and the plains). The foregoing will suffice to indicate what is the spirit of the book.

However rich in insights and comparisons of all kinds it may be, what must above all be retained from the book is the general conception. We have been able to assure ourselves that it is indeed a question of constituting a new science. Undoubtedly political geography is no new invention. But of all the branches of geography it was perhaps the most neglected until the most recent years. Above all, there was no other branch of it that appeared less conducive to a truly scientific formulation. A mere inventory of facts, it narrated, but did not explain anything. Ratzel aspires to discovering real laws. His undertaking is therefore one of great importance and, although he has his predecessors, his originality remains considerable. It is especially interesting for us to see how those disciplines once most removed from sociology are progressively drawing closer to it. Thus there is a dual movement, which is equally necessary: sociology is compelled to leave the realm of generalities in which up to now it has rooted itself, so as to enter into contact with the specialist sciences (this is what we are working at here). And the specialist sciences are of their own accord increasingly tending to enter into contact with sociology and take on a sociological form. Ratzel, an eminent geographer, would doubtless not refuse his designation as a sociologist.

Thus understood, political geography appears in one sense to be a branch of — and even another name for what we have called — social morphology, since it deals with the territorial forms that society assumes. However, the conceptualization that Ratzel makes of it is still very vague and indeterminate. We pointed out this indeterminateness at the outset, but we must come back to it. The author wavers between two very different conceptions. First he seems clearly to propose that the object of political geography should be the forms that societies acquire for themselves as they settle upon the earth — and this is social morphology proper.

Then he assigns as its aim the determination of the effect that the material features of the earth (rivers, mountains, seas, etc.) have on the political development of peoples. Yet there can be nothing more distinct. Indeed what imparts to one society one form or another, what causes frontiers to be equipped with fortresses, or whether societies are definite or not, whether the means of communication are more numerous or less so, the urban groupings more, or less important, the territory more vast, or less so — these are social causes, and consequently of a moral order. So are also the state of economic progress, the unequal capacity of religious ideas to spread themselves over broad surfaces, etc. It is possible that the facts of physical geography have also some part in it, but they are only one of the causes that contribute to bringing about the phenomena studied. On the contrary, they become the essential and almost the sole cause that one takes into consideration if one sets oneself the exclusive object of investigating how they affect the development of the State. The author clearly adopts the first point of view when he is studying political frontiers and their evolution, the system of exchange, and social density, etc. Moreover, as he goes along he does not fail to invoke causes that are entirely non-geographical. However, at the same time what demonstrates that the second point of view preoccupies him, even predominantly, is that he sees the earth as the basis of all collective life, the bond that unites men. By this he means the earth as it exists naturally, before any social institutions arise, since social institutions are held to find in this their prime condition for existence. Furthermore, one has only to read the titles of the chapters about rivers and seas, etc. This ambiguity does not exist without engendering a confusion that upsets the reader.

Likewise the method might be reproached for its insufficient rigour. The comparisons are made up of illustrations rather than methodical comparisons. The contrary facts are rarely examined and, however rich the scholarship of the author, one cannot fail to be struck by the gap that exists between a number of his assertions and the proofs on which they rest. But these are imperfections inherent in any science at its beginnings.

2

Democracy and Political Representation

The absence of corporative institutions . . . creates in the organization of a society like ours a void whose importance it is difficult to exaggerate. What is lacking is a complete system of agencies necessary to the functioning of social life. This structural defect is evidently not a localized failure, limited to one part of society; it is a malady *totius substantiae*, affecting the whole organism. Consequently, any attempt to put an end to it cannot fail to produce the most far-reaching consequences. It is the general health of the social body which is in question here.

That does not mean to say, however, that the corporation is a sort of panacea for everything. The crisis which we are experiencing is not to be traced to any one specific cause. In order to overcome it, it is not enough to establish some sort of regulation where it is needed. This regulation must be just. Now, as we shall say further on 'as long as there are rich and poor at birth, there cannot be just contract,' nor an equitable distribution of social goods. But while corporative reform must be accompanied by other reforms, it is the primary condition for these others to be effective. Let us imagine that the primordial state of ideal justice were achieved; let us suppose that men enter life in a state of perfect economic equality, which is to say, that wealth has completely ceased to be hereditary. The problems with which we are now struggling would not thereby be solved. Evidently there will always be an economic apparatus, and various agencies cooperating in its functioning. It will still be necessary to determine their rights and duties for each form of industry. In each occupation a body of rules will have to be established which fix the quantity of work expected, equitable rates of payment for different workers, their duties toward each other and toward the community, etc. We shall face a *tabula rasa*, just as now. Because wealth will not be inherited any longer, as it is today, it does not follow that the state of anarchy will disappear, for it is not a question of the ownership of wealth, but of the regulation of the activity to which this wealth gives rise. It will not regulate itself by magic, as soon as it is necessary, if the forces which can generate this regulation have not been previously aroused and organized. . . .

Since a body of rules is the specific form which is assumed by spontaneously established relations between social functions in the course of time, we can say, *a priori*, that the state of anomie is impossible wherever interdependent organs are sufficiently in contact and sufficiently extensive. If they are close to each other, they are readily aware, in every situation, of the need which they have of one another, and consequently they have an active and permanent feeling of mutual dependence. For the same reason that exchanges take place among them easily, they take place frequently; being habitual, they regularize themselves accordingly, and in time become consolidated. As the smallest reaction is transmitted from one part to another, the rules which are thus created express this directly: that is to say, they embody and fix, in detail, the conditions of equilibrium. But if, on the other hand, they are not clearly visible to each other, then only stimuli of a certain intensity can be communicated from one organ to another. The relationships being infrequent, they are not repeated often enough to become fixed; they must be established anew each time. The channels cut by the streams of movement cannot deepen because the streams themselves are too intermittent. If a few rules, at least, do come into existence, they are nevertheless too abstract and diffuse, for under these conditions it is only the most general outline of the phenomena that can become fixed. The same thing will be the case if the contiguity, although sufficient, is too recent or has not existed for long enough.

In a general way, this condition is realized in the nature of things. A function can be divided between two or several parts of an organism only if these parts are fairly close to each other. Moreover, once labour is divided, since these elements are dependent upon one another, they naturally tend to lessen the distance separating them. That is why as one goes up the evolutionary scale, one sees organs coming together, and, as Spencer says, being introduced in the spaces between one another. But, in unusual circumstances, a different situation can be brought about.

This is what happens in the cases we are discussing. In so far as the segmental type is strongly marked, there are nearly as many economic markets as there are different segments. Consequently, each of them is very limited. Producers, being near consumers, can easily calculate the range of needs to be satisfied. Equilibrium is established without any difficulty and production regulates itself. On the other hand, as the organized type develops, the fusion of different segments draws the markets together into a single market which embraces almost all society. This even extends further, and tends to become universal, for the frontiers which separate peoples break down at the same time as those which separate the segments of each of them. The result is that each industry produces for consumers spread over the whole surface of the country or even of the entire world. Here the contact is broken; the producer can no longer take in the market at a glance, or even conceptualize it. He can no longer have an idea of its limits, since it is, so to speak, limitless. Accordingly, production becomes unchecked and unregulated. It can only operate haphazardly, and in the course of these gropings, it is inevitable that it will be out of proportion, either in one direction or the other. From this come the crises which periodically dislocate economic life. The growth of local, restricted crises — or business failures — is in all likelihood an effect of the same cause.

As the market extends, large-scale industry appears. This has the effect of changing the relations between employers and workers. An increasing fatigue of the nervous system joined to the contagious influence of large concentrations of population increase the needs of the workers. Machines replace men; manufacturing replaces hand-work. The worker is regimented, separated from his family throughout the day. He always lives apart from his employer, etc. These new conditions of industrial life naturally demand a new organization, but as these changes have been accomplished with extreme rapidity, the interests in conflict have not yet had the time to become equilibrated. . . .

An occupational activity can be effectively regulated only by a group close enough to it to know how it operates, what its needs are, and how it is likely to change. The only one that meets all these conditions is the one which might be formed by all the agents of the same industry united and organized into a single body. This is what we call the 'corporation' or 'occupational group'.

Now, in the economic order, the occupational group does not exist any more than occupational ethics. Since the eighteenth century suppressed the old corporations, *not without reason*, only fragmentary and inadequate attempts have been made to reestablish them upon new foundations. To be sure, individuals working at the same trade have contacts with one another, because of their similar occupation. Their very competition puts them in relationship. But these relationships are not permanent; they depend upon chance meetings, and have, very often, an entirely personal aspect. A particular industrial worker is found in contact with a colleague; this does not result from the industrial body of this or that speciality united for common action. In rare cases, the members of the same occupation come together as a group to discuss some question of general interest, but these meetings are only temporary. They do not survive the particular circumstances which bring them into being, and consequently the collective life which they stimulate more or less disappears with them.

The only groups which have a certain permanence today are the unions, composed of either employers or workmen. Certainly there is here the beginning of occupational organization, but still quite formless and rudimentary. For, first, a union is a private association, without legal authority, and consequently without any regulatory power. Moreover, the number of unions is theoretically limitless, even within the same industrial category; and as each of them is independent of the others, if they do not federate or unify there is nothing intrinsic in them expressing the unity of the occupation in its entirety. Finally, not only are the employers' unions and the employees' unions distinct from each other, which is *legitimate and necessary*, but there is no regular contact between them. There exists no common organization which brings them together, where they can develop common forms of regulation which will determine the relationships between them in an authoritative fashion, without either of them losing their own autonomy. Consequently, it is always the rule of the strongest which settles conflicts, and the state of war is continuous. Save for those of their actions which are governed by common moral codes, employers and workers are, in relation to each other, in the same situation as two autonomous States, but of unequal power. They can form contracts, as nations do through the medium of their governments, but these contracts express only the respective state of their military forces. They sanction it as a condition of reality; they cannot make it legally valid.

In order to establish occupational morality and law in the different economic occupations, the corporation, instead of remaining a diffuse, disorganized aggregate, must become — or rather, must again become — a defined, organized group; in a word, a public institution. . . .

What the experience of the past proves, above all, is that the framework of the occupational group must always be related to the framework of economic life: it is because of this dislocation that the corporative regime disappeared. Since the market, formerly localized in the town, has become national and international, the corporation must expand to the same degree. Instead of being limited only to the artisans within one town, it must grow in such a way as to include all the members of the occupation throughout the country, for in whatever area they are found, whether they live in the town or country, they are all interdependent, and participate in a common activity. Since this common activity is, in certain respects, independent of any territorial basis, the appropriate agency must be created that expresses and stabilizes its operation. Because of the extensiveness of those dimensions, such an agency would necessarily be in direct contact with the central agency of collective life; for events which are important enough to interest a whole category of industrial enterprises in a country necessarily have very general implications, which the State cannot ignore. This leads it to intervene. Thus, it is not without reason that royal power tended instinctively not to allow large-scale industry to operate outside its control when it first appeared. It was impossible for it not to be concerned with a form of activity which, by its very nature, can always be capable of influencing the whole of society. But while this regulatory action is necessary, it must not degenerate into direct subordination, as happened in the seventeenth and eighteenth centuries. The two related agencies must remain distinct and autonomous; each of them has its function, which it alone can execute. While the function of formulating general principles of industrial legislation belongs to the governmental assemblies, they are not able to diversify them according to the different forms of industry. It is this diversification which is the proper task of the corporation. This unitary organization, representing the whole country, in no way excludes the formation of secondary agencies, comprising workers of the same region or locality, whose role would be to further specify the occupational regulation demanded by local or regional conditions. Economic life would thus be regulated and determined without losing any of its diversity.

For that very reason, the corporative system would be preserved from the tendency towards stagnation that it has often been criticized for in the past, for this was a defect rooted in the narrowly communal character of the corporation. As long as it was limited to the town, it was inevitable that it become a prisoner of tradition, like the town itself. In so restricted a group the conditions of life are almost invariable, habit has complete control over people and things, and anything new comes to be feared. The traditionalism of the corporations was thus only an aspect of the traditionalism of the local community, and showed the same properties. Once it had become ingrained in the mores, it survived the factors which had produced and originally justified it. This is why, when the material and moral centralization of the country, and large-scale industry which followed from it, had opened up new wants, awakened new deeds, introduced into tastes and fashions a changeability heretofore unknown, the corporation, which was obstinately attached to its established customs, was unable to satisfy these new demands. But national corporations, in virtue of their dimension and complexity, would not be exposed to this danger. Too many different men would be involved to lead to a situation of unchanging uniformity. In a group formed of numerous and varied elements, new combinations are always being produced. There would then be nothing rigid about such an organization, and it would consequently be adapted to the changing equilibrium of needs and ideas.

INDIVIDUALISM AND POLITICAL FREEDOM[2]

The condemnation of individualism has been facilitated by its confusion with the narrow utilitarianism and utilitarian egoism of Spencer and the economists. But this is very facile. It is not hard, to be sure, to denounce as a shallow ideal that narrow commercialism which reduces society to nothing more than a vast apparatus of production and exchange; and it is perfectly clear that all social life would be impossible if there did not exist interests superior to the interests of individuals. It is wholly correct that such doctrines should be treated as anarchical, and we fully agree with this view. But what is unacceptable is that this individualism should be presented as the only one that there is, or even could be. Quite the contrary; it is becoming increasingly rare and exceptional. The practical philosophy of Spencer is of such moral poverty that it now has hardly any supporters. As for the economists, even if they once allowed themselves to be seduced by the simplicity of this theory, they have for a long time now felt the need to modify the severity of their primitive orthodoxy and to open their minds to more generous sentiments. M. de Molinari is almost alone, in France, in remaining intractable and I am not aware that he has exercised a significant influence on the ideas of our time. Indeed, if individualism had not other representatives, it would be quite pointless to move heaven and earth in this way to combat an enemy who is in the process of quietly dying a natural death.

However, there exists another individualism over which it is less easy to triumph. It has been upheld for a century by the great majority of thinkers: it is the individualism of Kant and Rousseau and the spiritualists, that which the Declaration of the Rights of Man sought, more or less successfully, to translate into formulae, which is now taught in our schools and which has become the basis of our moral catechism. It is true that it has been thought possible to attack this individualism by reference to the first type; but the two are fundamentally different, and the criticisms which apply to the one could not be appropriate to the other. It is so far from making personal interest the aim of human conduct that it sees personal motives as the very source of evil. According to Kant, I am only certain of acting properly if the motives that influence me relate, not to the particular circumstances in which I am placed, but to my equality as a man *in abstracto*. Conversely, my action is wrong when it cannot be justified logically except by reference to the situation I happen to be in and my social condition, class or caste interests, my emotions, etc. Hence immoral conduct is to be recognised by the sign that it is closely linked to the individuality of the agent and cannot be universalised without manifest absurdity. Similarly, if Rousseau sees the general will, which is the basis of the social contract, as infallible, as the authentic expression of perfect justice, this is because it is a resultant of the totality of particular wills; consequently it constitutes a kind of impersonal average from which all individual considerations have been eliminated, since, being distinct from and even antagonistic to one another, they are neutralised and cancel each other out. Thus, for both these thinkers, the only modes of conduct that are moral are those which are applicable to all men equally: that is to say, which are implied in the notion of man in general.

This is indeed far removed from that apotheosis of pleasure and private interest, the egoistic cult of the self for which utilitarian individualism has validly been criticised. Quite the contrary: according to these moralists, duty consists in turning our attention from what concerns us personally, from all that relates to our empirical individuality, so as to pursue solely that which is demanded by our human condition, that which we hold in common with all our fellow men. This ideal goes so far beyond the limit of utilitarian ends that it appears to those who aspire to it as having a religious character. The human person, by reference to the definition of which good must be distinguished from evil, is considered as sacred, in what can be called the ritual sense of the word. It has something of that transcendental majesty which the churches of all times have accorded to their gods. It is conceived as being invested with that mysterious property which creates a vacuum about holy objects, which keeps them away from profane contacts and which separates them from ordinary life. And it is exactly this characteristic which confers the respect of which it is the object. Whoever makes an attempt on a man's life, on a man's liberty, on a man's honour, inspires us with a feeling of revulsion, in every way comparable to that which the believer experiences when he sees his idol profaned. Such a morality is therefore not simply a hygienic discipline or a wise principle of economy. It is a religion of which man is, at the same time, both believer and god.

But this religion is individualistic, since it has man as its object; man is, by definition, an individual. Indeed there is no system whose individualism is more uncompromising. Nowhere are the rights of man affirmed more energetically, since the individual is here placed on the level of sacrosanct objects; nowhere is he more jealously protected from external encroachments, whatever their source.

A verbal similarity has made possible the belief that *individualism* necessarily resulted from *individual*, and thus egoistic, sentiments. In reality, the religion of the individual is a social institution like all known religions. It is society which provides us with this ideal as the only common end which is today able to offer a focus for men's wills. To remove this ideal, without replacing it with any other, is therefore to plunge us into that very moral anarchy which it is sought to avoid.

Nonetheless we must not consider as perfect and definitive the formula with which the eighteenth century gave expression to individualism, a formula which we have made the mistake of maintaining in an almost unchanged form. Although it was adequate a century ago, it today needs to be enlarged and completed. It presented individualism only in its most negative aspect. Our forerunners were concerned solely with freeing the individual from the political shackles which hampered his development. Thus they regarded freedom of thought, freedom to write, and freedom to vote as the primary values that it was necessary to achieve — and this emancipation was indeed the precondition of all subsequent progress. However, carried away by the enthusiasm of the struggle, and concerned only with the objective they pursued, in the end they no longer saw beyond it, and made into something of an ultimate goal what was merely the next stage in their efforts. Now, political freedom is a means, not an end. It is worth no more than the manner in which it is put to use. If it does not serve something which exists beyond it, it is not merely fruitless, it becomes dangerous. If those who handle this weapon do not know how to use it in productive struggles, they will not be slow in turning it against themselves.

It is precisely for this reason that it has fallen today into a certain discredit. Men of my generation recall how great our enthusiasm was when, twenty years ago, we finally succeeded in toppling the last barriers which we impatiently confronted. But alas, disenchantment came quickly; for we soon had to admit that no one knew what use should be made of this freedom that had been so laboriously achieved. Those to whom we owed it only made use of it in internecine conflicts. And it was from that moment that one felt the growth in the country of this current of gloom and despondency, which became stronger with each day that passed, the ultimate result of which must inevitably be to break the spirit of those least able to resist.

Thus, we can no longer subscribe to this negative ideal. We must go beyond what has been achieved, if only to preserve it. Indeed, if we do not learn to put to use the means of action that we have in our hands, it is inevitable that they will become less effective. Let us therefore use our freedoms to discover what must be done and in order to do it. Let us use them to soften the functioning of the social machine, still so harsh to individuals, so as to put at their disposal all possible means for the free development of their faculties in order finally to progress towards making a reality of the famous precept: to each according to his works!

THE CONSTITUTION ACCORDING TO PLATO, ARISTOTLE AND MACHIAVELLI: REVIEW OF W. LUTOSLAWSKI, *ERHALTUNG UND UNTERGANG DER STAATSVERFASSUNGEN NACH PLATO, ARISTOTELES UND MACHIAVELLI* (BRESLAU, 1888)[3]

This little work is made up of two parts. In the first part the author expounds and discusses the theory of Aristotle concerning revolutions. In the second he compares it to the corresponding theories of Plato and Machiavelli.

Two questions dominate the whole of Aristotle's doctrine: how do revolutions arise, and how can they be prevented? In other words, what causes constitutions to perish? What causes them to last?

To resolve these two related questions, Aristotle works out a veritable psychology of the revolutionary spirit. We need not reproduce here the details of that delicate analysis, which Lutoslawski has summarized very methodically and clearly. Let us come immediately to the conclusions that he draws from his exposition and to the way that he interprets and evaluates Aristotelian theory.

Firstly, concerning method, it seems to the author that, contrary to prevailing opinion, Aristotle, as in his *Politics* generally, proceeded deductively in this matter. According to this interpretation, the facts cited in the work in abundance are there only as examples, and it is a mistake to see in them the integrating elements in a scientific induction. The whole political doctrine of Aristotle is stated to consist solely of a deduction made from his psychology, logic and ethics. He is alleged to have proposed exclusively to construct the plan for the ideal State from elements borrowed from these three disciplines. If the author does not confine himself to these purely ideological speculations, if moreover he analyses carefully the other types of political constitution met with in the course of history, if he describes the particular revolutions to which each one has been exposed, it is because in his view the wise political scientist must not only know how to construct a new constitution *ab initio*, but how to make use of existing ones, after improving them. In order to do this one must know them, and consequently it is not possible to leave them out of account. Yet if for practical purposes experience cannot be omitted, the pure science, the theory, cannot be discovered by the induction of historical facts. It can only be obtained through 'an immediate knowledge of the motives for all actions, through a sensitive and developed consciousness.' Thuriot had already pointed out the very misunderstood character of Aristotelian politics. Lutoslawski takes up the same idea, stressing it even more, and concluding that Aristotle's method in his *Politics* is purely *a priori*. Moreover, he does not make this out to be a criminal matter. On the contrary, he believes that it is a substitute for scholarship, and can suffice for everything. As we shall see, he has practised it himself. We cannot indulge in a merely incidental discussion of such an important assertion. We can readily believe that what has been called the experimental spirit of Aristotle has occasionally been exaggerated and misunderstood. Aristotle is essentially a metaphysicist and remains one in the social and moral sciences. But it is also really extravagant to make him out to be a pure *a priori* thinker, particularly in political science. When, as he does, one declares so firmly that society predates the individual, when one has such a strong feeling for the reality of the social being, and of its individual character, which is *sui generis*, one cannot admit that social facts are simply transformed psychological ones, or that sociology is a deduction from and an application of psychology. In brief, all we mean is that the procedures and method of Aristotle are too complex and too personal to be defined by words as simple and vague as induction or deduction.

Since Aristotle's theory has no other basis than the knowledge of the human spirit in general, one should expect that it could be applied to all countries and all ages. However, the author acknowledges that this is not the case at all, and that it could not be fitted to the types of society that exist at present. In fact, today there exists not a single one of the constitutions that Aristotle analysed. The constitutional monarchy and the republic are phenomena entirely different from the democracy, oligarchy or aristocracy described by Aristotle. However, one should not think because of this that the political science of Aristotle is false and inapplicable to our times. The difference between the societies distinguished by Aristotle and contemporary societies is not so profound as at first sight it may seem. The former societies are no less than the blueprints for the latter, which can be deduced from them. To construct them it suffices to take as a basis the societies described by Aristotle and to modify them, so as to make them conform to the great new phenomenon that separates modern times from Antiquity. That phenomenon was the abolition of slavery. Whilst slavery is characteristic of small ancient societies, the liberty and equality of citizens are the distinctive hallmark of the great contemporary societies. If one takes this new fact into account one will understand how the constitutions of Antiquity have been transformed so as to become what they are.

Through this example one can see that the author's sociology is somewhat superficial. Thus all the changes that have come about in social life since the disappearance of the Greco-Roman world would allegedly have no other cause than the abolition of slavery. The explanation is extremely simplistic, and the method no less so. A few brief pages suffice for the author to deduce the series of transformations through which societies have successively passed, and to state their causes. The example of Aristotle that is invoked is not enough to legitimize such a rapid process.

Having brought out the *a priori* tendencies of Aristotle, Lutoslawski is led naturally to compare more than has normally been done the political science of Aristotle with that of Plato. In particular, on the question of revolutions he juxtaposes a certain number of important propositions taken from these two authors, and from this parallel it would seem to emerge that the disciple owes more to his master than he would care to admit. It is indeed true that Aristotle was the first to establish a theory of revolution, but he found the elements and subject-matter in Plato.

The work concludes with a comparison of the same kind between Aristotle and Machiavelli. A fair number of comparisons tend to demonstrate that there are many points where these two political doctrines coincide. Should one conclude from this that Aristotle's book was truly a source for Machiavelli? Despite what Ranke has stated, nothing is less likely, for in *The Prince* are to be found none of the historical examples met with so frequently in the *Politics*, and which Machiavelli would certainly have used if he had had them before him. The author therefore supposes that Aristotelian political science had, before Machiavelli, already been elaborated and set out in a derivative work, which alone was available to the Italian philosopher.

Summing up, there is to be found in this book, which is methodically planned and clearly written, an historical exposition that is very worthy of our attention. But the sociological views that are interspersed with it are not of equivalent merit.

SOCIAL PROPERTY AND DEMOCRACY: REVIEW OF
ALFRED FOUILLEE, *LA PROPRIETE SOCIALE ET LA DEMOCRATIE*
(PARIS, 1884)[4]

Through all the revolutions in his thought Fouillée remains faithful to his method of conciliation. Opposites have something that attract this refined dialectician, whose lively mind nowhere finds itself so perfectly at ease than amid the conflict of systems. Where we perceive only contradictory doctrines, between which we must resolutely choose, Fouillée sees merely exaggerated opinions, but which complement each other and even suppose the other's existence. Thus he has successively combined in scholarly synthesis determinism and freedom, idealism and realism, Rousseau's morality and modern sociology. This time it is individualism and socialism that he has undertaken to reconcile.

I

Personal property is naturally not only advisable for reasons of self-interest, but has its rational basis; it is the very law of life. With the individual the living cell must find sustenance for the force that it expends in movement. Otherwise it exhausts itself and dies. Similarly, under pain of death the labour of the social cell must sooner or later be returned to him, and in equivalent form. Thus if there somewhere exists an object entirely created by one man, it wholly belongs to him. This much may be conceded to individualism. But absolute ownership, without reservation or restriction, is not thereby justified, for of our own strength alone we can create nothing. We produce only forms, and all our efforts are applied to matter supplied by nature. This resource is not our handiwork; why then should we own it in perpetuity? The reply is made that natural riches lack all value so long as they are not made fecund by human labour. But what would human labour produce if it were wasted in the void? Moreover, one finds it very difficult to admit that fertile land has neither more nor less value than barren land, or that 'a pond full of fish has neither more nor less value than a pond in which fish cannot live'. And even if this inordinate thesis were proved, one would still have to acknowledge that in each product, beyond the labour of the individual, is to be found a certain quantum of social labour. If a great highway is constructed to pass in front of my house, it immediately doubles in value. I have not given any more of my effort, I have merely profited from the labour of others. By what right? And this fact is not an exception selected for the necessities of proof. If we search within ourselves for what we owe only to ourselves the sum is quickly totalled; our personal baggage does not weigh very heavily. The physical person is commonly represented as a kind of impregnable island, where the individual reigns as sovereign, from which he emerges only if he so desires, into which one penetrates only with his permission. This is why the individualist holds nothing more dear than the capacity to protect himself against any encroachment upon that proud independence. In vain his efforts. Whilst he withdraws into himself so as to escape from any kind of influence, there infiltrates within the environment in which he moves, the air he breathes, the society surrounding him. It stamps its mark upon him, kneading and fashioning him without his seeing or feeling it, and above all without his having cause for complaint, for it is in this way that is shaped the best part of himself.

Thus in all property, beyond the share belonging to the individual, there is that of nature and the nation. Orthodox economics is wrong not to acknowledge this cooperation. Yet for similar reasons socialism is no less false. If the individual does not do everything, it is through him that all is done. He has undoubtedly numerous ancillaries, but he is the essential agent of production. Production will not flourish unless he is stimulated to produce. In vain the soil may be fertile, the people intelligent, science in a state of progress. If nothing comes to set in motion that last but indispensable lever, individual activity, not one jot of value will be created and all these riches of nature and the intelligence will be as if they did not exist. But socialism turns society into an army of civil servants on more or less fixed salary. From then on each worker, having no longer any interest in his task, will perform it only in mechanical fashion. Exactness, but not zeal can be required of him. Absorbed into society, he will feel of too little consequence to dare to undertake anything. What use is it to wear himself out in efforts that, anonymous and unseen, will be lost in that enormous mass of the State? The State is moreover too massive a machine for all these operations, very delicate as they are. How could it adapt production to the thousand adjustments in demand? How could it fix the value of objects and the share to be allocated to each individual?

But if the State is not everything we must not conclude that it is nothing. It should not do everything, but it should not let everything be done. It has economic functions and set obligations. If it cannot itself produce or distribute wealth, it can at least, and must, regulate the circulation of wealth. Its duty is to watch over the well-being of society. But in every living creature the equilibrium of forces, the just balance between the parts is the condition for health. It is therefore wrong that here wealth should abound, there be absent, and the State must erect obstacles in the path of such a monstrous inequality. To do this, what measures are appropriate for it to take? According to circumstances, this is what will be decided by the wisdom of governments. However, the author believes he can point to some reforms that appear to him to be useful and practical at this present time. If the rent paid for real estate cannot be abolished, the profit accruing from it could at least be reserved for the State — namely, everybody. Towns could buy back wholly or in part the lands on which they are built, the State could enlarge its domains. This *ager publicus* could not be exploited by the community but would be divided up into lots leased out for a hundred or a hundred and fifty years. After a few generations society would repossess its property, whose value would have increased, and it would benefit itself from the additional value. It is true that there is another form of revenue against which the State is less well armed, that from capital. But here the evil is disappearing spontaneously; returns on it are tending more and more to decrease. An improved taxation base would furthermore allow the nation to recover the share in these profits that is legitimately its own. Finally, the State could easily increase its income by strict legislation regulating property very severely and restricting to close relatives natural inheritance arising from the absence of a will.

This collective wealth might 'constitute a fund of universal assistance and insurance, a sort of Lake Moeris that, having received the overflow, could in case of need provide what is necessary'. This is because for the State charity is a strict duty of justice; it is one of the tacit clauses of the social contract. Society can only require respect in its acquisition of property if it ensures for everyone some means of existence. It is true that it will be objected that philanthropy is exercised in the reverse manner to selection, and runs counter to its salutary efforts. It is said that it protects the weak and incapable, allowing them to perpetuate themselves, and thus gradually lowers the physical and moral level of the race. But again a distinction must be drawn. There can be no question of letting die without assistance a worker that a chance illness deprives of his strength. Thus it is only from the sickly that society should withhold pity. But these are very, very few in number, scarcely marry, and in any case legal barriers could be placed upon their marriage. Thus public charity has no serious disadvantages; on the contrary, it affords great and serious advantages. It lessens the excesses of inequality among men; it often preserves the life of intellects that are valuable; finally, and above all, it acts as an excellent mentor for the soul, which it opens up to sympathy and pity.

II

But material power is not the only kind in which the masses wish to have a share. Political power constitutes a kind of social fund whose distribution must be regulated. This problem is everywhere tending to have a similar solution. Everywhere democracy, with universal suffrage, which distributes this collective capital equally between everybody, is carrying the day. The nations are being swept along on a broad democratic current that it would be absurd to seek to resist. Moreover, although one may agree not to make universal suffrage an absolute dogma, it can be justified for good and solid reasons. Society is made up of free individuals: universal suffrage allows a common life, without infringing on that freedom. Society is an association, a kind of joint-stock company in which all concerned should be consulted concerning the management of the undertaking. Universal suffrage is merely the exercise of that right. Finally, society is an organism that must know itself in order to steer its course: universal suffrage is the best means at the nation's disposal for becoming aware of itself. 'By the vote, it might be said, all the cells of the body politic are called upon to play their part in intellectual and voluntary life, and in some respects to become conscious, directing cells like those of the brain.' At the time of voting the elector fulfils a function; he represents the entire nation.

Unfortunately, like all things that are relative, universal suffrage is full of contradictions: contradiction between the majority and the minority, contradiction between the quantity and quality of the votes. Education alone can smooth out these antagonisms. The majority must be instructed so as to learn modesty and moderation. To reconcile numbers with intelligence, education must become widespread. Everyone can participate in political power without endangering it, when everyone has his share of that other collective good, intellectual capital.

However, we must never lose sight of what is the goal of public education. It is not a matter of training workers for the factory or clerks for the warehouse, but citizens for society. The teaching must therefore consist essentially of moral instruction — to sever minds from selfish views and material interests, to replace a vanishing religious piety by a kind of social piety. But it is neither by the rule of three nor by Archimedes' principle that one will ever inculcate morality in the masses. Only aesthetic culture can act in so profound a fashion upon the human spirit. Under the influence of art minds are lifted up, hearts are warmed and soften, becoming thus more accessible to one another and consequently more fitted for life in common. Thus even in the primary school it is appropriate to initiate the child into the love of the beautiful. However, this purely literary education plainly cannot suffice. In addition the future citizen must be equipped with exact notions of politics and social economics. In secondary education the teaching will have to become still broader and more liberal. Instead of that mishmash of knowledge with which we clutter up the memory of our pupils nowadays, we should make increasing room for the philosophy of the sciences, the arts and history, and above all for social and political philosophy. Finally, it would be timely to create a higher form of civic education. In our university faculties there should be established chairs for the teaching of the social sciences. In this respect Germany has been ahead of us for a long time, and yet public opinion, because with us it is more powerful, has a greater need to be enlightened in this way.

III

From this exposition one can see the infinite variety of questions touched upon in this little book. All those problems that today preoccupy the public consciousness are treated in succession, and this with a rare independence of mind. Economists of the orthodox school have as their ideal a cult that is sometimes superstitious: liberty has become for them a kind of idol, to which they willingly sacrifice all else. Fouillée does not hold this exclusive faith. He most certainly cares deeply about liberty, but he also believes that social life would not be the worse if it were more regulated and balanced. He has great confidence in individual initiative, but it seems to him that things would not go any the worse if we produced less and loved one another more. He recognizes that the individual must belong to himself and make of himself what he will. But he does not forget that children need education and discipline, and that men are too often merely grown-up, naughty children. In short, unless one relies a great deal upon Providence, as Bastiat did, it seems difficult to him for there miraculously to emerge a harmony of interests from the spontaneous interplay of individual egoisms.

Everything has already been said about the charm that his brilliant dialectic imparts to Fouillée's books. He advances not a single step without an opponent arising and a fight being launched. A gleam like the flash of swords passes before our eyes, and then everything ends in reconciliation. But this procedure is not a mere dramatic device for our author; it is above all a scientific method. According to him it is the best means of forestalling opinions that exclude all others, as well as absolute judgements. Indeed the sociologist cannot mistrust simple solutions enough, for no mind is sufficiently powerful to encompass in its gaze the infinite complexity of social events. But neither must it be forgotten that the wealth of detail, the variety of forms, the diversity of colours nowhere precludes the unity of the whole. When the reality becomes more complex that unity only becomes more skilfully articulated. Far from disappearing, it is among superior individuals that it manifests itself most brilliantly. What above all is to be feared are not so much absolute principles but arid, dry ideas, immutable as the rocks, incapable of living and evolving. A system of thought is intended to represent a system of things. It must therefore be alive, as ideas are, growing and developing as do living creatures. This is why the system must arise from a seed, namely, an idea of simple origin, but one that gradually divides up and differentiates itself, awakening life around it, bearing along in its precipitant wake those ideas and facts that fall within its sphere of action, becoming organized and fully constituted, until it arrives at a state of equilibrium, which however can never be anything other than temporary.

Nevertheless it is somewhat difficult to reconcile this economic eclecticism with the theory that Fouillée so strongly upheld in his *Science sociale contemporaine*. In this he acknowledged the organic character of society; from there he was, it appears to me, logically led to socialism. It is true that Spencer denies that this is the consequence that follows from his doctrine. He remains faithful to the old English liberalism, but this is through a contradiction that is the radical defect in his latest works. For the individualist, society is a meeting of autonomous beings, equal in freedom, exchanging their services between one another, but without ever depending upon one another. It is therefore a mechanical assemblage and not a living organism. But, states Spencer, the animal brain never intervenes in the internal life and merely directs those organs charged with linking up with others. The socialists do not ask either that the brain of the nation, that is, the State, the government proper, should itself direct production or the distribution of values: they merely desire that the great social functions should be unified and centralized, just as are the corresponding animal functions. In the body there is only one digestive system, only one circulation system. The blood globules do not belong to some privileged cells, but to all without distinction. The same should hold good for wealth, the blood that nourishes society. In vain does Fouillée invoke the conscious and voluntary character of the social organism. What does that matter? Socialism also will be voluntary and conscious. Only authoritarian communism believes that one can do without reflective thinking and free consent, which it replaces by constraint.

Fouillée, it is true, seems to admit that by definition all socialism is despotic, the enemy of liberty and individual initiative. In support of this accusation he cites on several occasions Schaeffle and his monograph on the quintessence of socialism. But it is not in that little book, destined as propaganda, that one must look for the economic theories of Schaeffle. It is in his *Gesellschaftliches System der menschlichen Wirtschaft* and in the third volume of *Bau und Leben des sozialen Körpers*. In the latter work Schaeffle rejects with horror a State that would aspire to, and absorb within itself, all the activity of a nation, one in which the mass of citizens would be no more than pliable, docile clay in the hands of an all-powerful government. Such a conception appears to him as monstrous as that of an organism in which, in order to circulate round the body, the blood would ask for instructions from the brain, or in which the stomach would digest to order. But that is not socialism. It is only excessive administrative centralization, and Schaeffle denounces it himself, not as a coming evil that must be foreseen and prevented, but as a present evil from which we must cure ourselves. At every occasion he repeats that collective life cannot be created ready-made by a decree imposed from on high. It is a resultant force, the repercussions within a common centre of those millions of elementary lives that vibrate scattered throughout the organism. He wishes to coordinate them, not stifle them. Undoubtedly in his system the individual preserves no other property save that of the means of consumption. But he remains the essential mainspring of economic evolution. He it is who, by making known his needs to governing bodies, which take cognizance of them, regulates production accordingly. He it is who chooses the kind of work he likes. Finally, it is he again who determines its value. Indeed Schaeffle attempts to show how the current value of products can vary according to needs and follow the fluctuations in demand. Thus he undertakes to resolve a serious question that his monograph left unanswered. This is not the time to expound or discuss his doctrine. But so long as it has not been answered, one has no right to say that socialism has been refuted.

As for the remedies propounded by Fouillée, we believe them to be scarcely effective. If land is a monopoly, it will not change in nature by becoming more easily transferable. It will not be more equitably distributed because it circulates more rapidly, or less so. One would still need to place people in a position to be able to take their fair share. But would society at least profit from the amounts of value added? Unfortunately the yearly revenue from land does not increase in a regular manner. It has its ups and downs. It may therefore reach its maximum at some point during the lifetime of the concessions so that it is not the State that will benefit from it. As for stock market capital, we have seen that Fouillée perceives no way of regulating how it circulates. He relies, it is true, upon a progressive decrease in the return on stocks and shares. But nothing is so little justified as this vague hope. Interest only goes down in times when the industrial arts remain stationary. Thanks to new discoveries, new capital funds end up by finding a use that is no less productive than formerly. Thus all these reforms would not reduce the inequalities between fortunes. All that would have changed would be that the State would have been plunged into the maelstrom of interests and would upset the regular functioning of the social mechanism. It would weaken its natural springs without supplanting them. It would perhaps succeed in slowing down the functioning of the machine, but it would not make it more efficient.

Like his economic doctrines, Fouillée's political science seems to us to mistake the organic nature of society. It is said that the elector should represent the nation? But is this possible? I can certainly agree that the cells in my arm are conscious of themselves; perhaps they feel vaguely the cells that are immediately their neighbours, but they perceive nothing beyond this. The citizen in isolation cannot likewise be conscious of that immense society of which he perceives and knows only an infinitesmal part. How then could he become its authorized substitute? Is faith put in the benefits of education? But however effective it may be, it cannot perform miracles. It will never succeed in rendering the average mind powerful enough and broad enough to be able to encompass satisfactorily a representation of the vast system of social action and reaction. Moreover, if society is an organism, labour within it is divided up. Each individual has his special task and at any given moment all individuals cannot fulfil equally successfully the same function. Yet let us suppose that the ideal society of which Fouillée dreams has been realized. On voting day the sum content of each individual consciousness is identical. Each consciousness resembles all others, and is of equal value. But then the social organism would collapse. Instead of there being living cells subordinated to one another, there would be no more than atoms in juxtaposition, located on the same level.

It is true that this prospect may hold nothing displeasing for our author. In the end the perfect society, according to him, would be one in which each individual would possess exactly enough means to provide for himself through his labour; enough intelligence to understand what were his immediate duties; enough feeling not to fail to take an interest in others. Social harmony would result from a spontaneous accord of individual wills. It would be a kind of gentle, enlightened democracy in which, despite the inequality in condition, each and every natural superiority would be gratefully accepted as splendid, happy exceptions. This somewhat tempting dream resembles that imagined by the Socialists of the Chair across the Rhine. Unfortunately there is every reason to fear that such an organization would be very precarious. Sentiments, excellent as they may be, constitute fragile links. A society that was not more solidly cemented together would risk being swept away at the first storm.

3

The Concept and Nature of Socialism

One can conceive of two very different ways of studying socialism. It can be seen as a scientific doctrine concerning the nature and evolution of societies in general, and more especially, of the most civilized contemporary societies. In this case the investigation that one makes of it does not differ from that to which scientists subject the theories and hypotheses of their respective sciences. It is considered in the abstract, divorced from time and space, outside the historical process, not as a fact whose origin one undertakes to discover, but as a system of propositions that express or are deemed to express facts. One asks oneself what is true or false about the system, whether it conforms to social reality, and to what extent it is consistent with itself and with things. . . . This will not be the point of view we adopt. This is because, without belittling in any way the importance and interest of socialism, we cannot acknowledge that it has any truly scientific character. Indeed, no enquiry can be termed scientific unless it has an object that is actual and realized, and whose purpose it is merely to translate it into intelligible language. A science is a study that deals with a given segment of reality that must be known and if possible understood. To describe and explain what is and what has been is its sole task. Speculations concerning the future are not its affair, although its ultimate object is to make them possible.

Now, quite to the contrary, socialism is wholly future-oriented.

Above all it is a plan for the reconstruction of present-day societies, a programme for a collective life that does not yet exist or does not exist as it has been imagined, one that is put before men as worthy of their preference. It is an ideal. It deals much less with what is or what has been than with what should be. Undoubtedly, in its most Utopian forms it has never disdained to call up facts in its support and in most recent times it has even affected a certain scientific posture. It is indisputable that in this way it has perhaps rendered greater service to social science than it has received. For it has awakened reflection, stimulated scientific activity, provoked research and posed problems, so much so that at more than one point its history has mingled with that of sociology itself. Yet how can we not be struck by the huge disproportion that exists between the scarce and meagre facts that it borrows from the sciences and the vastness of the practical conclusions that it draws from them, and that are nevertheless at the heart of the system. It aspires to a complete reshaping of the social order. Yet in order to know what can and should become the family, property and the organization, whether political, moral, juridical or economic, of the peoples of Europe, even in the near future, it is indispensable to have studied that host of institutions and practices as they were in the past, to have sought out how they have varied throughout history, and the principal conditions that have determined these variations. Only then will it be possible to ask oneself rationally what they should become today, given the present conditions of our collective existence. But all such research is still in its infancy. Several studies have scarcely been undertaken, and those that are most advanced have not yet gone beyond a very rudimentary phase. And moreover, since each of these problems represents a world, the solution to them cannot be found in a moment, simply because of the fact that the need to do so has been felt. The bases for methodical inductions concerning the future, above all for inductions on such a scale, have not been established. The theorist must construct them himself. Socialism has not taken the time to do so — one may even say that it had no time to do so.

That is why, to speak precisely, there can be no scientific socialism. This is because, were such a socialism possible, sciences that have not been invented and yet cannot be improvised would be necessary. The only attitude that science permits when faced with these problems is one of reserve and circumspection, and socialism can hardly sustain it without deceiving itself. In fact, it has not done so. Consider even the work that is the most powerful, the most systematic and the richest in ideas that the school has produced: Marx's *Capital*. How many statistical facts, historical comparisons and studies would be indispensable to resolve any one of the questions that are dealt with in it? Need we recall that a whole theory of value is established in a few lines? The truth is that the facts and observations assembled in this way by theorists anxious to document their statements are hardly there save to figure as arguments. The research that has been carried out has been undertaken to establish a doctrine the notion of which had been conceived in advance, and one that is far from having resulted from their research. Almost all had their position already worked out before asking science for the support it could give them. Strong feelings have inspired all such systems. What gave rise to them, and what constitutes their strength, is a yearning for a more perfect form of justice, pity for the misery of the working classes, a vague sentiment of disquiet that pervades contemporary societies, etc. Socialism is not a science, a miniature sociology, it is a cry of pain and occasionally of anger uttered by men who feel most acutely our collective malaise. To the facts that arouse it, it is comparable to the groanings of the sick person to the illness from which he is suffering and to the needs that torment him. But then what would we say of a doctor who took the replies or desires of his patient for scientific aphorisms? Moreover, the theories that are normally advanced against socialism are no different in kind and no more deserve the status that we refuse them. When the economists demand laisser-faire, asking that State influence should be reduced to zero and that competition should be freed from all barriers, they do not base their claims any the more on laws that have been scientifically induced. The social sciences are still much too young to be able to serve as a basis for practical doctrines that are so systematic and so vast in scope. It is needs of another kind that sustain these other doctrines: a feeling that is jealous for individual autonomy, the love of order, the fear of innovation — misoneism, as it is called today. Individualism, like socialism, is above all a passion strongly asserted, although it can if needs be produce reasons to justify itself.

If this is so, to study socialism as a system of abstract propositions and a corpus of scientific theories, and to discuss it from the standpoint of doctrine, is to view and demonstrate an aspect of it that is only moderately interesting. Whoever is conscious of what social science should be, the lengthiness of its procedures, the laborious investigations that it presumes in order even to resolve the most limited problems, cannot show much interest in such hasty solutions and such vast systems that are so cursorily sketched out. One feels too acutely the gap that exists between the simplicity of the methods employed and the broad nature of the results, and one is consequently inclined to disdain these results. Yet socialism may be examined from a completely different viewpoint. If it is not a scientific expression of social facts, it is itself a social fact of the highest importance. If it is not the work of science, it is the object of science. Science should not concern itself with it in order to borrow some ready-made proposition from it, but in order to know about it, to know what it is, whence it comes and whither it is tending.

For a double reason it is interesting to study it from this viewpoint. Firstly, we may hope that it will help us to understand the social conditions that have given rise to it. For precisely because it derives from them, it manifests and expresses them in its own way, and by this very fact gives us an additional means of ascertaining them. It is most certainly not true that it reflects them exactly. On the contrary, for the motives we have stated above, we may be certain that it involuntarily refracts them, giving us only an inaccurate expression of them, just as the sick person misinterprets the sensations that he feels and attributes them very often to a cause that is not the real one. But these very sensations, such as they are, are interesting, and the clinician notes them with care and takes them seriously into account. They are an element in the diagnosis, and a very important one. For example, it is not unimportant to know in what spot they are felt and when they began. Likewise it is of the utmost importance to determine when socialism began to appear. We said that it was a cry of collective distress — well, it is essential to determine the moment when that cry was first uttered. One might view it as a recent phenomenon that relates to entirely new conditions in the life of the collectivity, or on the other hand as a mere repetition, at the very most a variation on the complaints that the wretched in all ages and in all societies have voiced, the eternal demands made by the poor against the rich. According to these lights, one will judge very differently the tendencies that socialism manifests. In the second case, one will be inclined to think that they can no more achieve anything than that human misery itself can come to an end. They will be viewed as a kind of chronic sickness of humanity that from time to time, in the course of history and under the influence of passing circumstances, seems to become sharper and more painful, but which always in the long run ends by subsiding. In that case one will be solely intent on seeking out tranquillizing drugs in order to send it to sleep once more. If, on the other hand, we find that it is of recent origin, that it relates to a situation unparalleled in history, we can no longer conclude that it is chronic, and it is less easy to resign oneself to it. But it is not only for determining the nature of the sickness that such a study of socialism bids fair to be instructive; it is also in order to discover the appropriate remedies. Certainly we can be sure beforehand that it will not be precisely any of those that the systems clamour for, just as the drink demanded by the fever-wracked patient is not the one suitable for him. But, on the other hand, the needs that he feels do not fail to act as a guide to his treatment. They are never without some cause, and it can even occasionally happen that the best course is to satisfy them. In the same way and for the same reason it is important to know what new social dispositions, i.e. what remedies the suffering masses of society have spontaneously and instinctively thought of, however unscientifically they have been worked out. This it is what socialist theories express. The information that can be gathered on this matter will be particularly useful if, instead of locking oneself into a system, one makes a broadly comparative study of all the doctrines. For then one has a greater chance of eliminating from all such aspirations what is necessarily individual, subjective and contingent about them, so as to sort out and retain only their most general characteristics, those that are most impersonal and consequently most objective.

Not only does such an investigation have its usefulness, but it seems indeed to be more fruitful in a different way from that to which socialism more usually is submitted. When one studies it only in order to discuss it from a doctrinal viewpoint, since it rests solely on a very imperfect science, it is easy to demonstrate how it goes beyond the very facts on which it relies, or to match them against opposing facts, in short to highlight all its theoretical imperfections. Thus one can without much difficulty undertake a survey of all systems; there is not one that cannot be relatively easily refuted, because none are based upon science. Nevertheless, however scholarly, however well conducted it may be, such a critique remains superficial, for it leaves on one side what is the essential. It concentrates solely on the external and visible form of socialism and consequently does not perceive what constitutes its stuff and substance, namely that collective tendency, that profound malaise of which individual theories are only the syndromes, as it were, and spasmodic superficial manifestations. When one has done battle with Saint-Simon, Fourier or Karl Marx, one is nevertheless not informed about the social conditions that gave rise to them, what was and still is their *raison d'être*, which tomorrow will give rise to other doctrines if the former ones fall into disrepute. Thus all these fine refutations are a real labour of Penelope, continually to be restarted, for they only touch socialism from the outside, and what is inside eludes them. They tackle the effects and not the causes. But it is the causes that must be arrived at, even if only to understand thoroughly the effects. Yet to do this socialism must not be considered in the abstract, outside all conditions of time and place. On the contrary, we need to link it with the different social environments in which it arose. It should not be subjected to dialectical discussion, but its history should be surveyed.

This is the viewpoint where we shall take up our position. We shall visualize socialism as a thing, as a reality, and attempt to understand it. We shall strive to determine in what it consists, when it began, through what changes it has passed, and what has determined those changes. An investigation of this kind therefore does not differ appreciably from those we have undertaken in previous years. We shall study socialism as we did suicide, the family, marriage, crime, punishment, responsibility and religion. The sole difference is that this time we shall find ourselves confronted with a social fact that, since it is very recent, has had only a very short period in which to develop. The result is that the range of possible comparisons is very limited. This makes the phenomenon more difficult to understand thoroughly, all the more so because it is very complex. Thus in order to arrive at a more complete understanding, it will be useful to compare it with certain data that we owe to other research. For that social state to which socialism corresponds does not present itself to us for the first time. On the contrary we have encountered it whenever we have been able to follow down to modern times the social phenomena that were our subject, at the end of each of our previous studies. It is true that in this way we have only been able to penetrate to this state of society piecemeal. In a sense might not socialism even allow us to know it in its entirety, because, so to speak, it expresses it as a whole? Nonetheless we shall be able on occasion to use the partial results we have obtained.

Yet, to be able to undertake such a study, above all else we must determine what shall be its subject. It is not enough to state that we shall consider socialism as a thing. We must also indicate the signs by which that thing can be recognized, i.e. provide a definition of it that will allow us to identify it wherever it occurs, and not confuse it with what it is not.

How shall we proceed to such a definition?

Would it be sufficient to reflect attentively upon the idea of what we conceive socialism to be, to analyse it, and to express the fruits of that analysis in as clear a language as possible? Indeed we have certainly not waited for sociology to pose methodically this question in order to attach a meaning to the word 'socialism', which we use repeatedly. Would we therefore only have to withdraw into ourselves, questioning ourselves carefully, apprising ourselves of the notion we have of it, and developing it into a precise formulation? Proceeding in this way, we might indeed be able to succeed in knowing what we understand personally by socialism, but not what socialism is. Since everyone understands it in his own way, according to mood, temperament, habits of mind and prejudices, we would thus obtain only a subjective and individual notion that could not be used as the subject-matter for a scientific investigation. By what right should I impose upon others the way I personally perceive socialism, and by what right should others impose theirs upon me? Shall we better succeed by eliminating from these conceptions, which vary according to the individual, what is individual about them, so as to retain only what they have in common? In other words, to define socialism, might this not entail expressing, not the idea that I have of it, but the average idea that men of my time have? Shall we therefore not call it, not what I do, but what it is generally designated as? Yet we know how indeterminate and inconsistent these common, average conceptions are. They are made up day by day, empirically, without any logic and method. The result is that soon they apply equally to very different things, or on the contrary exclude those very closely related to the ones to which they are applied. Ordinary persons, in forming their concepts, let themselves at one time be guided by external resemblances, which are deceptive, and at another time let themselves be deceived by apparent differences. Consequently, if we were to follow this course we would run a grave risk either of calling all sorts of opposing doctrines socialism or, conversely, of excluding from socialism doctrines that have all its essential features but are not so called by the mass of people, who have not become accustomed to doing so. In the one case, our study would deal with a confused mass of heterogeneous facts lacking unity, and in the other it would not include all the facts that are comparable, and of a kind that would throw light upon one another. In both cases, the study would not be in a good position to achieve success.

Moreover, in order to realize what this method is worth, it is sufficient to see its results, i.e. to examine the definitions of socialism that are most usually given. Such an examination is all the more useful because, since these definitions express those ideas about socialism that are the most widespread, and the most common ways of conceptualizing it, it is important to rid ourselves immediately of those prejudices that otherwise could only prevent us from reaching agreement and would hinder our research. If we do not free ourselves from them before proceeding further, they will form a barrier between us and things and will cause us to see these differently from what they are.

Of all the definitions, the one that generally perhaps comes most constantly into people's minds every time the question of socialism is mooted is the one that makes it out to consist purely and simply of a negation of individual property. . . . For example, let us consider that doctrine which most limits private property, the collectivism of Karl Marx. It certainly does remove from individuals the right to own the instruments of production, but not to own all kinds of wealth. Individuals preserve an absolute right over the products of their labour. Can this limited assault on the principle of individual property at least be regarded as a characteristic of socialism? But our present economic organization presents restrictions of the same kind and in this respect is only distinguishable from Marxism by a difference of degree. Is everything that is directly or indirectly a State monopoly not withdrawn from the private domain? Railways, the postal service, tobacco, the minting of money, explosives, etc. — all these cannot be exploited by private individuals, or can only be so through an express concession granted by the State. Should we say that socialism effectively begins where the practice of monopolies does? Then socialism would be everywhere; it is of all ages and of every country, for there has never been a society without monopoly. This means that such a definition is much too broad. There is something else; far from denying the principle of individual property, socialism can claim not without reason that it is its most complete affirmation, the most radical that has ever been made. In fact, the opposite of private property is communism. And there is still in our present-day institutions one vestige of the old family communism: this is inheritance. The right of relatives to succeed one another in the ownership of goods is only the last trace of the ancient right of co-property that in former times all members of the family possessed collectively over the whole of the domestic fortune. Now one of the articles that occurs most frequently in socialist theories is the abolition of inheritance. Such a reform would therefore have the effect of freeing the institution of individual property from any tincture of communism, and consequently make it more truly what it should be. In other words, one can reason as follows: for it to be possible to say that property is really individual, it must be acquired through the work of the individual, and his work alone. But the patrimony transmitted by inheritance has not this character: it is merely a collective store appropriated by an individual. Individual property, one may say, is that which begins and ends with the individual. But what he receives through the right of succession existed before him and was built up without him. In reproducing this reasoning, moreover, I do not seek either to defend the socialist thesis, but to show that communism exists also among its adversaries and that consequently this is not how it is possible to define what it is.

We shall say as much about the no less widespread conception according to which socialism allegedly consists of the close subordination of the individual to the collectivity. 'We can define as socialist', states Adolphe Held, 'any tendency that demands the subordination of individual wealth to the community.' Roscher also, but mingling a judgement and a criticism with his definition, terms those tendencies socialist 'which demand an esteem of the common good above what human nature allows.' But there has been no society in which private goods have not been subordinated to social ends, for such a subordination is the very condition of all common life. Shall we say, as does Roscher, that the abnegation socialism demands of us has as its characteristic that it is beyond our power? This is to evaluate the doctrine and not to define it, and such an evaluation cannot serve as a criterion to distinguish it from what it is not, for it allows too much latitude for the arbitrary. This extreme limit of sacrifices that the egoism of the individual can bear cannot be objectively determined. Each person, depending on his mood, will go beyond or fall short of it. Consequently each person would be free to interpret socialism in his own way. There is something more: this subjection of the individual to the group is so little part of the thinking of certain schools of socialism, among them the most important, that their tendency is rather towards anarchy. This is notably the case with Fourierism and with Proudhon's 'mutualism', in which individualism is pushed to its most paradoxical consequences. Does not Marxism itself propose, according to the famous phrase of Engels, the destruction of the State as the State? Rightly or wrongly, Marx and his disciples esteem that from the day when the socialist organization has been set up, it will be able to function by itself, automatically, without any form of constraint, and we find this idea already in Saint-Simon. In short, if an authoritarian socialism exists, there is also one that is essentially democratic. How indeed could it be otherwise? It has, as we shall see, emerged from revolutionary individualism, just as the ideas of the nineteenth century have emerged from those of the eighteenth, and consequently it cannot fail to bear the mark of its origins. It is true that the question remains of knowing whether these different tendencies are capable of being logically reconciled. But for the time being we have not to weigh up the logical value of socialism. We are only seeking to know of what it consists.

But there is one last definition that appears more adequate for the object to be defined. Very often, if not always, socialism has had as its main aim the improvement of the condition of the working classes by introducing more equality into economic relationships. This is why it is called the economic philosophy of the classes that suffer. But this tendency alone does not suffice to characterize socialism, for it is not peculiar to it. The economists also aspire to less inequality in social conditions. They merely believe that this progress can and must occur by the natural interplay of supply and demand and that any intervention through legislation is useless. Shall we then say that what distinguishes socialism is that it wishes to obtain this self-same result by other means, that is, through legal action? This was the definition of Lavelye. 'All socialist doctrines', he states, 'aim at introducing greater equality into social conditions and, secondly, at realizing these reforms through the operations of the law or of the State.' But from one viewpoint, if this objective is effectively one of those pursued by the doctrines, it is far from being the only one. The linking to the State of large-scale industries, the large economic undertakings that, through their importance, embrace the whole of society — mines, railways, banks, etc. — has as its aim to protect the collective interest against certain individual influences, but not to improve the lot of the workers. Socialism goes beyond the question of the workers. In certain systems it even occupies only a somewhat secondary place. This is the case with Saint-Simon, i.e. the thinker who, it is agreed, is considered the founder of socialism. It is the case also for the 'Socialists of the Chair', who are much more preoccupied with safeguarding the interests of the State than with protecting those ill-favoured by fortune. On the other hand, a doctrine does exist that aims to realize that equality much more radically than does socialism: this is communism, which denies all individual property and, by this very fact, all economic inequality. Now, although the confusion has often occurred, it is impossible to make it out to be a mere variety of socialism. We shall shortly have to return to this question. Plato and Thomas More, on the one hand, and Marx on the other, are not disciples of the same school. Even *a priori* it is not possible for a social organization thought of for the industrial societies that we have at present to have been conceived when these societies were not yet born. Finally, there are many legislative measures that one could not regard as exclusively socialist ones, and yet whose effect is to reduce the inequality in social conditions. The progressive tax on inheritance and income has necessarily this result, and yet it is not an apanage of socialism. What should one say about scholarships granted by the State, and the public institutions for welfare and savings, etc.? If they are termed socialist, as sometimes happens in current discussions, the word loses all meaning, so much does it acquire an extended and indeterminate usage.

The pitfalls to which one is prone can be seen when, in order to discover the definition of socialism, one confines oneself to expressing with some preciseness the idea held of it. One then confuses it with some or other special aspect or special tendency in certain systems, simply because for some reason one is more struck by this peculiarity than by others. The only way not to fall into these errors is to practise the method that in such circumstances we have always followed. Let us for the moment forget the idea we have of the object to be defined. Instead of looking within ourselves, let us look outside; instead of interrogating ourselves, let us interrogate things. There exists a certain number of doctrines concerning social things. Let us observe and compare them. Let us classify together those which present common characteristics. If among the groups of theories formed in this way there is one that reminds us sufficiently through its distinctive characteristics of what is normally designated as socialism, we shall apply that appellation to it without any change. In other words, we shall term socialist all those systems presenting these characteristics. Thus we shall have the definition we seek. It is doubtless very possible that it does not include all the doctrines that are commonly so designated, or on the contrary includes some which in present-day discussions are termed differently. No matter. These divergences will only once again prove how roughly drawn are the classifications that form the basis of the terminology we use — but this we already knew. The essential is for us to have before us an order of facts that forms a clearly circumscribed unity, and to which we may apply the term 'socialism' without doing violence to the language. For under these conditions our study will be possible, since we shall have as its subject-matter things that are determinate in nature. Moreover, it will elucidate the common idea of socialism, in so far as it can be clarified, i.e. to the extent that it is consistent or expresses something definite. Conducted in this way research will then answer adequately everything that we can logically ask when we pose the question: what is socialism?

Let us apply this method.

Social doctrines may be divided at the outset into two main types. Some seek solely to express what is or what has been; they are purely speculative and scientific. Others, on the contrary, have above all as their object to modify what exists; they propose not laws but reforms. These are the practical doctrines. What has been stated above suffices to warn us that, if the word socialism corresponds to something capable of definition, it is to the second type that it must belong.

Now this type includes species. The reforms thus proposed deal sometimes with politics, sometimes education, sometimes administration, and sometimes economic life. Let us stop to consider this last species. All the signs justify our presumption that socialism forms part of it. Doubtless we may say that broadly speaking there is a political socialism, a pedagogical one, etc. We shall also see that in the nature of things it extends to these various domains. However, it is certain that the word was coined to designate theories aimed above all at the economic condition, and that demand its transformation. Nevertheless we should guard against believing that this observation is sufficient to express its character. For the individualist economists also protest against the present organization, demanding that it should be freed from any form of social constraint. The reforms demanded by de Molinari in his *Evolution économique* no less undermine the present social order than do those to which the most violent form of socialism aspires. We must therefore push our classification further and see whether, in the economic transformations demanded by the different reformist sects, there are not some that are distinctive to socialism.

In order to understand fully what follows some definitions are necessary.

Normally it is said that the functions exercised by the members of one society are of two kinds: some are social, and the others private. Those of the State engineer, the administrator, the Member of Parliament, the priest, etc. belong to the first category; commerce and industry, i.e. the economic functions — with the exception of monopolies — belong to the second. Truth to tell, the designations used in this way are not beyond criticism, for in one sense all functions of society are social, and economic functions like the rest. Indeed, if the economic functions do not operate normally, the whole of society feels the effect and, conversely, the general state of social well-being affects the functioning of the economic organs. However, the distinction between types of functions, leaving aside the terms in which it is expressed, remains well founded. Indeed the economic functions are peculiar in not entertaining well-defined and regulated relationships with the organ entrusted with the task of representing the body social as a whole and of directing it, i.e. what we commonly call the State. This absence of relationships can be noted also in the way in which our industrial and commercial life acts upon the State, just as the latter acts upon it. On the one hand, what occurs in large-scale manufacturing, in factories, and in private shops in principle remains a sealed book to the State. It is not directly or especially informed about what is produced. In certain cases it can indeed feel the repercussions, but it is not alerted about it in any other way, nor in conditions any different from the other organs of society. Hence the economic state must be somewhat seriously disturbed for the general state of society to be appreciably modified by it. In that case, the State suffers, and consequently is vaguely conscious of it, just as are the other parts of the organism, but not in any different way. In other words there is no special line of communication between the State and this sphere of collective life. In principle economic activity lies outside the social consciousness; it functions silently; the centres of consciousness do not feel it so long as it is functioning normally. Likewise they do not affect it in any particular and regular fashion. There is no determinate system of organized channels through which the influence of the State can be brought to bear upon economic activity. In other words, there is no system of functions entrusted with the task of imposing on it any action proceeding from the higher centres. With the other functions the case is entirely different. Everything happening in the various administrations, the local assemblies meeting for discussion, the public education system, the army, etc., is likely to reach what has been termed the social 'brain' through ways specially designed to ensure communication between them, so that the State is kept informed without the other surrounding parts of society being alerted. Similarly, there are other channels of the same kind through which the State conveys its actions to these secondary centres. Between them and itself there are continual and varied exchanges. Thus we can say that these latter functions are organized, for what constitutes the organization of a living body is the setting up of a central organ and the linking of that organ with secondary organs. By contrast, we may say of the economic functions, in their present state, that they are diffuse, and that their diffuseness consists in the absence of organization.

Once we have postulated this it is easy to prove that there are among economic doctrines some that demand the linking of industrial and commercial functions to the conscious directing functions of society, and that these doctrines are opposed to others that by contrast demand a greater diffuseness on the part of the first kind of functions. It would appear indisputable that by dubbing the first of these doctrines socialist we shall not be doing violence to the ordinary meaning of the word. For all the doctrines normally termed socialist agree about this demand. Certainly this linking is conceived of differently depending on the schools of socialism. According to some, it is all the economic functions that should be linked to the higher centres; according to others, it is enough for some of them to be. For these this link-up should take place through intermediaries, i.e. secondary centres invested with a certain autonomy, occupational groups, corporations etc. For others, the link must be direct. But all these differences are secondary and consequently we can fix upon the following definition that expresses the characteristics all theories have in common:

> Any doctrine is termed socialist that demands the linking of all the economic functions, or certain of them that are at present diffuse, to the conscious, directing centres of society.

It is important to note straight away that we say 'linking', and not 'subordination'. This is because in fact this bond between economic life and the State does not imply, in our view, that all action should proceed from the latter. On the contrary it is natural that it should receive as much as it imposes. We can foresee that industrial and commercial life, once it has been placed in permanent contact with it, will affect its functioning, and will contribute to determining the manifestations of its activity much more so than it does today, playing a much more important role in government life. This explains how, whilst they fit the definition we have just worked out, there are socialist systems that tend towards anarchy. This is because, according to them, this transformation should have the effect, far from placing them in State hands, of making the State dependent on the economic functions.

BELOT AND SOCIALISM[2]

The definition that not unreasonably a reader of the *Revue* demands seems to me to be devoid of interest unless it expresses something other than a particular view held by the mind, that is, it needs to be a definition of a thing and not of a concept. It is important to know not what our particular doctrine of socialism is, but what constitutes the objective fact called socialism as it is evolving before our gaze. On this condition alone will we be able to judge it and foresee what it will become, indeed what it must become, in the future. If arguments that revolve around it daily are not to be mere conflicts of passions and interests, for them to assume a truly scientific character, we must above all else establish the nature of the thing being discussed. The definition demanded must satisfy this logical necessity.

To resolve the problem if it is posed in this way, Belot's dialectical method, which he advocated in the interesting note he published on the subject in these pages for our August issue,[3] clearly cannot be used. To analyse, as this method would have us do, the idea of socialism is to analyse the idea we each individually have of it, but it is not to analyse socialism itself. The subject of that logical analysis is a conception of the mind whose objective value cannot in any way be guaranteed. Thus Belot starts from the idea that socialism is 'the opposite of individualism', whereas this alleged antimony is anything but demonstrated.[4] What is more, so greatly is it a matter of expounding the author's own personal socialism that he supports his definition with all sorts of very disputable propositions, or in any case ones much argued about. In these few pages are to be found, rapidly sketched out and demonstrated, a theory about society in general, another about the State, yet another about the social contract — theories that are the very basis for the formulation advanced, and yet ones far from being universally accepted. It is true that this formulation is presented as expressing the essence of socialism, but on what authority? The essential properties of a thing are those to be observed wherever the thing exists, and which are peculiar to it alone. Thus if we wish to know of what the essence of socialism consists we must sort out those traits found to be the same in all socialist doctrines without exception. Now the socialism peculiar to one sociologist or another is never more than one of the countless varieties of the species; it is not the species itself. Let us even concede that it is the only true kind, that all other forms of socialism are erroneous and are, so to speak, unhealthy varieties. We have nevertheless no right to omit the latter in a definition of the phenomenon. An erroneous socialism is still socialism. By systematically omitting it we incur the risk of conceiving a truncated notion of the reality we are studying, because it is based upon observations that are not complete. In the living order we cannot know what constitutes the essence of a fact unless we take into account the abnormal and pathological forms that it presents, as well as the normal forms. This is a truth that is fundamental to the new methods of psychology and that holds with no less authority for the sociologist.[5]

However, since allegedly 'we recognize a doctrine historically as being idealist, pantheist, socialist, etc. it is because, independent of history, we have some general idea of the tendencies that these words represent, and they are categorized in the mind *in abstracto* with greater or less preciseness.'[6] Thus it would seem that we have only to evoke this idea in our consciousness and express it in terms that are clear and definite. Yet it is a mistake to think this precedes any knowledge of the doctrines. Quite the opposite is true: it arises from them. How indeed could it have any other origin? There do not exist ready-made in the mind as many special categories as there are schools of philosophy or sociology. The truth is that the idea has gradually taken shape, as we have correspondingly been initiated into the different forms that each system presents historically. It reproduces their most striking characteristics, or rather those that have struck us most forcibly. It is, so to speak, the generic image. The dialectical method, if it is used for the analysis of these ideas, therefore applies to notions derived empirically, and consequently the results to which the method leads have no other value than that of the notions themselves. But they have been formed in such a way that they cannot be at all scientific. Indeed they have been constituted not according to any system, but through chance events, dictated by myriad circumstances that bear no relationship to the intrinsic reality of the object to which they correspond. In fact, we do not know whether the particular doctrines we know about exhaust all possible variations in the system. Above all, we can have no assurance that the characteristics that have struck us most forcibly are the most vital ones. On the contrary, inevitably passions and prejudices of every kind have intervened to distort our observation, causing some secondary characteristic or other to stand out, or effacing artificially some fundamental trait. For we have taken none of those preventive measures to eliminate this source of error that constitute the very method of science. This is why we may be certain that such an idea of socialism bears the same resemblance to the scientific notion of the phenomenon as the common or garden representation of the sun or earth bears to the conception held of them by the astronomer. Thus it is not by such an analysis of the notion that we shall ever be able to define precisely that thing which the notion so inaccurately expresses. On the contrary, to arrive at that definition we must return to the thing itself, seeking to attain it by some more methodical process.

It is true that afterwards Belot attempts to validate the conclusions arrived at by the dialectical method, using the historical and empirical method. Yet in reality this verification is conducted in the same spirit and according to the same principles as the very proof it is intended to check. In fact, it tends merely to establish that the definition put forward corresponds to socialist doctrines that have had an historical existence, and not that all manifestations of socialist thought without exception conform to it. The effect of this is therefore that the author is obliged to omit from his formulation almost the whole of German socialism. Yet this is no negligible factor.

From the foregoing we may discern the method to be followed if the question is to be dealt with historically.

A certain number of doctrines exist that may be termed socialist, and term themselves socialist. We may legitimately deem them to be various expressions of that general tendency called the spirit of socialism. Thus if there exist among all these doctrines common characteristics that it is possible to discover, then we will be justified in making these the substance of the definition we are searching for.

To arrive at this we would have to compare all such doctrines, from the most timorous version of the 'Socialism of the Chair' to the most revolutionary form of collectivism; we would have to classify them into kinds and species, and then compare the types thus constituted so as to bring out what they have in common. The mere exposition of this method sufficiently demonstrates that, in this brief note, we cannot put it into practice with the logical precision and exactness that are desirable. Yet without plunging rigorously into this analysis and classification it is not impossible to discern and point up the various tendencies that are to be found in all socialist doctrines we know of. This is what we shall attempt to do.

The first characteristic that all doctrines without exception exhibit is that they inveigh against the present state of the economy and demand its transformation, whether abruptly or progressively. Although marginally, as well as from its etymology, the term 'socialism' may be understood in a wider sense, in fact theories bearing the socialist label relate essentially to that particular sphere of collective life which is termed economic. Moreover, this does not assert that the social question is one of wages. On the contrary, we are among those who think that it is above all moral. Yet the moral transformations to which socialism aspires depend upon transformations in the economic organization. Later we shall have occasion to point out how the former are linked to the latter.

We see already how the meaning of the word is becoming more limited and more determinate. But among all the transformations demanded by the various socialist factions what do they have in common?

The characteristic of the present state of economic functions is their dispersed state. This dispersion is, so to speak, at two levels.

First, they are dispersed in the sense that they lack any definite organ as their base. In fact, enterprises in competition devoted to identical or similar purposes are not grouped together in a manner that forms them within society into a body possessing any unity.

For instance, there is no single collective undertaking to which, branching out into the different regions, is entrusted the task of exploiting the coal mines, or the production of cereals, or the manufacture of cloth, etc., for the whole country. On the contrary, each individual firm is entirely independent of the others. They may undoubtedly have links with one another, may act and react upon one another, but they lack a common purpose. Each works on its own behalf, pursues for itself its own interests, and those of no other. It may well happen that they are affected similarly by the same event — a famine, for example, or war. Yet because they all react in the same way when influenced by the same cause, it does not follow that this coalescence possesses a life of its own. *Each institution has its individuality, the whole has none.* Now an organ consists of an association between a certain number of anatomical parts, united by a bond of solidarity in such a way that the society so constituted has truly a 'persona' within the organism, whether it be individual or social. Thus we may legitimately state that the scattered enterprises are like the pieces and substance of an organ. But the organ as a whole does not exist — not because these are not physically in contact, but because they do not form any kind of moral community.

Second, in another sense also the economic functions are dispersed: they are not systematically attached to the central regulatory organ, i.e. to the State. Undoubtedly they are not sheltered against all social influences; we have ourselves shown how law exerts a moderating influence on all these kinds of relationships.[7] But this action itself is diffuse. The legislator has defined the normal type of exchange for the main combinations of circumstances arising in the usual course of events. In fact, for the majority of the average cases this type is imposed upon the actors in an exchange. However, they still remain free to depart from it by mutual agreement, nor does the State intervene directly to force them to submit to it. No special body of public officials exists with a more or less broad authority to ensure the administration of economic life. Indeed if here and there such an administration is beginning to emerge, it is still only rudimentary, and moreover it is under the influence of socialist ideas that it has made its appearance. As a general rule, the State takes no cognizance of the regular, normal working of industrial and commercial functions, which in consequence are not directly set in motion by it. It is patently clear that, in an organism where the division of labour exists, functions can only remain dispersed, and can only be said to be organized when they enjoy a close relationship with some central organ. This is because it is only through that organ that they can participate in the common life, because it is especially responsible for it. We need not discuss whether it is good that this should be so. We must merely state the fact, which is indisputable.

This established, it is easy to affirm that all schools of socialism agree unanimously in protesting against this state of dispersion, and in demanding that it should end. All require the organization of economic functions. It is true that the type of organization stated to be needed by the various schools of thought is not the same. For some it would be almost sufficient to increase the State's authority in economic matters. This is the case for certain 'Socialists of the Chair'. On the other hand, others demand that those special organs of economic life that are lacking should be built up on a solid foundation. This means giving to groups of occupations that individuality they do not possess, whilst moreover linking them to the organ of government. Among such thinkers are to be found fresh points of difference, as to whether the secondary organs constituted in this way should be granted a greater or lesser degree of autonomy, and the State more or less power. There are also divergencies as to whether each group of firms should be conceived of as an independent corporation or as a kind of public administration, and whether these transformations are expected to occur by violent or peaceful means. But these are only shades of difference, so that one may conclude by stating:

> Socialism is a tendency that causes economic functions to move, either abruptly or progressively, from the dispersed state in which they exist, to an organized state.

One may say that this is also an aspiration towards the more or less complete socialization of economic forces.

We can now understand why such a revolution cannot take

place without profound moral transformations. In fact, to socialize economic life is to subordinate individual and selfish ends that still predominate in it to ends that are truly social and consequently moral. Thus it means to introduce a higher morality into it. This is why, not unjustifiably, it has been possible to say that socialism tends to bring about greater justice in social relationships. Yet, although such moral consequences are included in the definition of socialism, they cannot serve to define it, for it extends well beyond this.

We believe this definition is one capable of casting some light on the questions that socialism raises.

In the first place it demonstrates that, in spite of very real differences that separate the various schools of thought, they are all, from the mildest to the most radical, imbued with the same spirit. There exists a socialism common to all specific forms of socialism that subsumes them all. This observation is by no means unimportant. Indeed this variety of doctrines has sometimes been adduced to remove all importance from the increasing spread of the socialist idea. What does the number of supporters it recruits matter if they are distributed among a host of irreconcilable churches? A current seems less strong if it is made up of a number of small streams, independent of one another, whose waters nowhere intermingle. On the contrary, socialist claims have increased authority once we recognize that dissension begins only at a certain point, but up to then agreement exists. The significance of this movement can no longer be denied, at least as regards its essentials, once its general nature is no longer hidden.

Secondly, the formulation set out above prevents us from confusing, as has occurred many times, present-day socialism with primitive communism. Because of this alleged identity, orthodox thinkers have thought it possible to arrive at a refutation of socialism. For it is patently unreasonable to try to impose upon the most complex and most advanced societies an economic organization borrowed from the simplest and least advanced types. But such an objection rests upon a confusion. Far from being the revival of ancient communism, socialism is rather its opposite. Communism is possible only where social functions are common to all, and where the mass of society, in a manner of speaking, included no differentiated parts. In fact, under such conditions property is naturally held collectively, because the collective 'persona' is the only one to have developed. As soon as special organs break away from what was originally a homogeneous mass, communal life becomes impossible, because each of these organs possesses its own specificity and its own interests. Socialism, on the contrary, implies that labour is extremely divided up, since it tends to link specific functions to specific organs, and these latter to one another. Communism corresponds to the historical phase when social activity is at the peak of dispersion, and consists of that very dispersion, whereas the object of socialism is to impart to that activity the highest form of organization possible. We find the model for communism in those unorganized societies of medusoids in which one creature cannot eat unless the others eat at the same time. On the contrary, the most perfect examples of socialism are afforded us in the higher animals, with their multiple organs that are autonomous but nevertheless solidly linked to one another and to the central organ that both epitomizes the organism and ensures its unity.[8]

Far from being a retrograde step, *socialism as we have defined it* really appears part and parcel of the very nature of higher societies. Indeed we know that the more history advances the more social functions that were originally dispersed become organized and 'socialized'. The army, education, public assistance, the communications and transport network, etc. have already undergone this transformation. In the book already cited we have attempted to prove that changes that occurred in a parallel development concerning the constitution of the social environment made this necessary. Thus if the basic conditions upon which historical development depends continue to evolve in the same direction, we may anticipate that this socialization will become ever more complete, and that it will spread gradually to functions it has not yet attained. There seems to be no privileged position for economic functions that would make them solely capable of successfully resisting this movement.

4

Socialism and Marxism:
Critical Commentaries

REVIEW OF GASTON RICHARD:
LE SOCIALISME ET LA SCIENCE SOCIALE (PARIS, 1897)[1]

The object of this book is to constitute what the notion of socialism is and to compare it with the results of comparative sociology.

Richard seeks the elements of his definition in the great works of the masters and not from the programmes of political parties or discussions at workers' congresses. According to him socialism is diminished if it is reduced to a mere catalogue of workers' demands, whether long or short, and the practical reforms designed to do justice to them. If the doctrine is considered only in this light, it is simple to demolish it. It is easy to demonstrate that the different methods recommended by the various systems as sovereign remedies for the woes that we are suffering are either inapplicable to the facts or would not have the result we expect, etc. A general, abstract formula is by nature too distant from reality to be able to penetrate it immediately, without encountering resistance. The immediate inapplicability of a chemical law does not demonstrate that it is false. Likewise, from the fact that the applications that have been deduced from socialist theories are unrealizable or would run counter to their purpose, we have no right to conclude that those theories are false. Socialism is above all a certain way of conceiving and explaining social facts, their past evolution and future development. This conception must therefore be examined by itself, apart from any considerations relating to the practical consequences that may follow from it.

Understood in this way, socialism, in spite of the undeniable variations that it has presented in history, is far from lacking in unity. However diverse may have been the forms it has successively assumed, at least there is one proposition on which all sects are unanimous: it is the affirmation that a new society, in which capital would no longer be the driving force of economic life and in which values would no longer be fixed through competition, must of necessity emerge from present-day societies. Richard therefore defines it in this way: 'Socialism is the notion of the coming of a society in which there is no competition, thanks to an organization of production without capitalist entrepreneurship and to a system of distribution in which the duration of work would be the sole measure of value'. Seen in this light, this is to reduce socialism to collectivism and almost to Marxism. Indeed the only interpreters of socialist thinking that the author tackles are Marx, Engels and Proudhon. He denies that designation to Saint-Simon and Fourier, as well as to agrarian or Christian socialism.

If certain of these exclusions can be perfectly well founded, there are others that one can find to be inadequately justified. If Christian asceticism has nothing in common with socialism, this does not hold good for Saint-Simonism. For our part we reckon that the essence of socialist doctrine is to be found in the philosophy of Saint-Simon. Yet, after all, any author is the arbiter for constituting the object of his research as he understands it, and for limiting it as he wishes. Nevertheless, thus defined, socialism evokes discussion about two basic questions, one concerning the past and the other looking to the future. In fact it implies a certain theory as to how capital has been accumulated, and another regarding the direction in which social evolution is tending. What is the value of these theories?

According to Marx, the capitalist regime is a mere transformation of the feudal system, and the wages system a new and debased form of serfdom. Formerly the serf worked openly for his master for a part of the week. Today the worker labours for his boss for a part of the day. Yet the exploitation is less apparent. His salary, if one looks solely to appearances, represents his labour — in reality it merely represents a fraction of it. The rest is profit for the employer.

Now, states Richard, this historical conception is doubly mistaken. Firstly, it is untrue that the wages system arose out of serfdom. The serf of former times has become, not the industrial worker or the wage-earning proletarian, but the small farmer and petty landowner of today. The ancestor of the worker is the journeyman of the Middle Ages. It was from the corporation that capitalist entrepreneurship emerged, just as the corporation itself emerged from the domestic workshop. All such comparisons therefore between extra labour and forced labour are objectively devoid of all foundation. Secondly, this evolution, far from having made worse the condition of the employee, 'corresponds to a real increase in personal liberty'. The corporation is the system of hereditary monopoly under the control of authority. The master craftsmen hold the journeymen dependent upon them, in the same way as they are dependent upon the political authority. Capitalist organization develops at the same time as does individual personality. It is the instrument through which the individual has emancipated himself from the collective and hereditary yokes. It is true that Marx only invokes these historical considerations to confirm his theory of value, which forms the basis of his whole system. Yet this theory implies a contradiction. Value cannot, as Marx would wish, be expressed as a function of the duration of work and of that alone, unless one leaves out of account its capacity. Or rather, if one tries to evaluate the capacity itself in terms of duration one would have to take as the middle term the difficulty of the work. But the difficulty of the work cannot raise the remuneration of the workers unless competition is made more difficult. Yet if we return to competition what remains of the doctrine? Richard goes so far as to accuse the theory of extra labour of leading to the negation of saving. Is not to save to build up capital, that is to employ the fruits of labour not in consumption goods, but in more work, or — and this comes down to the same thing — into the instruments of work?

The author then moves on to the second question. Whatever

one may think about the origins of capitalist society, are there reasons to believe that it is destined to give birth to a new society in which capital would no longer form the basis of economic undertakings?

According to Marx it is a law of history that capital is concentrated into fewer and fewer hands, from which he concludes that in the end it must pass into the hands of the community. But in reality this alleged law of evolution has been worked out from observing one single case. His history of the progressive accumulation of capital is above all, and on his own admission, the economic history of England. One cannot imagine a comparison whose basis is more narrow and which, above all, contrasts more with the extremely general character of the law that has been induced. We cannot read the future of Europe in the past of England alone. All this philosophy of history is moreover nullified by the celebrated dogma of economic materialism, which is devoid of any scientific value. It is not the economic organization that has determined the other social institutions. This is proved by the fact that the Incas of Peru were communists just as was the Iroquois confederation, and yet the basic constitution of these two societies was very different. Moreover, it is untrue to state that the functions of nutrition and reproduction enjoy the preponderant role attributed to them. It is functions of relationship, that is, representative functions, which are the essential factors in human development.

But let us consider the law of accumulation of capital by itself. If capital really was being concentrated into increasingly fewer hands, we should see the surplus value of capital diminish correspondingly. For since, by virtue of the theory, workers cannot buy back all the product of their labour, the excess that eludes them can only have as its consumers the capitalists themselves. Outlets would therefore necessarily decline in number if those holding the common fortune really did become increasingly fewer. Moreover this accumulation is only possible through coercive measures that would impose upon the worker an ever-increasing amount of extra labour. But where can one perceive the slightest sign of this constraint? Is not history an increasingly perfect liberation of the individual? Statistics confirm the induction from history. The number of owners is forever increasing.

Yet to justify its predictions socialism brings in not only the economic but also the political history of humanity. It is claimed that the present social condition arises from the splitting of society into hostile classes, a split that itself is due to the present organization of market production: the first split cannot therefore disappear without the other. Yet this organization, Richard contends, is solidly linked to the division of labour in society. If socialism is internally logical it must therefore arrive at the conclusion that the division of labour is likewise destined to disappear. This comes down to rebelling against history. What is more, in fact, regarding the law that the class spirit develops with capitalism, that spirit grows weaker as economic life becomes organized on the basis of private enterprise. The advance of the bourgeoisie runs parallel to that of science and free investigation. Everything therefore goes to prove that societies are tending in a direction very different from that assigned to them by the socialists. It is certainly necessary for competition to grow weaker and it is a matter of urgency that juridical regulation of contracts should put a stop to what are indisputably abuses. The weak, and in particular women and children, must be protected. Yet in order to accomplish these results it is not necessary to overthrow the present economic organization. Quite the contrary: if the destruction of capitalism were to come about it could only make such results impossible.

These are the main arguments that Richard advances against socialism. Whatever one may think of his discussion, it has one merit that one cannot deny without doing him an injustice; it is a merit that in such a subject already possesses originality. This is the ardent desire to introduce into controversies that arouse so much passion a calm, scientific impartiality. Thus we can find both surprising and regrettable the violent attacks of which he has been the object from the authorized representatives of socialist doctrines. Yet it seems to us that socialism has every advantage in affording a different kind of welcome to those who, whilst discussing it, treat it with the deference and consideration due to any system of ideas that has played an important role in the history of the human mind. We all even have an interest in seeing that discussions are henceforth conducted on both sides more impartially and without that mutual animosity that is the rule today, and which deprives them of any scientific character. At the very least this would be a first step towards a return to calm, and this is the service that science in such matters can most directly render to practical affairs.

Moreover, there is something novel in the point of view adopted by Richard, and one which deserves to be retained. Leaving on one side all the traditional objections concerning the possible applicability of socialist theories, he has demonstrated, we believe, a scientific spirit. Indeed there is nothing more vain than all the dialectic in which passion has free rein. We are more easy about the future precisely because it does not yet exist and we can conceive it somewhat how we will. Depending on whether a measure attracts us or otherwise, we readily find it either practicable or chimerical. There has been no reform which has not been said to be impossible on the very eve of when it was to become reality. Although philosophers and statesmen have been warned through experience of the stupidity of this dialectical method, as it is the easiest and the most readily available to everybody, it is the one to which recourse is most freely had. Yet if we want to work to good purpose it is towards the past and not the future that we must turn. There at least, because the reality is a fact, is a field for objective research and consequently for understanding.

There are also to be found in Richard's book a number of ingenious and interesting views. The author has deployed those qualities as a logician which already distinguished his *Essai sur l'origine de l'idée du droit*. It is true that occasionally his argument has a somewhat formal character about it. It is perhaps because he has not adopted towards socialism the sole attitude that is fitting for a sociologist. Of socialism conceived as a theory of social facts, sociology has one thing alone to say: it must, because of its method and in order to retain its inner harmony, refuse to see socialism as a scientific undertaking. If it must not concede it this scientific character, it is because the propositions that it enunciates are too widely pitched. It is a complete system of society, considered in the past, in the present, and through their repercussions, in the future. Yet it is impossible that so broad a system can be scientifically constructed. At present, science can only establish partial laws, limited in scope and weakly linked to one another. Consequently it requires the greatest circumspection for anything that deals with practicalities. To be able to pronounce judgements as categorical as those of the socialists about the whole of our social institutions we would need to know somewhat better what those institutions consist of, what causes gave rise to them, to what needs they correspond, and what connections they maintain with one another. But for this all kinds of research are necessary, research that has hardly begun. Speaking precisely, socialism cannot therefore be scientific. It can only use certain facts of science that are incomplete and fragmentary in the service of a cause that it upholds for reasons foreign to science, for socialism goes beyond it. For example how many observations, how many comparisons, statistical, historical, and ethnographical are assumed in the smallest theory of *Capital*. Yet Marx had not only failed to carry out these studies, but they have mostly still to be done. This is not to say that the book does not contain some very stimulating philosophical views. But we must not confuse fine, fruitful intuitions with well-defined laws that have been methodically demonstrated. The task of the scientist is not that of the philosopher. Moreover, of all the criticisms Richard has made of Marx, the strongest seems to us to be the one that limits itself to highlighting the gap that lies between the fundamental proposition of the system and the observations on which it relies.

Yet from the above it by no means follows that sociology should, in our view, treat socialism as a negligible quantity, leaving it out of account. If it is not a scientific theory of social facts, it is a social fact of the utmost importance that sociologists must seek to understand. Whatever one may do, it exists, and not without reason; it expresses a state of society. Undoubtedly we can be sure in advance that it does not express it faithfully. It is not sufficient for the sick person to question himself about the pains that he experiences in order to discover their cause, their nature and the remedy for them. Now socialism is above all a way in which certain social strata particularly adversely affected by the ills of the collectivity represent those ills to themselves. Yet at least it attests to the existence of a social malaise and, although it does not express it adequately, it can help us to understand that malaise because it derives from it. In this regard it is of the greatest interest. But from this viewpoint it matters little what scientific value can be attached to the way in which it justifies its doctrines. They are no more than symbols. We must remove all that apparatus of logic in order to reach the underlying reality. So long as we do not proceed in this way, however ingenious the arguments advanced may be, it is difficult for them not to appear a little artificial and to smack of the scholar, for they do not deal with anything real but only with the external form of reality. Moreover, is not this objective study the only one that is useful in practice? For, when we have refuted the reasons that socialism advances in support of its assertions, we are no more informed about the causes that gave rise to it almost a century ago, or about the needs, whether normal or not, to which it corresponds. But is it not this that is important? It is true that to resolve this question the parties have ready-made answers. But these hasty solutions have no more value when they deny socialism than when they affirm it. To succeed in knowing what socialism is, what it is made up of, and on what it depends, it is no more sufficient to question the socialists than their opponents, but we need research, information and methodical comparisons, for which the muddled and passionately felt intuitions of the common consciousness cannot be a substitute.

REVIEW OF A. LABRIOLA: *ESSAIS SUR LA CONCEPTION MATÉRIALISTE DE L'HISTOIRE* (PARIS 1897)[2]

The object of this book is to reveal the principle of historical philosophy that is at the basis of Marxism, to submit it to a fresh elucidation with a view not to modifying it, but to explain it, rendering it more precise. This principle states that in the last analysis historical development will depend upon economic causes.

This is what has been termed the dogma of economic materialism. Since the author believes that the best formulation of it is to be found in the *Manifesto of the Communist Party*,[3] it is this document that is used as the theme of his study. This comprises two parts: the first expounds the genesis of the doctrine, the second gives a commentary on it. An appendix contains the translation of the *Manifesto*.

Normally the historian sees only the most superficial part of social history. Individuals, who are the actors in history, represent to themselves the events in which they participate in a certain way. So they can understand their behaviour, they imagine they are following some aim or another that appears desirable to them, and they furnish reasons to prove to themselves and, if needs be, to others, that this aim is worthy to be so desired. It is these motives and reasons that the historian considers as having been the really determining causes of historical development. If, for example, he succeeds in discovering what goal the men of the Reformation intended to attain, he believes he has explained at the same time how the Reformation came about. Yet these subjective explanations are worthless because men do not perceive the true motives that cause them to act. Even when our behaviour is determined by private interests, which, since they concern us more nearly, are easier to perceive, we can only distinguish a very small part of the forces that cause us to act, and these are not the most important. This is because the ideas and reasons that develop in our consciousness, the conflicts between which constitute the debates going on inside us, derive very often from organic states, hereditary tendencies and ingrained habits of which we are not aware. This is consequently even more true when we are acting under the influence of social causes which elude us even more because they are more remote and more complex. Luther did not know that he was 'one instant in the development of the Third Estate'. He thought he was working for the glory of Christ and did not suspect that his ideas and actions were determined by a certain state of society, and that the relative position of the social classes required a transformation of old religious beliefs. 'All that has happened in history is the work of man, but was only very rarely the result of a critical choice or a reasoned act of the will'.

Thus if we wish to understand the true linkage between facts we must abandon this ideological method. We must set aside that superficial view of ideas in order to reach the deep matters that they express with greater or less accuracy and the underlying forces from which they derive. In the author's words, 'we must strip the historical facts from the covers in which those facts cloak themselves whilst in the process of evolving.' The only rational and objective explanation of events consists in discovering the way in which they have really been engendered and not the idea of their origins that those who have been their instruments conceived them to be. It is this revolution in historical method that the materialist conception of history has allegedly brought about.

In fact, according to Marx and his disciples, by proceeding in this fashion we are assured that social evolution has as its vital source the state in which technology finds itself at any given moment in history, that is, 'the conditions of the development of labour and the instruments that are appropriate for it'. It is this which constitutes the deep structure or, as our author puts it, the economic infrastructure of society. Depending on whether production is agricultural or industrial, and whether the machines employed oblige it to be concentrated in a small number of large-scale enterprises or, on the other hand, facilitate their dispersion, etc., the relationships between the classes of producers will be very differently determined. It is on these relationships, i.e. the frictions and antitheses of every kind that result from this organization, that all the rest depends. Firstly, the State is a necessary consequence of the division of society into classes subordinate to one another, for a balance cannot be maintained between these entities, which are economically unequal, unless it is imposed by violence and repression. This is the State's role; it is a system of forces employed 'to guarantee or perpetuate a mode of association whose foundation is a form of economic production'. Its interests are therefore bound up with those of the ruling classes. Similarly, the law is never more than 'the defence, whether customary, authoritarian or judicial, of a particular interest'; 'it is only the expression of those interests that have triumphed', and consequently, 'it comes down almost immediately to the economy'. Morality is the whole of the dispositions and habits that social life, depending on how it is organized, develops in the consciousness of individuals. Finally, even the products of art, science and religion are always related to the particular economic conditions.

The scientific value of this viewpoint, so it is stated, is that its effect is to 'naturalize' history. It is 'naturalized' solely because in the explanation of social facts there are substituted for those inconsistent ideals, those phantoms of the imagination that were up to now held to be the springs of progress, forces that are definite, real and resistant, namely the distribution of people into social classes, which is itself linked to the state of economic techniques. Yet we must take care not to confuse this naturalist sociology with what has been termed political and social Darwinism. This consists simply in explaining the development of institutions by the principles and concepts adequate for explaining zoological development. Since animal life is carried on in a purely physical environment that no labour has yet modified, this simplistic philosophy accounts for social evolution by causes that are not social at all, namely the needs and appetites already to be found in the animal creation. According to Labriola, the theory that he is defending is entirely different. It seeks the motivating causes for historical development not in the cosmic circumstances that may have affected the organism, but in the artificial environment that the labour of men associating together has created from nothing and added to that of nature. It makes social phenomena dependent not upon hunger, thirst or the desire for procreation, etc. but upon the state that human artefact has reached, the ways of life that have resulted from it, in short, upon the works of the collectivity. Doubtless men, like the other animals, had originally only the natural environment as their sphere of action. Yet history is not obliged to go back as far as that hypothetical era, about which we can now make no empirical representations. It begins only when an environment going beyond nature, however rudimentary that may be, has arisen, since only then do social phenomena begin to appear. It has not to concern itself with the way — which in any case is not determinable — by which humanity has been led to raise itself in this manner above the pure state of nature and build up a new world. Consequently we may say that the method of economic materialism can be applied to the whole of history.

From these abstract principles revolutionary socialism logically flows. Great changes have come about in industrial technology since a century ago. There must consequently result from them changes of equal importance in the social organization. Since everything concerning the nature and form of production is fundamental and substantial, the upheaval that has occurred in this way is not a local and limited affliction that piecemeal corrections in our collective economy can halt. Of sheer necessity it is a sickness *totius substantiae* that can only be cured by a radical transformation of society. All the old frameworks must be broken, all the social substance set free so that it may be poured into new moulds.

Such is the summary of this work which, not without reason, Sorel in a preface presents as an important contribution to socialist literature. We may undoubtedly deplore the extreme diffuseness in its development, the patent insufficiencies in its composition, and a certain linguistic violence that is out of place in a scientific discussion. Yet, so far as we know, it is one of the most rigorous efforts that has been made to bring Marxist doctrine back to its elementary concepts and to go into them in depth. The thought does not attempt, as too often happens, to hide behind indecisive shades of meaning. It presses straight ahead, with a kind of freshness about it. The author has no other preoccupation than to perceive clearly the principle that underlies the beliefs, all of whose logical consequences he resolutely accepts in advance. Thus this exposition of the system is singularly apt to bring out both fruitful insights and weaknesses.

We believe it to be a fertile idea to explain social life not by the conception that those participating in it have of it but by those deeper causes that elude consciousness. We also think that these causes must be sought mainly in the manner in which individuals associating together are grouped. It even seems to us on this condition, and on this condition alone, that history can become a science, and consequently sociology can exist. For, so that collective representations can be intelligible, they must indeed proceed from something. As they cannot constitute a closed circle, the source from which they derive must be found outside themselves. Either the *conscience collective* is floating in a vacuum, a sort of unrepresentable absolute, or it is joined to the rest of the world by an intermediate substratum on which it consequently depends. On the other hand, of what can this substratum be made up unless it is the members of society, as they are socially combined together? This proposition appears to us to be crystal clear. But we see no reason at all to link it, as does the author, to the socialist movement, from which it is totally independent. For our part we arrived at it before we had read Marx, whose influence we have not undergone in any way. Indeed this conception is the logical outcome of the entire historical and psychological movement over the last fifty years. For a long time historians have perceived that social evolution has causes that the authors of historical events are unaware of. It is under the influence of these ideas that one tends to deny or restrict the role of great men and that, underlying the literary or juridical movements, etc. is to be sought the expression of collective thinking that no one definite personality embodies completely. At the same time individual psychology has above all come to teach us that the individual consciousness very often merely reflects the underlying condition of the organism, and that our successive representations are determined by causes that are not imagined by the subject. From then on it was natural to extend this conception to collective psychology. But we cannot perceive what part the sorry class struggle we are at present witnessing may have had in the elaboration or development of this idea. Doubtless it came at an appropriate moment, when the necessary conditions for it to appear were fulfilled. This could not be possible at any time. But we need to know what these conditions are. When Labriola affirms that the idea arose 'because of the wide, conscious and continuous development of modern technology, and the inevitable suggestion of a new world in the process of being born', he states as self-evident a thesis that is in no way proven. Socialism was able to use the idea to its advantage, but it did not give rise to it, and, above all, it is not implicit in it.

If, as our author postulates, it is true that this objective conception of history is all of a piece with the doctrine of economic materialism, since the latter certainly has socialist origins[4] one might believe the former to have been constituted under the same influence and inspired by the same spirit. *But this confusion has no basis at all and it is vital to dispel it.* There are no solid links between the two theories, whose scientific value is singularly unequal. Just as it appears to us to be true that the causes of social phenomena must be sought outside the representations of the individual, so it seems false to us that they can in the last resort be ascribed to the state of industrial technology or that the economic factor is the mainspring of progress.

Without even contradicting economic materialism with any precise facts, how can we not be aware of the insufficiency of the proofs on which it rests? Here is a law that claims to be the key to history. But in order to demonstrate it one is content to quote a few isolated, disconnected facts, which do not constitute any kind of systematic series and whose interpretation is far from settled. Primitive communism is cited, the struggles between patricians and plebs, between the Third Estate and the nobility, which are explained in economic terms. Even when to these rare documents, which are rapidly surveyed, are added a few examples taken from English industrial history, one will not have succeeded in demonstrating so broad a generalization. On this point Marxism is at odds with its own principle. It starts by declaring that social life depends on causes that elude both the consciousness and the reason in the reasoning process. Yet then, in order to arrive at the causes, procedures are necessary that are at least as intricate and complex as those employed in the natural sciences. All sorts of observations, experiments and laborious comparisons must be required to uncover some of these factors in isolation, and there is no question of gaining at the present time any unified representation of them. Then in a flash all these mysteries are cleared up and a simple solution given to these problems into which human intelligence seemed to be able to penetrate only with such great difficulty. Will it be said that the objective conception that we have just summarily expounded is not proved adequately either? This is absolutely certain. But it does not propose either to assign to social phenomena a definite origin; it confines itself to affirming that there are causes for them. For to state that they have objective causes has no other meaning, since the collective representations cannot have their ultimate causes within themselves. Thus it is merely a proposition intended to guide the enquiry, and consequently continually suspect, for in the last resort it is experience that must decide. It is a methodological rule, and not a law from which one may justifiably deduce important consequences, whether theoretical or practical.

Not only is the Marxist hypothesis not proven, but it runs counter to facts that appear to be well established. Sociologists and historians are tending more and more to come together in affirming that religion is the most primitive of all social phenomena. It is from religion that have emerged, through successive transformations, all the other manifestations of collective activity — law, morality, art, science, political forms, etc. In the beginning everything was religious. But we are aware of no way in which religion can be reduced to economics, nor of any attempt really to effect this reduction. No one has yet demonstrated what were the economic influences under which naturism emerged from totemism, nor through what modifications in technology it became in one place the abstract monotheism of Jehovah, and elsewhere Greco-Latin polytheism. We have strong doubts that such an undertaking could ever be successful. More generally, it is undeniable that originally the economic factor was rudimentary, whereas religious life was, by contrast, luxuriant and all-pervading. How therefore could religion emerge from it, and on the contrary is it not probable that economics depend upon religion rather than the opposite?

Moreover, one should not push the ideas outlined above to extremes where they would lose all truth. Psychophysiology, having indicated that the basis of psychological life lies in the organic substratum,, has often fallen into the error of denying all reality to the latter. From this has emerged the theory that reduces the consciousness to a mere epiphenomenon. The fact has been lost from sight that, if the representations originally depend upon organic states, once they have been constituted they are by this itself realities *sui generis*, autonomous, and capable of becoming causes in their turn and of producing new phenomena. Here sociology must carefully guard against falling into the same error. If the different forms of collective activity have also their substratum, and if in the last instance they derive from it, once they exist they become in their turn original sources of action, having their own efficacy, and reacting upon the very causes upon which they depend. Thus we are far from maintaining that the economic factor is an epiphenomenon: once it exists, it has its own special influence, and can partly modify the very substratum from which it has emerged. But there is no reason to confuse it, in some way, with that substratum, so as to build it up into something that is particularly fundamental. On the contrary, everything leads us to believe that it is secondary and derived. Hence it follows that the economic transformations that have occurred during the course of this century, the replacement of small-scale by large-scale industry, do not in any way necessitate the overthrow and complete renewal of the social order. It follows also that the malaise from which European societies can suffer does not have its origin in these transformations.

REVIEW OF SAVERIO MERLINO:

FORMES ET ESSENCE DU SOCIALISME (PARIS, 1897)[5]

For some while some interesting work has been in progress in the socialist party. Practically everywhere, and especially in Germany, Belgium and Italy, the need has been felt to renew and enlarge formulas within which for too long people had remained imprisoned. The doctrine of economic materialism, the Marxist theory of value, the iron law [of wages], the prime importance assigned to the class struggle, — all such postulates, which still serve as propaganda for the party, are beginning to appear somewhat old-fashioned. Anyone who is well informed about the state of the sciences and the direction they are taking can hardly be satisfied by them. Thus it was natural to seek to disentangle the *socialist idea* from these questionable, outmoded hypotheses, which compromise that idea, and to work towards harmonizing it more with the recent progress in science. It is in this task of rejuvenation that Merlino has taken it upon himself to carry out in the book we are going to review.

The method he employs in order to do so is certainly the surest and most radical one. Is not the best means of revitalizing socialist thought to aim in some way at its very heart, at its source, by divorcing it from the specific systems that claim to express it, and to rethink it anew? This is to some extent what the author wished to do. There are, he states, two kinds of socialism: the socialism of the socialists and the socialism of things. The first kind is to be found in the works of the theorists and in party programmes. In general, it comprises a certain number of formulations, whose contours are relatively well defined, having been systematized more or less logically. The socialism of things consists of that confused drive, half unconscious of itself, that is at work in societies today and that stimulates those societies to seek a fresh reorganization of their forces. It is these needs, these aspirations to a different moral, political and economic regime, that arise from the present conditions of collective life. The first kind of socialism merely interprets, with more or less accuracy, the second kind; it is the reflection of the latter, but always a somewhat pale one. Thus it is this objective, basic socialism that it is essential for us to know. We must successfully take hold of it, and not through the formulations that are advanced which, because they are too narrow, both truncate and denature it. Once we know of what it consists we shall have to do no more than seek the most appropriate means of realizing it. This entails bringing to the light of the present day once and for all those trends and needs that even now exist in more than pure thought.

According to Merlino, this objective socialism can be reduced in essence to the two following tendencies, which are moreover closely related and solidly linked to each other:

1 The tendency towards a political regime in which the individual would be freer, no longer subject to the cumbersome hierarchy that at present oppresses him, and one in which the governance of society by itself would finally become a reality;

2 The tendency towards an economic regime in which contractual
relationships would be truly equitable, and which presumes a
greater equality in social conditions. Indeed any relationship
between individuals that takes place under unequal social
conditions is necessarily unjust. This is because constraint
is exercised by the more favoured of the two contracting parties over the other, thus falsifying the conditions of exchange.
The rich man obtains from the poor man more than the
latter can obtain from the former, because they are not fighting
with equal weapons; one receives more than he gives. Yet
retributory justice can only be realized in so far as the services
exchanged are equivalent. Thus it excludes any idea of a
monopoly. 'It is fair that all men should have equal access to
natural goods' and, more generally, to all the sources of labour.
Interpreted in this way, the social problem appears to be a
juridical one. The question is how to incorporate into positive
law, transforming it into institutions, that ideal of justice that
is today acknowledged by the moral consciousness of civilized
peoples.

Having set out this objective, what will be the means?

The method employed by Merlino to deal with this practical
problem is by no means revolutionary. On the contrary, it is
inspired by a very strong feeling for what are the historical
realities. Society, he says, is no pure abstraction or purely ideal
relationship; it is a concrete, living thing. Its material basis
comprises an accumulation of elements that have been brought
together to perform its functions. Society is made up of a set of
organs 'as indispensable to the life of a civilized people as housing
and clothing are to the life of present-day man'. Thus there
can be no question of razing the social edifice to the ground
in one day of revolution and then erecting another *ab initio* upon
the ruins of the first. What is needed is to develop and expand
what exists. The new grows upon the old; institutions need not be
melted down and remoulded in order that they can serve new
purposes. They are transformed under the pressure of needs.
Socialism's role is to hasten and guide this transformation, and
not to carry out a work of destruction that would shatter the very

tools needed for its realization. To proceed otherwise is to halt the forward march of the movement, under the pretext of speeding it on. Social life is a perpetual act of becoming. Thus it is much more important to determine what it is in the process of becoming, what it should and can develop into in the near future, than to seek to divine that final ideal towards which it is moving. Moreover, a pure ideal is unrealizable precisely because it takes no cognizance of the exigencies of reality. There can never be a perfect balance between services that are rendered and the remuneration for them. There are actions that exceed all possible recompense, such as acts of devotion and scientific discoveries. And then, as regards material products, it is impossible to split them up into the factors of every kind that have contributed to their production, etc.

This is what both collectivism and anarchic socialism have been unable to comprehend. They have undertaken to achieve the ends they are pursuing by leaving out of account the permanent conditions of 'social complicity'. Thus the first has thought feasible a society from which all competition would have been eliminated; the second, one in which there would be a lasting agreement of human wills without their being subjected to any common discipline. Now, however we proceed, the respective value of things, i.e. the reason for which exchanges occur, will always require to be determined by the spontaneous equilibrium achieved by supply and demand. There are no regulations flexible enough to keep up with the continual variations in tastes and needs, and which can cater for an infinite diversity of special circumstances. From another viewpoint, however perfect solidarity may be, the interest of the individual can never coincide exactly with that of society. The sole means of controlling the disagreements that would inevitably arise from these divergences is to install a stable organization that would overrule individual interests in the name of collective needs. Moreover, these unilateral conceptions, even if we assumed they were realizable, could not become concrete without becoming at odds with one another, precisely because they unduly simplify the given facts of the problem. Thus the main aim of collectivism is to emancipate the individual — yet, by its excessive centralization it would end up by becoming a veritable despotism. For the opposite reasons anarchism would lead to the same result. For if there were no collective organization superior to arrangements between individuals, there would be nothing to prevent the inequalities naturally inherent in things and people from producing their logical consequences. Monopolies would once again arise of their own accord. This is the danger to which we expose ourselves if we fail to seek in the past the seeds of the future. On the other hand we should not hope either to satisfy the fresh demands of the public consciousness by leaving the old organization intact. If it is chasing a will o' the wisp to desire to construct a new society from a *tabula rasa*, it is not through ancient institutions retained in unmodified form that social life can be renewed. Yet it is this task, replete with contradictions, that has tempted the 'socialism of the chair', which might also be termed conservative socialism, and which is no less powerless than its adversary, revolutionary socialism, but for opposing reasons.

In order to introduce into our societies more retributory and more distributive justice, and to make the individual more free, there is no need to upset from top to bottom the entire system of property, production and exchange. Whatever one might do, private property can never be abolished, for in property there is something inherently personal, and the individual nature of property likewise entails that of production. Also, there can be no reason why the private enterprise system cannot be modified so as to make exchanges sufficiently equitable. It would suffice so to organize it that monopolies were rendered impossible. Merlino argues that this result might be arrived at by the following means:

1 Land, and the large-scale means of production, transport and distribution would be owned by the collectivity.
2 The collectivity would itself exploit those industries most liable to become important monopolies, but only these. As for the others, the initiative in production and exchange would be left to individuals and private bodies. It would be competition that would decide in whose hands should be placed the instruments of labour; the collectivity would accord them to whoever

offered the best conditions for them. By this process the most capable would be self-selected. It would only remain to establish detailed rules so as to ensure impartiality in the granting of concessions, etc. On the other hand, through the charges paid, the rent, i.e. the surplus income deriving from the inequality of natural conditions, would not profit individuals, but the collectivity. In this way that source of inequality would be extinguished.

3 Yet, in order for this moral equity to be real, society would ensure that all its members enjoyed the means of education and work. Moreover, out of a spirit of solidarity it would provide them free of charge with certain facilities, and would come to the help of those unable to cope.

Under such a system, there would accordingly be *private management* of industries since, once they had paid the rent to the collectivity, individual and private bodies would have the full enjoyment of the fruits of their labour, and could exchange them as they thought fit, etc. Yet this private management would not be at all *capitalist*, since capital could not be a monopoly. Nonetheless it will be objected that the collectivity would exercise a very striking ascendancy as regards the individual and his liberties. But our author believes he can obviate this disadvantage through his conception of the political organization of such a society.

Theoretically this conception is an anarchic one. Individuals should not be subjected to any form of domination by another individual, class or party. 'No governmental power. The people cannot reign over the people.' All that it can and must do is to administer its own affairs. Consequently the whole system of government must give place to an administration for public affairs. Or rather, since social interests are very diverse, and no one has the necessary ability to administer them all at the same time, a plurality of autonomous administrative bodies is necessary, charged with the different domains of social activity. If we have understood clearly the author's thinking there would be as many bodies as there are groups of workers and principal collective functions. Yet, from certain passages in his work, it would appear that the basis of this administrative organization would be territorial. Perhaps the idea is that these two types of groups would function simultaneously. These various administrations would be formed on the model of producers' cooperatives. Their members would be chosen from those rivalling with one another who showed the greatest ability, and they would choose their technical directors and administrators from among their number. Precautions would be taken to give them effective responsibility, for one of the faults of the present regime is the lack of a sense of responsibility among public officials, particularly among those elected to office. It is a matter of urgency to ensure that the idea of justice penetrates into the domain of public life.

Such autonomous organizations would be linked by communicating organs that might be permanent or temporary (congresses, conferences, federal commissions), whose task would be to administer those interests common to a multiplicity of groups, or to all groups. Yet these commissions would also be only administrative. In no circumstances would there be any general legislative body, for a permanent organ of that kind would rapidly subject individuals to its authority. Technical legislation would be discussed by each group concerned. Questions of a general nature would be resolved by the collectivity itself, if numbers were not too great, or by *ad hoc* temporary assemblies for each particular case. In brief, society would consist of a vast constellation of autonomous groups, each legislating on its own behalf, and setting up common assemblies only when necessary, for precise purposes that were found to require such gatherings.

Although we may legitimately find the documentary evidence in this book to be somewhat slim, the argument above all dialectical, and the authorities cited sometimes far from scientific (cf. particularly the importance ascribed to Tolstoy's theory of government in the work), we cannot applaud enough the effort the author makes to rid socialism of all kinds of doctrine, which for him are no more than encumbrances. In particular, it would be a considerable step forward, one from which everybody would benefit, if socialism finally abandoned confusing the social question with that of the workers. The first includes the other, but extends beyond it. The malaise from which we are suffering is not rooted in any particular class; it is general over the whole of society. It attacks employers as well as workers, although it manifests itself in different forms in both: as a disturbing, painful agitation for the capitalist, as discontent and irritation for the proletariat. Thus the problem reaches infinitely beyond the material interests of the two classes concerned. It is not a question of merely reducing the share of one group so as to increase that of the other, but one of refashioning the moral constitution of society. This manner of posing the problem, whilst it corresponds more to the facts, would have the advantage of causing socialism to lose that aggressive and hate-ridden character for which it has often been justly reproached. For then it would address, not those feelings of anger that the less-favoured class harbours against the other, but feelings of pity for society, which is suffering in all classes and in all its organs.

On the other hand, it cannot be denied that the main objective ascribed to the reform is one of those that should really be pursued. It is true that we may doubt whether the problem of contract possesses the kind of preponderance that is attributed to it. Yet it is certainly one of those that are posed in the most pressing manner, and it is evident that the present state of our law of contract no longer satisfies the requirements of our moral consciousness. No longer does a contract appear equitable merely because it has been agreed upon. It must also be one where the contracting party does not enjoy such a superiority over the other that he predominates and is able to impose his wishes.

Yet what we see as requiring the most categorical reservation concerns the programme of the means the author suggests in order to realize what he terms the *essence of socialism*. Here also we should doubtless praise his justifiable mistrust of unilateral solutions. It is absolutely certain that in the future societies, of whatever kind they may be, will not be based upon one single principle: former social forms always survive in new ones, and not without reason. For the older forms could not have been constituted unless they corresponded to certain needs, and these needs cannot suddenly have disappeared. New necessities may relegate them to the background but cannot eliminate them root and branch. Consequently, however future society is organized, it will include, in a state of coexistence, the most varied types of economic management. There will be room for all kinds. But the anarchic nature of the political theories Merlino expounds seem to us to constitute a veritable sociological heresy. The more societies develop, the more the State develops. The State's functions become more numerous, and penetrate increasingly all other social functions, which by this very process it concentrates and unifies. Progress towards centralization runs parallel to the progress of civilization. If we compare the State as it is today in a great nation such as France, or Germany or Italy, with what it was in the sixteenth century, and what it was then with what it was in the Middle Ages, it can be seen that it is moving entirely continuously in the same direction. Equally so, was not the State, even in the Greek and Italian cities considered at the peak of their development, rudimentary as compared with what it has become among the peoples of Europe? One may say that there is no historical law that is better established. Hence how can we suppose that in the societies of tomorrow an abrupt regression, moving us backwards, will occur? Is not such a hypothesis contrary to all likelihood?

The reasons advanced by the author as to why this impossible step backwards appears desirable have moreover no better justification. The State is esteemed to be the adversary of the individual, and seemingly cannot develop save to his detriment. There is no greater figment of the imagination than this alleged antagonism, for which Merlino has borrowed, very wrongly, the idea from orthodox economics. The truth is that the State has in fact rather been the liberator of the individual. It is the State that, as it has increased in strength, has freed the individual from specific local groups that tended to engulf him — the family, the city, the corporation, etc. In history individualism has advanced hand in hand with Statism. This does not mean that the State cannot become despotic and oppressive. Like all the forces of nature, if it is not limited by some collective power that restrains it, it will develop out of all proportion and in turn become a threat to individual liberties. Hence it follows that the social force within it must be neutralized by other social forces acting to counterbalance it. If secondary groups can easily become tyrannical when their effects are not tempered by those of the State, conversely those of the State, to remain at a normal level, require in turn to be moderated. To arrive at this result there needs to be in society, outside the State although subject to its influence, more restricted groups (for the moment it does not matter whether these are of a territorial or occupational nature). But they must be powerfully constituted and endowed with an individuality and with sufficient autonomy to be able to resist the encroachments of the central authority. What liberates the individual is not the abolition of any central regulatory force, but for such groups to be numerous, provided these multiple centres are all coordinated and subordinated to one another.

We can understand that this fundamental error seriously affects the whole system set out by Merlino, since in the end it boils down to his mistaking the true nature and role of social discipline, that is, what constitutes the vital knot of collective life. Thus the society portrayed in his plan has something about it that is essentially tenuous and unsolid. For socialism to renew itself and progress, it has not merely to rid itself of its exclusive obsession with the question of the working class and include the present malaise in all its dimensions. It must also free itself from the anarchist trend that has deformed the ideas of its greatest thinkers. It must succeed in understanding that a more perfect and complex justice can reign only in society if that justice has an organ and consequently can develop. Far from the State's moral role being about to end, we believe that it can only continue to grow. Not that by this we mean to justify what Merlino terms conservative socialism. It is very plain that the State cannot be equal to the tasks that confront it unless it undergoes a profound transformation. Yet it must first exist.

A DEBATE ON CIVIL SERVICE UNIONS (1908)[6]

JEANNENEY: On the one hand, the union movement proceeds from the conviction held by trade unionists, and the hope they entertain, that they have already, if you like, of possessing a sovereign remedy against the arbitrary acts and favouritism that nobody denies exist. In this order of ideas I should like someone to tell me what are the superior merits of a trade union as compared with the ordinary professional association. In other words, what is specifically the superiority of the trade union over the professional association? This is the first clarification that I should like to see given by the militant trade unionists that are here.

On the other hand, trade unionism declares its ultimate purpose to be the rational organization of the public services through corporative action. It seeks the democratization and even the socialization of the public services. This is an idea that is distinct from the previous one and which deserves to be treated separately. I should like it to be given the full discussion it requires, after the other one.

DURKHEIM: It seems to me that the problem was beginning to be presented with a certain clarity. We all acknowledge that the complaints of civil servants are too often justified. Moreover, one may admit that the trade union, because of the ideas that it evokes, and the prestige that the term enjoys *sui generis*, is more suitable than an association for obtaining the redress of certain of the lapses that have been pointed out.

At the very least, I see no use at all in concentrating the controversy on this point. But once these postulates are granted, the question remains entirely unresolved. For after all, even when it is established that the trade union is a good means of obtaining satisfaction for civil servants we must nevertheless not lose sight of the fact that above and beyond the interest of civil servants, there is something else: the general interest of the country. Now I am afraid that trade unionism in the public administration would result in imposing upon it a framework that is in no way suitable for it, and thus would run the risk of seriously disorganizing those social functions that are most essential. Speaking in this fashion, it is true I may appear to align myself with the purely conservative viewpoint. But I believe the trade union movement nonetheless runs counter to our general direction in historical evolution.

Despite its revolutionary aspect, there is something retrograde about it.

To prove this proposition I must return to an idea that I already expressed at the last *Entretien.*

During the nineteenth century there was born an idea to which many of us are certainly attached. It is that between jobs in the private and public sectors there is, in the final analysis, no difference in kind. This is because, to a varying degree, we are all 'civil servants' of society.

Trade unions have been the means of introducing to some extent this idea into our economic life. In fact, in the economic domain the social character of functions is only slightly felt; indeed, it is only indirectly so. It brings only individuals into relationships with one another, and in the service of individual interests. But the interests of individuals are naturally opposing: hence the painful and continual conflicts, and the chaotic aspect of economic relationships. Through trade unions it was hoped to introduce a little order into this anarchy. In fact, the trade union groups together workers in the same occupation, if only approximately, as are grouped, for each branch of the administration, employees within the same public department. When all workers in the same industry unite permanently for common action, they are much more capable of becoming aware of, and communicating to everybody, a feeling for the social character of that occupation. They can better understand, and make others understand, that they also constitute an organ in society. We may hope that in these conditions the notion of the social interests which that occupation serves will be more readily discernible, and capable of taking precedence over individual interests that up to now have been preponderant.

Thus the trade union has been a means of lessening the gap that in this respect separated economic from public functions, and of imprinting upon the former a more patently social character. There can be no question of being able to blend them completely. Whatever changes may occur in the future, between these two forms of activity there will remain differences whose rationale is inherent in the very nature of things. But the once striking contrast that existed between them is no longer in accord with our present-day ideas, nor with the present state of the economy. It was necessary to make the contrast less marked. Thus, in the final resort, the trade union is only a poor and imperfect image of what the administrative organization is.

Yet here we are now wanting to fashion the model upon the copy! We wish to impose upon functions that are social to the highest degree a form of organization that has been devised for those whose social nature is least apparent. We aspire to a time when strikes in industry would be rare, and even one when they would be compulsorily referred to arbitration tribunals, when wages would be more stable and less dependent upon bargaining, capriciousness and circumstances. And such evils, which we seek to combat even in our economic life — here we are now talking about introducing them into those public services that have been free from them! It is true that all the advocates of a trade union do not go so far as to demand the right to strike. But there are also many others who are less moderate. And then, the trade union has practices that are inherent in its nature and that it would be very difficult to avoid.

This is why I say that trade unionism in the public administration seems to me a retrograde move. Thus I fear that it would be a remedy worse than the evil itself. I am afraid that, in order to redress the grievances, which are moreover legitimate, of a special category of citizens — one very limited in number — we would throw into disarray the most vital mechanisms in the social organism.

Again, if an improvement in the present situation could only be brought about in this manner! But why not require that improvement from a reform of the present system of administration? The real problem seems to me to discover what modifications can and should be introduced into it in order to prevent the very real ills that have rightly been denounced.

BERTHELEMY: I completely approve of what Durkheim has just said. Let me add that what the trade unionists are demanding will only tend to introduce a new method of recruiting leaders.

What will be the outcome of the trade union campaign? Logically it will be the introduction of a system of election for the allocation of the higher posts.

Now, until the contrary has been demonstrated to me, I consider that any system that substitutes an elective system for appointment by competitive examination would be fatal. Election may be indispensable, but everywhere that it is practised, it substitutes intrigue for merit. It places a premium upon boastfulness. Above all, in the end it subjects the person elected (who should govern) to the elector (who should obey). In the realm of politics an elective system can avoid the worst evils. In the realm of administration election can only be destructive of any reasonable authority.

Yes, doubtless in certain cases, trade union resistance has been able to achieve good results. The question is to know whether these results weigh more in the balance than the bad practices that the trade unions have brought about. Against the facts that have been cited I could state other, opposing ones that are quite to the contrary, and nothing but a condemnation of trade union agitators. I have had occasion to cite at other meetings the shameful results that the excise department union has extracted from the weakness of M. Merlou. A few days ago M. Clemenceau passionately denounced the 'demands' — which were as incorrect in the form they took as they were of little worth in their substance — that were drawn up by the prison warders' union. I refrain from going into detail, because one fact proves nothing. Civil servants have legitimate protests to voice against the abuses of favouritism; trade unionism has given them the power to speak. That is no reason to close one's eyes and sing the praises of a method that is destructive of all authority. When I have been shown the uselessness of authority in the functioning of the public services, I shall become a trade unionist. Until this proof has been vouchsafed I am and will remain radically opposed to a campaign of agitation that is as ill-considered in its aim as it is incorrect in its methods of action.

DURKHEIM: I think it would be advantageous not to deal at the moment with the question of the elective system. For if we grant that a reform of the administrative system is necessary it is difficult not to give the elective principle some place in that reform. The capital question that, it seems to me, should dominate the discussion and from which it would be inappropriate to stray is this: should we strive to make the purely private contract more similar to that of the public contract, or should we reduce the public contract to the inferior forms of the private contract?

BOISSE: Does Durkheim at least concede that in its present state the trade union can be a useful instrument of struggle in the democratic organization of certain branches of the administration? Without allowing that it should be an *end in itself*, or that it has any ultimate value, can we consider its action as being at least *temporarily* necessary? However interesting speculation may be about the economic and political future of societies, it may perhaps be appropriate to restrict our gaze to present realities, and even in certain cases to the immediate present.

DURKHEIM: I have already replied to that. It is possible that a trade union in the public administration can serve special interests that are moreover respectable, namely, those of the civil servants concerned. But at the same time I am afraid that it would disorganize social life, preventing it from functioning normally, and this is an ill for which no compensation is possible.

PAUL DESJARDINS: Waroquier, it is you who consider a civil service trade union as a means of ultimately transforming the whole administrative system, and as the embryo of that future system or a prototype on which it should be modelled. Your thesis is precisely what Durkheim has just called into question. Would you care to state to us the reasons why you are opposed to him on that point?

WAROQUIER: Durkheim's line of argument is certainly very impressive. However, I believe that the creation of trade unions with the aim that he has stated is not a retrograde tendency or a return to the past.

Durkheim's thesis seems to me to be purely nominal. Basing itself upon the evolution of the forms of private institutions towards a continuous accentuation of their institutional and public character, it seems to me, however, not in accordance with a rigorous interpretation of that evolution.

Considering the matter from the standpoint of a struggle between interests, of whatever kind these may be, one notes that individual law and individual action have no longer either virtue or use, and are being progressively replaced by collective law and action. In order to set that law in motion and allow scope for that action to unfold, collective organizations are necessary. In the event, it is a trade union type of organization. This is my reply to the historical and sociological criticism of the observations made by Durkheim.

DURKHEIM: I do not see how an answer has been given to the question I put: how will we be able to elevate the so-called private functions to the dignity of public functions if, on the other hand, we lower the latter to the level of the former?

You speak of a future society in which all branches of public administration would be trade unions. I think that if you were to clarify the idea you have of these trade unions as you imagine them in the future you would see that they have nothing in common save the name with what we today term unions. They would doubtless be huge administrative corporations, strongly organized and unified, which would differ from our present-day administration only because the elective principle would play a greater part. Today our trade unions have neither that unity nor that strong organization. They are private, individual groupings. For a single occupation you can have as many as you wish. It is this absence of unity in organization and of hierarchy that renders them unsuitable for the task that it is wished they should fulfil. When one speaks of trade unions and their role in administrative life, we mean unions as they are at the present time, and not unions as they might be in some vague future.

PAUL DESJARDINS: Waroquier considers the union to be the means whereby our society evolves on a democratic path, is that not the case?

WAROQUIER: Exactly.

PAUL DESJARDINS: Which comes down to saying that the elective principle which is predominating more and more in all forms of organization, leads to the public administration union recommended by Waroquier . . .

DURKHEIM: It is clear that administrative reform must consist in introducing more fully the elective principle into administration. But in order to introduce this principle why should it be necessary to overturn the organ of administration, even to destroy it, in order to substitute some new organism? Why destroy life where it exists, instead of reforming it?

WAROQUIER: Allow me, Durkheim, to put the question to you in another form. In principle, do you consider the system of cooperative development superior to the system of capitalist development? If so, you should make its value general and not restrict it solely to the economic sphere.

DURKHEIM: First of all, one would need to know what you mean by 'cooperatism'.

WAROQUIER: Naturally, I would suppose that cooperation has been realized.

DURKHEIM: This term 'cooperatism' would need to be defined. What is more, why should not cooperation, to the extent that it is legitimate, not be introduced into the administrative system?

WAROQUIER: I consider that the economic system of cooperation is superior to the present system of production.

On the other hand, from the point of view of experience, it is certain that if you wish to maintain authority, as it exists, it would be for reasons of competence: your criticism seemed to me to bear on this point.

DURKHEIM: On the contrary, I avoided steering the discussion toward details like these.

BERTHELEMEY: No, it was I that made the criticism.

WAROQUIER: Ah, then I beg your pardon: poor old trade unionism is being so attacked on all sides that I can no longer remember where all the assaults have come from. (Smiles) In my little life as a civil servant, which up to yet has not been very long, I have noticed that the greater the latitude given to subordinates as well as heads of departments, the better the service proceeded. The experience has been somewhat local, I agree . . .

But at the time of the postal crisis did you not notice that the plan for the reorganization of the service came from the postal and telegraph association, and that the higher echelons of the administration were too incompetent to provide a plan of such high quality?

Now here were people whose corporative consciousness had not yet been awakened, who have not yet reached the stage of development that we require for the establishment of that system, and yet who show themselves almost the equals of the central authority.

DURKHEIM: Many individual examples of that kind could be put forward, without carrying conviction or progress being made on the problem.

WAROQUIER: I do not believe that there is such disparity between the competence of higher officials and those occupying subordinate posts.

DURKHEIM: You are missing out an entire element in administrative life that is essential, which is authority and hierarchy. Centres of command must exist. One cannot conceive that authority, which has proved indispensable in all known societies, is suddenly going to prove useless.

WAROQUIER: Yes, we admit that there is a hierarchy of functions, with the natural prerogative of hierarchy, which is the right to give orders and to control, but not a hierarchy of a personal character. There is a hierarchy of functions, but not of persons.

DURKHEIM: Precisely. There are only functions. Why do you not wish to put the following question: what must be changed in the administrative system in order to harmonize it with the present state of affairs? What struck me especially about what we were told a little while ago concerning the railway union was the fact that considerable improvements were obtained as soon as employees' delegates officially had seats on the boards that decide upon promotion. Since in the end we must come to some reform of this kind, why should it not be made the immediate goal of our demands? But to obtain it we must demand a statute, not unions.

5

Political Obligation, Moral Duty and Punishment

MORALITY AND OBLIGATION[1]

Moral reality, like every kind of reality, can be studied from two different viewpoints. One may seek to know and understand it, or one may set out to judge it. The first of these problems, which is entirely theoretical, should necessarily come before the second. It is the sole one that will be dealt with here. We will merely demonstrate at the end how the method followed and the solutions adopted leave untouched the right then to tackle the practical problem.

On the other hand, to be able to study moral reality theoretically it is indispensable to determine beforehand what constitutes a moral fact. In order to be able to observe it, we must needs know what characterizes it, and by what signs it can be recognized. It is this question that will be dealt with first. Next, we shall investigate whether it is possible to find a satisfactory explanation for these characteristics.

I

What are the distinctive characteristics of the moral fact?

Every morality presents itself to us as a system of rules of conduct. Yet all the techniques are likewise regulated by maxims which prescribe how the actor should conduct himself in certain set circumstances. What therefore makes moral rules different from other rules?

1 We shall show that moral rules are invested with a special authority, by virtue of which they are obeyed because they impart commands. Thus we shall discover once more — but by a purely empirical analysis — the notion of duty, which will be given a definition very close to that which Kant gave. Obligation therefore constitutes one of the prime characteristics of the moral rule.

2 Yet, contrary to what Kant has stated, the notion of duty does not exhaust the notion of morality. It is impossible for us to carry out an act solely because we are commanded to do so, regardless of its purport. For us to undertake to become the actor, the act should to some extent engage our sensibility, and in some respect appear *desirable*. Obligation or duty therefore expresses only one of the aspects, and an abstract one at that, of morality. A certain *desirability* is another characteristic, no less essential than the first.

However, something like the nature of duty is to be found in this *desirability* of the moral viewpoint. If it is true that the purport of the act attracts us, yet by its very nature it is one not capable of being accomplished without effort, without constraint being exercised upon oneself. The urge, which can even be one of enthusiasm, through which we are enabled to act morally, draws us out of ourselves, lifts us above our own nature — something which does not occur without difficulty and without our applying ourselves. It is this desirability *sui generis* that is commonly called goodness.

Goodness and duty are two characteristics upon which it is particularly useful to insist — without our wishing to deny that there may be others. We shall be especially eager to show that every moral act displays these two characteristics, although they can be combined together in variable proportions.

In order to give some idea of how the notion of the moral fact can present these two aspects, which are in part contradictory, it will be compared with the notion of the *sacred*, which manifests the same duality. The sacred being is, in a sense, the forbidden being, whom one does not dare to violate; it is also the being that is good, loved, and sought after. The comparison between these two notions will be justified:

1 historically, by their being akin and linked in their relationship to each other.
2 by examples drawn from our present-day morality. The human personality is sacred; we do not dare to violate it, we keep a distance from the ambit of the person, yet at the same time the supreme good is communion with others.

II

Once these characteristics have been determined we would like to explain them, that is, to find a means of allowing us to understand how there are precepts that we must obey because they give commands, and which demand from us desirable acts in the special sense that has been defined above. To tell the truth, a methodical answer to this question assumes as exhaustive a study as possible of the special rules the totality of which constitutes our morality. But without this method, inapplicable in the circumstances, it is possible to arrive at results that are not without value by a more summary procedure.

By interrogating the contemporary moral consciousness (whose answers can moreover be confirmed by what we know about the different moralities of all known peoples) we can agree on the following points:

1 In fact, the term 'moral' has never been applied to an act whose only object is the interest of the individual, or the perfection of the individual understood in a purely selfish way;
2 If the individual that I am does not constitute an end having *in itself* a moral character, the same necessarily holds good for those individuals who are like me and who differ from me only to a greater or lesser degree;
3 Hence we may conclude that, *if a morality exists*, it can only have as its object the group formed by a plurality of individuals

associating together, i.e. society, *on condition, however, that the society can be considered as a personality qualitatively different from the individual personalities that go to make it up.* Thus morality begins where there begins an attachment to a group of any kind.

Once this has been postulated the characteristics of the moral fact are explicable. Firstly, we will show how society is a good thing, desirable for the individual, who cannot exist outside it, who cannot deny it without denying himself; how, at the same time, because it goes beyond the individual, he cannot wish and desire it without doing some violence to his individual nature. Secondly, we shall then demonstrate how society, as well as being a good thing is a moral authority that, by communicating certain precepts of conduct which it particularly cherishes, endows them with the hallmark of obligation.

Moreover, we will apply ourselves to establishing how certain ends — the devotion of individuals to one another, the devotion of the scientist to science — that are not moral ends in themselves, nevertheless partake of that particular trait indirectly or derivatively.

Finally an analysis of the collective sentiments will explain the sacred character attributed to moral matters — an analysis that will moreover only confirm the previous one.

III

The objection will be raised to this conception that it subjugates the mind to the prevalent moral opinion. This is not so at all, for the society that morality bids us desire is not society as it appears to itself, but society as it is or tends to be in reality. The consciousness that society possesses of itself in or through public opinion can be inadequate in comparison with the underlying reality. It can be that public opinion is full of hangovers from the past and lags behind as regards the real state of society. It can be that, under the influence of temporary circumstances, certain principles that are even essential to existing morality for a while are thrust back into the unconscious and from then onwards become as if they were not there. The science of morality allows these errors . . . to be rectified.

ROUSSEAU AND HOBBES ON POLITICAL ORDER[2]

We can now appreciate the perfect continuity that the thoughts of Rousseau represent from the second *Discours* to the *Contrat Social*. The *state of nature*, as it is described in the first of these works, consists of a kind of peaceful anarchy in which individuals, independent of one another, and entering into no relationships among themselves, depend only upon the abstract force of nature. In the *civilized state*, as conceived by Rousseau, the situation is the same, but in a new form. Individuals are outside one another's ambit, sustaining among themselves as few personal relationships as possible. But they depend upon a new force, added to the natural forces, one which has nevertheless the same character of generality and necessity: this is the *general will*. In the same way, man in the state of nature submits of his own accord to the effect of natural forces and follows spontaneously the direction that they impose upon him, because he feels instinctively that he can do no better and that self-interest dictates his conduct. He wants to do what he does. In the civilized state he submits himself no less freely to the general will, because that general will is of his own making and by obeying it he is obeying only himself.

In this way the connections and differences between Rousseau and his two predecessors, Hobbes and Montesquieu, are discernable. For all three, society is something that is added on to nature proper. For Montesquieu himself the laws of the state of nature are distinct from those of the social state. The former are superimposed upon the latter by an express act of the legislator. Yet if there is agreement upon this fundamental point, there are very deep differences in the way in which these thinkers conceive the governance that man adds in this way to the rest of the universe.

For Hobbes it is an act of the will that gives rise to the social order, and it is an act of the will continually renewed that is its mainstay. Societies are formed because men wish, so as to escape the horrors of the state of war, to subject themselves to an absolute sovereign, and they are maintained because this sovereign prevents their dissolution. The sovereign it is who rules and it is the submission of men to his sovereign will that constitutes the entire social bond. He must be obeyed because he commands. Undoubtedly, if they agree to this dependence it is because they find it in their interest, but this interest does not constitute the basis of all the details of social organization. Once the State is set up it is the head of State who rules without accepting any control. Montesquieu's thinking was already very different. If civil law can only be drawn up by a legislator, the legislator cannot draw it up how he likes. For it to be as it should be it must be in conformity with the nature of things. So far as possible, it does not depend on what is arbitrary; the conditions prevailing in society necessarily determine it. It is not impossible for it to depart from them, but then it becomes abnormal. Rousseau is perhaps even more categorical on this point. What constitutes the foundation of the social system is the objective concordance of interests, and the state of opinion, morals, customs, and laws can only express that state of things. It is precisely this which makes it impossible for the general will to be represented by one individual. It is because it goes beyond the bounds of any individual will. These two kinds of things are heterogeneous, and the one cannot serve as a substitute for the other. Opinion has its natural basis in the whole and not the part. Thus Rousseau's preoccupation is much less to arm the sovereign with a power of coercion great enough to cause resistance to fall away than to shape minds so that no resistance is engendered.

Thus, whilst these thinkers are in agreement in affirming the heterogeneity of what is social and what is individual, we note an increasing effort to base the social being upon nature. Yet it is here that is to be found the weakness in the system. If, as we have shown, collective life, according to Rousseau, is not contrary to the natural order, there are so few links with it that one cannot see with any clarity how it is possible. Somewhere Rousseau says that the authority of the legislator, if it is to be respected, already assumes a certain social spirit. But the constitution of society assumes this even more so. If, however, it is formed among a few isolated individuals, so to speak in an atomic condition, one cannot see from where it can spring. If, moreover, Rousseau allowed the existence of a state of war, as does Hobbes, one can conceive that to put an end to it men would constitute themselves into an entity and would even go so far as to refashion their primitive nature. Yet even this reason cannot be granted him, since, according to him the state of war arises when life is lived in common. Just as he scarcely explains how society could arise, even in the imperfect forms it has assumed in history, so he has also great difficulty in showing how it is possible for it to be rid of its imperfections and to constitute itself in a logical manner. Its foundations are so far from being solidly based on what exists already that it appears like a building that is continually swaying, whose balance, excessively delicately poised, cannot in any case be stabilized and maintained save through an almost miraculous conjuncture of circumstances.

RELIGION, INDIVIDUALISM AND POLITICAL RITUAL[3]

. . . if religion is a product of social causes how can we explain the individual worship and universalist character of certain religions? If it has arisen *in foro externo*, how has it managed to penetrate into the inmost being of the individual, becoming ever more deeply enmeshed within him? If it is the creation of specific individualized societies how was it able to break away from them to such a point that it is conceived of as the common affair of humanity?

In the course of our investigation [*The Elementary Forms of the Religious Life*] we have encountered the first germs of individual religion and religious cosmopolitanism, and we have seen how they have been formed. Thus we possess the most general elements of the reply that can be given to this double question.

In fact we have shown how the religious force that inspires the clan, by embodying itself within the consciousness of individuals, itself becomes individualized. In this way secondary sacred beings are created; each individual possesses his own, made in his own image, associated with his inner life, linked solidly to his destiny: they are the soul, the individual totem, the tutelary ancestor, etc. These beings are the object of rites that the believer can celebrate by himself, outside any group. Thus this is indeed a first form of individual worship. It is certainly still only a very rudimentary form of worship, but this is because, since the individual personality is still not very specific and since little value attaches to it, the cult that expresses it still cannot be very developed. Yet as individuals differ increasingly from one another and the value of the person grows, the corresponding cult has itself loomed larger in the whole of religious life, whilst becoming more hermetically sealed off from the outside.

The existence of individual cults therefore implies nothing that contradicts or hinders a sociological explanation of religion, for the religious forces that individual cults address are only the individualized forms of collective forces. Thus even when religion seems to be wrapped up wholly within the inmost depths of the individual, it is still within society that is to be found the living source on which it feeds. We can now appreciate the significance of that radical individualism that would seek to make religion something that is purely individual: it fails to recognize the basic conditions of religious life. If radical individualism has remained up to now at the stage of theoretical inspirations that are never realized, it is because it is unrealizable. A philosophy can certainly be elaborated in the silence of inner meditation, but not a faith. For, above all, faith represents warmth, life, enthusiasm, the exaltation of every activity of the mind, the lifting of the individual beyond himself. But how, without transcending himself, can the individual increase the energies that he possesses? How could he go beyond himself through his own strength alone? The only hearth that gives off heat at which we can warm ourselves morally is that formed by the company of our fellows. The only moral forces by which we can sustain and increase our own forces are those that others impart to us. Let us even concede that there really do exist beings more or less similar to those presented to us in mythology. For them to be able to exert over human spirits the useful effect that is their *raison d'être* we must believe in them. But beliefs are active only when they are shared. We can certainly sustain them for some while by a wholly personal effort, but this is not how they arise or how they are acquired. It is even dubious whether they can be preserved under such conditions. In fact the man who has a true faith feels a supreme need to spread it; to do this he emerges from his isolation and draws closer to others, seeking to convince them, and it is the ardour of the convictions that he arouses which come to strengthen his own. It would quickly die away if it remained alone. . . .

Thus there is in religion something that is eternal which is destined to survive all the individual symbols in which religious thought has been successively cocooned. There can be no society that does not feel the need at regular intervals to maintain and strengthen the collective sentiments and collective ideas which constitute its unity and personality. But this moral restoration can only be obtained through meetings, assemblies and congregations, where individuals, drawing close to one another, reaffirm together their common feelings. Hence there arise ceremonies that in their purpose, in the results that they produce and the procedures employed in them, are no different in nature from religious ceremonies proper. What essential difference is there between an assembly of Christians celebrating the principal dates in the life of Christ, or Jews celebrating the exodus from Egypt or the handing down of the Ten Commandments, and a meeting of citizens commemorating the institution of a new charter of morality or some great event of national life?

If today we have perhaps some difficulty in picturing to ourselves what such festivals and ceremonies might be like in the future, it is because we are passing through a transitional phase, one of moral mediocrity. The great matters of the past, those which inspired the enthusiasm of our forefathers, no longer excite in us the same ardour, either because they have become part of our common practice to such an extent that we are not conscious of them, or because they no longer match our present aspirations. Yet up to now nothing has occurred to replace them. We can no longer feel passionately about the principles in whose name Christianity recommended masters to treat their slaves humanely; moreover, the conception that religion has of equality and human brotherhood appears to us nowadays to leave too much room for unjust inequalities. Its pity for the humble seems to us to be over-Platonic; we should like it to be more effective. Yet we still do not see clearly what it should be nor how it can be realized in concrete terms. In short, the ancient gods grow old and are dying, and new ones are not yet born. This is what rendered abortive Comte's attempt to organize a religion evoking ancient historical memories, artificially reawakened. It is from life itself, and not from a dead past, that a living religion can emerge. Yet this state of uncertainty and muddled confusion cannot last for ever. The day will come when our societies will once again know that creative ferment in the course of which new ideas will arise, and new doctrines evolve to serve for a while as a guide for humanity. Once they have passed through this stage men will feel spontaneously the need to relive them in thought from time to time, that is, to maintain the memory of them through festivals which breathe fresh life regularly into their fruits. We have already seen how the Revolution instituted a whole cycle of festivals to keep in a state of perpetual youth the principles that inspired it. If the institution quickly fell into decay, it is because revolutionary faith lasted only a time, and because disappointments and discouragement rapidly succeeded the first flush of enthusiasm. Yet, although the enterprise was abortive, it allows us to imagine what might have been under different conditions, and everything leads us to suppose that sooner or later it will be revived. There are no gospels that are immortal, and no reason to believe that humanity is henceforth incapable of conceiving new ones. As for knowing what will be the symbols through which the new faith will come to express itself, whether they will or will not resemble those of the past, whether they will be more satisfying in translating that reality which is their purpose, is a question that goes beyond human capacity to foresee and one which, moreover, is not fundamental to the matter.

PUNISHMENT, SANCTIONS AND LAW[4]

In the present state of the social sciences very often we can only translate the most general aspects of collective life into intelligible statements. We can doubtless in this way only arrive at sometimes rough and ready approximations, but these are not without their usefulness. They represent the first grasp on things by the mind, and however much in outline they may be, are the preliminary and necessary condition for arriving at more detail at a later stage.

It is with this reservation that we shall seek to establish and explain two laws that seem to us to dominate the evolution of the penal system. In this way we shall very clearly only arrive at the most general variations. But if we succeed in introducing a little order into this confused mass of facts, however imperfect that mass may be, our enterprise will not have been a vain one.

The variations through which punishment has passed in the course of history are of two kinds: the first is quantitative, the other qualitative. The laws that regulate each are naturally different.

I

The law of quantitative variations

This may be formulated as follows:

> The intensity of punishment is the greater to the degree that societies belong to a less advanced kind, and the central power is of a more absolute character.

Let us first explain the meaning of these terms. The first has no great need of definition. It is relatively easy to recognize whether a social species is more or less advanced than another. We have merely to ascertain the extent to which they are constituted entities and, if they are at the same level, whether they are more or less organized. Moreover this hierarchy in social species does not imply that the succession of societies forms a single linear species. On the contrary, it would certainly be better conceived of as a tree with a multiplicity of branches that grow to a greater or lesser extent apart from one another. But on this tree societies are placed at a higher or lower level and relocated at a greater or lesser distance from the common trunk.[5] On condition that one considers them from this viewpoint, it is possible to speak of a general evolution of societies.

The second factor we have identified should cause us more to pause. We say that governmental power is absolute when in the other functions of society it encounters nothing capable of bearing down upon it, effectively limiting it. In truth such complete absence of any limitation is nowhere encountered. We can even state it to be inconceivable. Tradition and religious beliefs serve as checks upon even the strongest governments. Moreover, there are always a few secondary social organs capable on occasion of making themselves felt and resisting. The subordinate functions upon which is applied the supreme regulatory function are never bereft of all individual strength. But it so happens that this *de facto* limitation carries no legal obligation for a government subjected to it. Although the government maintains a certain moderation in exercising its prerogatives, it is not bound to do so either by written or customary law. In that case it disposes of a power that may be termed absolute. Doubtless, if it allows itself to commit excesses, the social forces that it harms may form a coalition to react against and contain it. If it foresees such a possible reaction and forestalls it, it may even restrain itself of its own accord. But such an act of containment, whether through its own action or physically imposed upon it, is essentially a contingent one; it does not result from the normal functioning of institutions. When it arises from its own initiative, it is represented as a freely granted concession, as a voluntary renunciation of legitimate rights; when it is the result of collective acts of resistance it possesses a frankly revolutionary character.

Again we may characterize absolute government in a different way. Legal life gravitates in its entirety around two poles. The relationships forming their connecting link are either unilateral or, on the contrary, bilateral and reciprocal. These are at least the two ideal types around which these relationships fluctuate. The first set of relationships is made up exclusively of the rights attributed to one of the terminal points of its relationship over the other, with the latter enjoying no right that is on a par with its obligations. The second set, however, has on the contrary a legal tie that results from the perfect reciprocity existing between the rights conferred on each of the two parties. 'Real' rights — pertaining to things — and more particularly the right to property, represent the most complete form of relationships of the first kind: the owner has rights over his goods that they have not over him. A contract, and particularly the fair contract, that is, the one where a perfect equivalence exists between the social value of the things or services exchanged, is the type of reciprocal relationships. The more the relationships of the predominant power with the rest of society are of a unilateral character, the more they resemble those that link a person and the thing possessed, and the more absolute the government. It is conversely less so when its relationships with the other social functions are more completely bilateral. Thus the most perfect model of absolute sovereignty is the *patria potestas* of the Romans, as defined in ancient civil law, since a son was assimilated to a thing.

Thus that which makes the central power more or less absolute is the more or less radical absence of any countervailing force that is systematically organized with the intention of moderating that power. We can therefore predict that what gives rise to a power of this kind is the more or less complete gathering together in the same hands of all the directive functions in society. In fact, because their importance is vital, these functions cannot be concentrated in one and the same person without giving him an exceptional preponderance over the whole of the rest of society; it is this preponderance that constitutes absolutism. The wielder of such an authority is invested with a power that frees him from all collective restraint. It is a power that works so that, at least to a certain degree, he is dependent on no one other than himself, subject only to his own good pleasure and able to impose upon others his every wish. This excessive centralization unleashes a social force *sui generis* that is so intense as to dominate all others, subordinating them to itself. Such a preponderance is exerted not only in practice but in law, for the one enjoying such privilege is endued with such prestige that he seems superhuman. One cannot therefore imagine that he can be systematically subjected to obligations, as are common mortals. . . . [The sections in which Durkheim goes on to discuss the 'law of qualitative variations' are omitted here.]

PRIMITIVE PENAL LAW: REVIEW OF E. KULISCHER,
'UNTERSUCHUNGEN ÜBER DAS PRIMITIVE STRAFRECHT'[6]

Our analysis of this article must confine itself to its doctrines and leave on one side the numerous and closely-studied facts on which it is based. But we must point to the interest that the felicitous use of Russian sources gives it. The author seeks to correct two points regarding the common theory that sees the origin of punishment in vengeance.

1 Vengeance of one group upon another has only indirectly contributed to the formation of penal law. Vengeance is not a punishment; it resembles modern warfare; it could not be transformed into punishment since it universally tends to give rise to negotiation, and to the payment of damages. The group to which the offender belongs always takes up the cudgels on his behalf, and this precludes all judgement concerning the legitimacy or illegitimacy of his act. If groups do not chance to make common cause with those of their members that under certain conditions have harmed other groups, this can only be a secondary phenomenon. However, for them to profit from this, the State must already be in a position to free them from all responsibility, on condition that they break all ties with those among their members who have offended, and abandon them to the vengeance of their victims. If there were no higher authority to intervene, the principle of solidarity as regards responsibility would expose the groups to vengeance, whatever might be their real attitude towards the actual perpetrators of the aggression. It is only when independent groups have been forced, particularly in order to defend themselves against a common enemy, to draw closer together and keep the peace with one another, that a group was able to repress an assault by one of its members upon another group, or consider to be a legitimate punishment the vengeance that the latter group meted out. It is not the attack itself that is condemned, it is the 'breaking of the peace', which would involve it in a dangerous

war with its neighbour or oblige it to pay compensation if this is to be averted. For the murder of a stranger to be considered as a crime, the murder had to harm the only interest that several groups might share in common, namely, the peace that had been established.

2 The reaction with which the group responds to the crimes committed by one of its members has not the character of vengeance. Such crimes, very distinct from acts of war that require blood vengeance, consist mainly of treason, incest, sacrilege and the murder of a relative, which is in no way a general kind of murder but something quite different. They never entail vengeance or compensation. If the most ancient legal documents make no reference to them, this does not, however, mean that they were tolerated. But the most ancient legal codes are veritable international treaties, concluded between sovereign groups in order to ensure the peace. Thus they concern only acts that bear upon the relationships between groups, and that could consequently endanger that peace. The administration of justice within each group does not concern them. The sanctions for crimes committed within the group or against it consist of proscription and excommunication. All members of a group are united among themselves by close bonds of sympathy. This is a necessary condition for success in the constant struggle for existence. This explains why in lower societies the murder of a relative goes unpunished: the fellow-feeling experienced for the murderer himself is too strong for him to be punished. But in most cases the feeling is counterbalanced in part by that which the victim arouses, and even more by the feeling of danger that internal dissensions excite in a group forever threatened by the enemy from without. Nevertheless the fellow-feeling is too strong for the murderer to be killed as one would a stranger. Yet it is sufficiently weakened for the group to desire to no longer share in common anything with him, and to suffer no longer his presence. Proscription manifests both the horror that the murder arouses and the feeling still felt for the murderer. Texts show that very often they do not feel justified in killing him as one would do an enemy: they would think themselves to

be committing a further crime. And when the decision to do so is taken, by a kind of fiction a way is sought to avoid committing one. For example, a mode of execution is chosen that only indirectly results in death, or which does not allow the burden to fall upon a single individual (stoning). The execution is entrusted to a slave; it is preceded by excommunication, which renders the guilty person a stranger and enemy. Yet in all these cases, as well as those in which the person proscribed necessarily dies through lack of protection and resources, what essentially characterizes the social reaction is that it consists of proscription. The group that reacts has very often no intention of killing the guilty person, and never considers it has a duty to do so. Capital punishment may have arisen historically out of the *Friedloslegung*. The fact remains that proscription is in principle in no way a capital punishment, a mode of execution. Its essence consists of the violent and definitive expulsion of the guilty person, for whom remaining in the group, and all connexions with its members, are now forbidden. This is why very frequently it entails the destruction of the house of the person proscribed, and of his possessions. It was most possibly to the crime of treason that capital punishment proper was applied, as a substitute for proscription. In fact for the traitor proscription would not necessarily entail living excluded from every society, devoid of all protection, since he would naturally receive the hospitality of the hostile group that had profited from his crime: proscription was thus ineffective against him. Only in the case of treason would primitive societies have been led to put to death one of their members.

We have serious reservations about Kulischer's theories, and particularly on two points. Firstly, all the difficulties raised by the study concerning the punishment for murder within a group are far from being resolved. How can one explain that in societies apparently very akin to one another the murder of a relative sometimes entails rigorous proscription, and sometimes remains exempt from any sanction? The skill with which Kulischer groups the facts should not make us forget that the problem has aspects that he neglects. Secondly, we believe that what were properly crimes, acts that provoked a reaction among the group against one of its members, possessed essentially a religious character, which determined the equally religious character of the sanction, that of excommunication. In this respect alone Kulischer's theory, which explains proscription by a decline in sympathetic feeling, appears to us to lag behind the more complex conceptions of the religious origins of punishment that are tending to become established. But, having made these reservations, the fact remains that Kulischer's article cogently demonstrates that punishment has its origins not in vengeance but in the reaction of the group against its members. He undertakes, with more care than others up to yet have done, the study of that reaction. It is from the same principle that proceed the ideas that we have expressed on this subject in the *Année sociologique* ever since it was started. But although this principle has already inspired studies that we have reviewed, in this respect Kulischer's work is the most important of those on which we have had to report.

THE IDEA OF REPRISALS IN PENAL LAW: REVIEW OF L. GUNTHER, *DIE IDEE DER WIEDERVERGELTUNG IN DER GESCHICHTE UND PHILOSOPHIE DES STRAFRECHTES,* PART III, 1, (ERLANGEN, 1895)[7]

Although this work dates from 1895 we think it useful to mention it and to point out its general tendencies, because there is to be a further volume that we must present to our readers when it appears.

By reprisals (*Wiedervergeltung*) the author does not only mean talion proper. If we have understood his thought clearly, he designates by this word all the processes and characteristics of punishment that are merely the reflection and automatic reproduction of the processes and characteristics that correspond to the crime with which it is linked. In so far as it is intended to make the guilty party a better person or to intimidate possible imitators, there is no reason for it to resemble to any degree whatsoever the act that it represses. If we wish it to succeed in stamping out evil tendencies either in the criminal himself or in those predisposed to follow his example, the punishment must be conceived according to the temperament of the criminal and not the nature of the crime. But it very often happens to be constituted in such a way as to be solely a repetition, wholly or in part, of the injury inflicted upon the victim. All peoples have admitted to a varying degree that there is a kind of relationship between the crime and its repression. It is these peculiarities of punishment that Gunther attributed to the idea of reprisals, i.e. to the need to render evil for evil. In this respect reprisals are not to be confused with talion, although talion is its main form. In fact there is only talion when punishment is the exact and material reproduction of the crime (an eye for an eye, a tooth for a tooth). But it may be only a symbolic reflection of it, or it can bear a relationship in its extent without resembling it qualitatively, or the resemblance can be reduced to an analogy, etc.

This tendency to derive the punishment from the crime exists nowhere in the pure state; everywhere punishment displays properties that derive from a different origin. Its sole purpose has never been to satisfy the need for revenge. Other aims have always been assigned to it, and it has been conceived of accordingly. Yet this strand of revenge nevertheless exists. Since it depends upon causes that are peculiar to it, it possesses its own individuality and can in consequence be isolated from other strands and considered separately. This is what Gunther has set out to do. He has undertaken to trace the evolution of this strand back to its origins right up to the present day.

The first two parts of the work, one published in 1889 and the other in 1891, presented us with the development of the concept of reprisals among the civilized peoples of Antiquity up to the middle of the eighteenth century. In the third part, the first section of which we are about to consider, the author carries his study right up to contemporary peoples. What emerges from this exposition is that the notion of punishment-as-reprisals tends to vanish when confronted by other conceptions, without, however, entirely disappearing. Numerous legislative measures still bear its mark. The author first reports on all those prescripts by virtue of which the perpetrators of acts of violence, whether these are fatal or not, are totally or partially absolved when the criminal act has been the result of prior provocation. This is in fact an ultimate consecration of the right of reprisals. Gunther backs up this interpretation by citing the fact that among the least advanced peoples of Europe (Montenegro, Spain), absolution from the crime in such cases is much more complete than elsewhere. The persistence of the death penalty is likewise alleged to be a survival of the ancient rule according to which blood cries out for blood. The other vestiges of the same principle that Gunther picks out in contemporary law are as follows: those prescriptions whereby the perjurer or the crooked judge are sentenced to a punishment either equal or at least in proportion to that which has or might have been inflicted upon the innocent party; those prescriptions that measure the punishment pronounced against those who effect the escape of a prisoner or free him illegally in accordance with the very punishment that he was in the act of purging. Finally, in a great number of cases an effort is made by the law to make the punishment fit the crime. Thus crimes that connote base feelings are punished by humiliating punishments (female attire for the cowardly, the whip or the pillory); offences arising from greed by monetary punishments, etc. More generally, there is no European legal code that does not acknowledge that the gravity of the repression must be proportioned to the crime, namely, that there must be a quantitative link between these two terms.

This work can rightly be attacked for the over-ideological character of the method that is followed and in consequence the too great lack of precision in the notions, even those that are fundamental, that are used in it. Gunther postulates the idea of reprisals as one that is clear, but nowhere gives a precise definition of it. Yet it greatly needs to be spelled out in detail. Does it concern individual or collective reprisals? Doubtless both. But each is very different in its causes, its nature and by the effect it has had upon the evolution of the law. They must not therefore be confused by being placed in the same category. Still for the same reason, namely, because such a notion seems elementary to him, it seems very easy for him to discern what in the various penal systems can be attributed to this spirit of reprisals. In reality this distinction can only be obtained through observations,

comparisons and very complicated operations. A little intro-
spection and dialectic is not sufficient to evaluate each one of the
factors from which punishment arises. Thus the manner in which
he makes the evaluation is often very much open to question. He
considers as self-evident that the rule of talion, according to
which the punishment is the exact replication of the crime, has no
other origin. However, by themselves the sentiments of revenge
are not so easily satisfied; on the contrary, they tend to obtain
redress that goes beyond the offence. They demand death for a
mere insult. Thus it is not their influence alone that can explain
the homogeneous character of the two acts. Likewise it is very
doubtful whether the persistence of the death penalty is explicable
in the way that the author claims. From the very beginning it
exists for attacks upon religion, and in that case bears no
resemblance to the offences that it represses. Why should not its
survival not stem from the fact that blood crimes make the same
impression upon us as did upon our fathers crimes against the
gods?

Yet however well-founded such criticisms may be, the fact
remains that punishment is in part a function of the crime, and
not only of the criminal, as the Italian school would have it. The
relationship that links the extent of the one with that of the other
is perhaps best proof of this. And since this feature of punishment
is to be found, more or less veiled, in all ages of history, we must
believe that it is essential to it, and that it cannot totally vanish
without ceasing to be what it is. This is what makes Gunther's
volume a useful contribution to the sociology of punishment.
Moreover, he has made himself very well-informed on his subject,
and a wealth of information regarding the penal legislation of
different peoples from Antiquity to the present day is to be found
in the book.

6

The State, Education and Equality

EDUCATION AND HUMANISM[1]

The problem of secondary education, as it is usually stated, consists almost exclusively in embarking, more or less methodically, upon a comparison between the relative educational merits of the arts and sciences. Couched in these terms, it hardly bears of any objective solution, for it leaves too much room for personal feelings. Each individual leans in the direction his own temperament favours. This is why such discussions are most often reduced to contradictory pleading, depending on whether they emanate from minds more enthusiastic for literary niceties than scientific precision, more curious about the aesthetic emotions than about positive knowledge, or vice versa. We have seen that for us the problem is posed in totally different terms. We have not speculated whether teaching should be carried on through the literary rather than the scientific subjects, but rather what kinds of reality it was appropriate to teach. Indeed to shape the mind, that ultimate aim of secondary education, is not to train it in a vacuum through some formal gymnastics. It is to cause it to acquire the habits and attitudes that are indispensable for it to tackle with profit the various aspects of reality with which it is destined to come in contact, so that it can make reasonable judgements about it. But these attitudes cannot be acquired by the mind save when confronted with the things themselves, and when it undergoes their effects. It is by practising to apply itself to them that the mind will acquire the necessary dispositions.

This is why the chief question is to know to what objects it is appropriate to apply itself. There are two principal categories of things knowledge of which is indispensable for men: these are, firstly man himself, and then, nature. Hence the two great branches of education: human things, minds, consciousness and their manifestations, on the one hand; the physical world on the other.

It is superfluous to demonstrate that men should know about man. That necessity is so evident that until very recently it has been felt to excess, since even at the end of the eighteenth century secondary education was one exclusively related to what is human. Thus in this domain we have only to continue a tradition that has been hallowed by long usage. However, it must be continued, whilst being transformed so as to harmonize it with the progress in our knowledge and with present-day requirements. The humanist in the Jesuit colleges or the colleges of the university only taught his pupils about a simplified form of man, truncated and reduced to some very general feelings, and some universal, simple ideas. The real man is in a different way complex, and it is man in his complexity that must be taught. This does not mean that it is possible or useful to delineate all his facets, which are infinite in number. Such a task, which is moreover unrealizable, goes beyond the bounds of secondary education. Yet what is needful is to give the child some inkling of this complexity. We have seen how the history of the ancient peoples compared with our national history, or the study of ancient literatures compared with the study of modern literatures, have alone been able to awaken that feeling, without however a knowledge of the languages in which these literary records were written being indispensable. It is by learning to know about other ideas, customs, political constitutions, domestic organizations, moralities and forms of logic different from those to which he is accustomed that the pupil will acquire a consciousness of the richness of the life as contained within human nature. Thus it is only in history that we can realize the infinite variety of the aspects that human nature can assume. This is why it has seemed desirable to us that the historical horizon of the college should be as broad as possible. I would even go so far as to express the desire that the teacher should know about peoples other than the classical peoples, so that at least he could convey to his pupils the impression that beyond this special form of humanity there are others that are different again, less advanced, so it is said, and yet who also have a right to our interest, because they are equally forms of humanity. The opportunity to do so would naturally be afforded him by the very fact that classical societies have roots that push down into this allegedly lower humanity and bear its mark. Consequently how regrettable it is that in two out of the four branches of our present classical programmes (1902) the history and the literature of Antiquity have almost no place. The mere study of medieval and modern history and their corresponding literatures is no substitute for them. It is a gross mistake to believe that in order to know man it is enough to look at him in his most modern and most finished forms. We cannot know him save by analysing him; we cannot analyse him save through history. Thus in our present syllabuses there is a very serious gap that we must acknowledge and seek to fill.

THE ROLE OF THE STATE IN EDUCATION[2]

This definition of education allows us easily to resolve the much disputed question of the duties and rights of the State in education.

Against these are opposed the rights of the family. The child, it is maintained, belongs primarily to his parents: thus it is incumbent upon them to direct, in the way that they think fit, his intellectual and moral development. Education conceived of in this way is something that is essentially private and domestic. If this view is taken, one naturally tends to reduce to the least possible minimum State intervention in the matter. It is held that it should be limited to its acting as an auxiliary and surrogate for families. When these are incapable of carrying out their duties it is natural for the State to assume them. It is even natural that it should make the task of families as easy as possible by placing schools at their disposal where they can send their children, if they so desire. But it should confine itself strictly within these limits, and be forbidden to take any positive action that is designed to guide the minds of the young in any particular direction.

Yet it is far from true that its role should remain such a negative one. If, as we have attempted to establish, education has above all a collective function, if its purpose is to adapt the child to the social environment in which he is destined to live, it is impossible for society to stand aside from such an operation. How could it remain aloof, since it constitutes the reference point from which education should direct its operations? It thus falls to society to remind the teacher continually of the ideas and sentiments that must be impressed upon the child in order for him to be in harmony with the environment in which he is destined to live. If society were not always present and ever vigilant to constrain the teaching to be exercised in a social direction, that teaching would necessarily be applied to serve particular beliefs, and the great heart of our country would become divided up, disintegrating into an incohesive host of fragmented, petty creatures in conflict with one another. One cannot go more completely against the fundamental goal of all education. A choice must be made: if we attach some value to the existence of society — and we have just seen what it represents for us — education must ensure between citizens a sufficient communality of ideas and sentiments, without which any society is impossible; and for it to bring about this result, it must not be abandoned entirely to the arbitrary will of individuals.

As soon as education becomes an essentially social function, the State cannot but be interested in it. On the contrary, all that is educational must to some degree be subordinate to its action. This does not necessarily mean that it must monopolize schooling. That question is too complex for it to be treated in this way as incidental: we propose to reserve it for later. One may believe that progress in school is easier and more immediate where a certain margin is left to individual initiative; for the individual is more ready to innovate than the State. Yet the fact that the State, in the public interest, must allow to be opened schools other than those for which it has direct responsibility does not mean that it must wash its hands of what goes on in them. On the contrary, the education given in them must remain subject to its control. It is not even permissible for the function of educator to be undertaken by someone who does not possess special qualifications, about whose validity alone the State can be the judge. Undoubtedly, the bounds within which its intervention should be confined cannot easily be determined once and for all, but the principle of intervention is indisputable. There is no school that can claim the right freely to impart an anti-social education.

We must nevertheless acknowledge that the partisan spirit that at the present time divides people in our country makes this duty of the State a particularly delicate one, but at the same time one even more important. It is not indeed the State's mission to create that community of ideas and sentiments without which no society can exist. This must be constituted of its own accord, and the State can only confer its authority upon it, maintain it and make the individual more aware of it. Now it is unfortunately undeniable that in our country this moral unity is not in every respect all that it should be. We are divided between divergent conceptions that are sometimes even contradictory. Among these divergent views there is one fact that cannot be denied and which must be taken into account. There cannot be any question of acknowledging any right of the majority to impose its ideas on the children of a minority. The school cannot be the appurtenance of a party, and the teacher is failing in his duty when he employs the authority that he has at his command to drag his pupils down into the pitfalls of his own personal prejudices, however justifiable these appear to him to be. Yet, in spite of all disputes, nowadays there exists, at the very foundation of our civilization, a certain number of principles which, implicitly or explicitly, are common to everybody and which very few people in any case dare to deny openly and outrightly: the respect for reason and science, the ideas and sentiments which are at the basis of the democratic ethic. The role of the State is to distinguish these essential principles, to cause them to be taught in its schools, to take care that nowhere are children left in ignorance of them, and that everywhere they are spoken of with the respect that is due to them. In this connection there is a task to be carried out that will perhaps be the more effective the less aggressive and less violent it is, and the better it can confine itself within wise bounds.

THE POWER OF EDUCATION: THE MEANS OF ACTION[3]

After having determined the goal of education we must seek to determine how and to what extent it is possible to achieve that aim, namely how and to what degree education can be effective.

In every age this question has been one that has been much disputed. For Fontenelle, 'good education does not make a good character nor does a bad one destroy it.' On the contrary, for Locke and Helvetius education is all powerful. According to the latter, 'all men are born equal and with equal abilities; education alone brings about differences.' Jacotet's theory is close to the first theory. The solution that one gives to the problem depends on the conception that one has of the extent and nature of innate predispositions on the one hand and, on the other, on the power of the means of action that the educator has at his disposal.

Education does not create a man out of nothing, as Locke and Helvetius believed; it is applied to aptitudes that it finds already constituted. On the other hand, it may be generally conceded that these congenital tendencies are very strong, very difficult to destroy or to change radically, for they depend on organic conditions over which the educator has little control. Consequently, inasmuch as they have a definite purpose and influence the mind and character to narrowly determined ways of acting and thinking, the whole future of the individual is laid down in advance, and there is not much that education can do.

Happily, however, one of the characteristics of men is that these innate predispositions are very general and vague. Indeed the type of fixed, rigid and invariable predisposition that leaves hardly any room for action on it by external causes is instinct. But one may wonder whether there exists in man a single real instinct. Sometimes one speaks of the instinct of preservation, but the expression is incorrect. For an instinct consists of a system of predetermined movements that are always the same, which, once sparked off by a sensation, automatically follow upon one another until they arrive at their natural termination, without any reflective thought intervening at any stage. Yet the movements that we make when our life is in danger in no way have this predeterminate pattern and automatic invariability. They change according to the situation; we adjust them to the circumstances. This means that they do not occur without a certain conscious choice, however swift that may be. What we call the instinct of preservation comes down in the end to a general impulsion to flee from death, without the means whereby we seek to avoid it being predetermined once and for all. As much may be said about what are occasionally called, no less inexactly, the maternal, paternal and even the sexual instincts. They are urges in a certain direction, but the means through which these urges are activated change from one individual to another, and from one occasion to another. Thus there is plenty of room reserved for trial and error, for personal adjustments and, consequently, for the effect of causes which cannot make their influence felt until they have arisen. And education is one of these causes.

It is true that the claim has been made that a child sometimes inherits a very strong tendency to commit a certain act such as suicide, theft, murder, fraud, etc. But these assertions in no way chime with the facts. Whatever may have been stated, one is not born a criminal; even less is one destined from birth to commit a particular kind of crime. The paradox advanced by Italian criminologists does not nowadays have many who defend it. What is inherited is a certain lack of mental balance that makes the individual less amenable to consistent, disciplined behaviour. But such a disposition no more predetermines whether a man will be a criminal rather than an explorer who loves adventure, a prophet, a political innovator or an inventor, etc. As much may be said about all vocational aptitudes. As Bain remarks, 'The son of a great philologist does not inherit a single syllable; the son of a great traveller can be surpassed in geography by a miner's son.' What the child receives from his parents are very general abilities: some power of attention, a certain modicum of perseverance, a healthy judgement, imagination, etc. But each one of these faculties can serve all kinds of different ends. The child gifted with a fairly vivid imagination is able, depending upon the circumstances and the influences brought to bear upon him, to become a painter or a poet, an engineer with an inventive mind, or a daring financier. Thus the gap is considerable between natural qualities and the special form they must assume in order to be used in life. This means that our future is not narrowly determined by our congenital make-up. The reason for this is easily understood. The only forms of activity that can be transmitted through heredity are those that are duplicated always in a way that is sufficiently identical for them to be fixable in a rigid form within the tissues of the organism. But human life depends upon multiple and complex conditions that are consequently in a state of flux. Human life must therefore be being incessantly changing and modified. Thus it is impossible for it to become set definitively in a well-defined mould. But only very general and very vague tendencies expressing characteristics common to every individual experience can survive and be passed on from one generation to another.

To state that innate characteristics are for the most part very general is to say that they are very malleable and flexible, since they can lead to very different outcomes. Between the imprecise virtualities that go to make up a man at the moment of birth and the very distinctive person that he must become in order to play a useful role in society the gulf is therefore considerable. It is this gap that education must constrain the child to bridge. It can be seen that its action can be exerted over a vast field.

Yet in order to exert that effect does it have at its disposal means that are sufficiently powerful?

In order to give some idea of what constitutes educative action and to demonstrate its power, the contemporary psychologist, Guyau, has compared it to hypnotic suggestion. The comparison is not without foundation.

In fact, hypnotic suggestion supposes the two following conditions:

1 The state of the hypnotized subject is characterized by his exceptional passivity. The mind is almost reduced to a blank; a

kind of vacuum has been realized within the consciousness; the will is as if it were paralysed. Consequently the idea that is suggested, since it encounters no opposing idea, can take root with the minimum of resistance;

2 However, as the vacuum is never complete, the idea also needs to draw from the suggestion itself a particular power for action. For this the hypnotist must speak in a tone of command, with authority. He must say, 'I want.' He must indicate that any refusal to obey is not even conceivable, that the action must be carried out, that the thing must be seen as he has demonstrated it, and that it cannot be otherwise. If he weakens, we see the subject hesitate, resist, and even sometimes refuse to obey. If he merely enters into discussion, the hypnotist's power is lost. The more the suggestion goes against the natural bent of the person hypnotized, the more indispensable is an imperative tone of command.

These two conditions are in fact realized in the relationship that the educator enjoys with the child that undergoes his teaching. Firstly, the child is naturally in a passive state, one that is entirely comparable to that in which the hypnotized person is artificially placed. The child's consciousness still only comprises a small number of representations that are capable of fighting against those that are suggested to him. Thus his suggestibility is very easily aroused. For the same reason, he is very susceptible to the infectiousness of example, and very disposed to imitate. Secondly, the natural ascendancy that the teacher has over his pupil, because of the superiority of his experience and culture, will naturally give his teaching that effectiveness which is necessary.

This comparison shows how far the educator is from being without weapons, for the hypnotic power of suggestion is well known. If therefore the educative action possesses, even to a lesser degree, a similar effectiveness, much may be expected of it, provided that one knows how to use it. Far from our needing to be discouraged because of our lack of power, rather do we have grounds for being frightened at its extent. If teachers and parents more consistently felt that nothing can happen in front of a child that does not leave a mark on him, that his turn of mind and character depends upon those thousands of small, imperceptible actions that occur at every moment and to which we pay no heed because of their apparent insignificance, how much more would they guard their speech and behaviour. It is certain that education cannot achieve great results when it proceeds brusquely by continual fits and starts. As Herbart states, it is not by sternly admonishing the child now and then that one can exert a strong influence over him. When, however, education is given patiently and continually, when it seeks no immediate and striking successes, but is conducted slowly in a very clearly given direction without allowing itself to be diverted by external happenings and chance circumstances, it commands all the means necessary for leaving its mark deeply upon the pupil.

At the same time it can be seen what is the essential mainspring of teaching. What causes the influence of the hypnotist is the authority that he derives from the circumstances. By analogy we may already say that education must essentially be a matter of exercising authority. This important proposition can, moreover, be established directly. Indeed we have seen that the object of education is to superimpose upon the individual, non-social being that we are at birth an entirely new being. Education must lead us to go beyond our initial nature: it is upon this condition that the child will become a man. Now we cannot rise above ourselves save by an effort that is more or less strenuous. Nothing is more false and deceptive than the Epicurean conception of education, the conception of a Montaigne, for example, whereby human beings can be educated through play, without any motivation save the attraction of pleasure. If there is nothing dreary about life and it is criminal to make it artificially so in the presence of a child, it is nevertheless serious and earnest, and education, which is a preparation for life, should partake of that earnestness. In order that he may learn to keep his natural selfishness within bounds, to subordinate himself to higher ends, to submit his desires to the domination of the will and to place appropriate limitations upon them, the child must apply his mind intensively. Yet we only place constraints upon ourselves, we only force ourselves, for either one of the two following reasons: because physical necessity obliges us to do so or because we are morally compelled to do so. Yet the child cannot feel the necessity that physically imposes these efforts, for he is not directly in contact with the harsh realities of life that make such an attitude indispensable. He is not yet involved in the struggle. Whatever Spencer may say, we cannot leave him exposed to the over-rough reaction of things. His education must already be almost entirely complete when he finally comes up against things. Thus it is not their pressure on him upon which we can rely to make him resolve to strengthen his will and acquire the necessary mastery over himself.

There remains duty. The sentiment of duty — this is indeed what is for the child and even for the adult the supreme stimulus to effort. Self-esteem itself presupposes this. For in order to be sensitive, as is fitting, to both punishment and reward, one must already be conscious of one's dignity, and consequently of one's duty. But the child can only know duty through his teachers or through his parents. He can only know what it is through the manner in which they reveal it to him, by their speech and conduct. For him they must therefore be duty incarnate, duty personified. This means that moral authority is the dominant quality of the educator. For it is through the authority within him that duty is what it is. What is wholly *sui generis* in it is the imperative tone in which it speaks to the consciousness, the respect that it inspires in the will of others, which causes the latter to yield as soon as he has pronounced. Thus it is indispensable that an impression of the same kind be given through the personality of the teacher.

We need not show that authority, if understood in this way, has nothing violent or repressive about it: it consists wholly of a certain moral ascendancy. It supposes that with the teacher there has been fulfilled two main conditions. The first is that he possesses willpower. For authority implies confidence, and the child cannot give his trust to someone whom he sees hesitate, falter, and go back on his decisions. But this first condition is not the most essential one. What is important above all is that the authority which he must bring to bear should be really felt by him. It constitutes a force that he cannot manifest unless he effectively possesses it. From where can that force spring? Might it be from the material power with which he is equipped, the right to punish and reward? But the fear of punishment is something completely different from the respect for authority. It has moral value only if the punishment is acknowledged to be just by the one who undergoes it, which implies that the authority that metes out punishment is already recognized to be legitimate. This is precisely what is in question. It is not from any external source that the teacher can derive his authority but from himself; it can only come from an inner confidence. Doubtless he must believe not in himself, nor in the superior qualities of his intelligence or sensibility, but in his task and in the greatness of his task. What constitutes the authority that colours so easily the discourse of the priest is the lofty idea that he has of his mission, for he speaks in the name of a god in whom he believes, to whom he feels closer than the host of the profane. The secular teacher can and must have something of this feeling. He is also the instrument of a great moral entity that goes beyond him, that of society. Just as the priest is the interpreter of his god, the teacher is the interpreter of the great moral ideas of his time and his country. Let him be attached to those ideas, let him feel all their greatness, and the authority inherent in them and of which he is aware cannot fail to communicate itself to his person and to everything that emanates from him. Into an authority that springs from so impersonal a source there can enter no pride, vanity or pedantry. It is wholly made up of the respect that he has for his functions and, if we may speak in such terms, for his ministry. It is that respect which, through the mediation of word and gesture, passes from his consciousness to that of the child.

Sometimes liberty and authority have been posed as opposites, as if these two factors in education contradicted and limited each other. But this opposition is artificial. In reality these two terms, far from excluding each other, are implicit in each other. It is true that liberty is the daughter of authority, for to be free is not to do what is pleasing to one. It is to be master of oneself, to know and to act by reason, and to do one's duty. Now it is precisely in order to endow the child with that self-mastery that the teacher's authority should be employed. The authority of the teacher is only an aspect of the authority of duty and of the reason. Thus the child must be trained to recognize it in the words of the educator and to yield to its ascendancy. It is on this condition that he will later discover it in his own consciousness and defer to it.

A DEBATE ON EGALITARIAN IDEAS (1909)[4]

DURKHEIM: If I have understood Parodi correctly, he has set himself a twofold goal. Firstly, he seeks to justify egalitarian ideas, and then to base a certain conception of morality on that same justification. To clarify the discussion, I think there is an advantage in reversing the order followed by Parodi, first examining his general conception of morality. For in the end it is from this that there flows his special theory of the idea of equality.

Parodi postulates as a self-evident truth that morality has continued to become more rational as history has progressed. Such an assertion appears to me highly controversial. Every moral system has its own rationality. The Roman one had its reasons in Roman society just as ours has its reasons in the nature of European societies today. For it to be possible to accept Parodi's postulate, one would need to reduce morality, as he does, to a mere system of abstract notions, a geometry of a particular kind. In my view this would be gravely to misconceive what moral reality is. It consists, not in a system of concepts that might be constructed *sui generis* through logic, but in a system of forces, certainly not physical, but mental and moral, that draw all their power to act from representations, from states of consciousness.

I take an example from the field of law, since today we are talking about law. Janet somewhere defines law as *a moral power*. Imagine, he says, a child asleep on the edge of a precipice. There is within that child a force that, moral as it is, is none the less effective, for it prevents my throwing him in the abyss, even were it in my interest to do so. In fact, from every human person there emanate forces of this kind that forestall such assaults and determine positive acts on our part. To account for morality means to account for these forces, their genesis and functioning. We may doubtless assume they are not how we commonly represent them to ourselves, nor are they immanent in the person they protect, but are merely the objectified form of the sentiments to which the person gives rise. But — and this is what is of importance — it is certain that they are indeed forces, since they have the property of either inhibiting or stimulating action.

Once this is postulated, I cannot see how one can be justified in stating that the morality of a particular country or age is more rational than that of some other country or age. All moralities have their own rationality. All moral forces have their own reality. All are natural, and consequently rational, like the rest of nature. We can express them in notions, that is, study the science of them, just as we study the science of physical forces. But no morality exists that cannot be translated in this way into concepts. In this respect there is no distinction to be made between present-day morality and that of former times.

I see only two reasons that might cause us to believe in the progressive rationalization of morality:

1 Occasionally the belief is that rationality is defined by its quality of generality. Because at the present time our moral ideal is more humane than that of former times, because our morality is more impersonal, more abstract, more free of the contingencies of time and place, we conceive it to be valid for all humanity. From this very fact we conclude that there is something more rational about it. But this fails to acknowledge that the general has no virtues peculiarly its own. It is merely what has been abstracted from the particular. If this latter is irrational, the general will possess the same irrationality.

2 We are experiencing today, more insistently than ever before, a need to be in harmony with ourselves. This need possibly exerts a greater influence upon moral life. But we are totally ignorant of its extent. The converse need also remains at work. Without it I do not know how morality could have evolved, for to evolve and change one must not respect with over-narrow devotion the principle of identity. What nowadays is the part respectively played by these tendencies? It is indeed very difficult to say. Thus there is nothing that can justify the categorical thesis that serves Parodi as a postulate.

Let us now attempt to see how these general considerations are applicable to the problem of egalitarian ideas.

We are informed that the global inequalities between castes or classes, as they once existed, were less rational than our present inequalities. In what way, and why? I find it impossible to perceive any grounds for that assertion. Our present inequalities are founded on the nature of our present-day societies, just as those of India are on the nature of Hindu societies. The former are no more unintelligible than the latter. A biologist does not ask himself whether it is more rational to breathe through the lungs rather than through gills.

Conversely, let us consider the relative equality that is tending to emerge today. Is it really ascribable to a greater need for logical coordination, for a more complete systematization, which allegedly is manifesting itself in our contemporary societies? But firstly, to have grounds for affirming this relationship, we would have to show that it is indeed this logical impulsion which has been the cause determining egalitarian aspirations, such as they are manifest in the law or the contemporary moral consciousness. But I do not see how Parodi has even attempted to begin to prove that point.

However, lacking that proof, let us consider the question from the purely dialectical viewpoint.

It may be the need to categorize people according to a single criterion that inclines us toward egalitarian conceptions. By hypothesis such a classification would be purely logical. It would be a very logical way to represent people to oneself. But the equality that needs to be explained is a *moral equality*, namely, as I showed a moment ago, an *equality of rights and powers*. However, I find it impossible to see how Parodi passes from the one classification to the other. Because it is convenient for us to classify people according to one single criterion, it does not follow that we should attribute to them all an equal social value and endue them all with the same power.

So little do logic and rationality enter into this whole question, and so little do our egalitarian practices accord with our need to achieve harmony with one another that, as Parodi has himself pointed out, such practices rest in reality upon two contradictory conceptions.

On the one hand there is the conception that comes expressed in the formula: *to each according to his labour*, or, *to each according to his merit*, a formula that claims equal treatment for men of the same merit, and a different treatment for men whose worth is different. But, contrasting with this principle, there is another which requires that men, to a certain degree, should be treated equally despite their unequal worth. This principle is not only, as Parodi appeared to admit, the ideal goal — an almost Utopian one — of moral evolution. Even now we practise it in part; it affects our behaviour at every moment. Charity requires us to do good to those who are suffering, and that, up to a certain point, regardless of their possible merit. Time was when serious punishments were finely arranged, gradating them so that they corresponded to an inequality between criminal acts. We have abandoned such refinements. We no longer have punishments skilfully ordered in a hierarchy for all the possible types of major crimes. The decline in punishment, making the scale more simple, has resulted in the gap between the various gradations becoming much less. Thus there is a less exact correspondence between the seriousness of punishments and the gravity of the offences. This conception is entirely opposed to the preceding one, yet coexists with the latter in our moral consciousness. And we indeed feel that it has a place there. For there are cases when we should treat people according to their worth, and others when we must leave their worth out of our consideration. In all this it can be seen how little we are concerned to satisfy the needs of speculative theory or of putting our ideas in order, since our attitude when faced with this practical problem depends upon contradictory notions. It is in entirely different terms that the question should be couched.

PARODI: It seems to me that Durkheim's remarks do not go against what I said as much as at first sight it might appear. He concedes that in the individual there exists a certain need to continue, or to set oneself, in harmony. Why then should not this same need also constitute a social force? The idea of equality seems to me to have been linked to every attempt at social classification. Now, can one deny that, as soon as social classes are established, there appears, as it were, a need to clarify and define them, which is the proper task of law, and that this need in the long run reacts upon them, in fact helping to delimit them and distinguish between them more rationally? Is this not a positive element in collective evolution that the sociologist should not fail to acknowledge? Moreover, this in no way prejudges the importance of this factor in comparison with all others. There remains the question of how to evaluate its effectiveness, and I took good care not to claim that the power of logic was preponderant in such procedures.

Furthermore, Durkheim asks me what is my basis for declaring that global distinctions or anti-egalitarian organizations are less rational than the rest, since, just like these others, where they exist they are linked to a set of social conditions that determine them and would not allow for any other conditions at all. It seems to me that here a distinction must be made: all social regimes, egalitarian or anti-egalitarian, are rational by the same token for the scientist, in so far as they are effects linked to causes that he has attempted to distinguish. They are rational in so far as they are sociologically explained or explicable. But for an individual wholly located within a society of this kind who is seeking to understand the institutions within which he is living, not through their determining causes, of which he is very often ignorant, but through the utility of their ends, such a justification cannot suffice. If he has sufficient mental freedom to put the question to himself, he will not judge to be rational social distinctions that correspond to no real superiority or whose usefulness, direct or indirect, is not demonstrated to him, these being distinctions imposed solely through the force of tradition. . . .

DURKHEIM: As regards the role that logical necessity plays in our moral life, I have simply heard that we remain totally ignorant of its importance, and that in all likelihood it is even somewhat limited. A theory that rests upon the opposing postulate therefore appears to me to be a somewhat risky one.

But I come now to the two questions I have been asked:

Scientific explanations of social institutions, Parodi says, can be valid for a man who looks at the society in question from the outside, but not for one who is part of it, living its life. Why, therefore? Doubtless the latter might find, rightly, the historical explanations without much bearing if they were limited to demonstrating how the past weighs down unreasonably upon the present. But these institutions, and in this particular case, these inequalities, would not have lasted if they were not grounded in the very nature of things. How then could they seem irrational to one who is seeking to understand them, whether he considers them from the inside or from the outside? Historical explanations are not simple statements; in certain conditions they are justifications. These global inequalities of castes and classes have been realities. We no longer grant that they were able to establish themselves by artifice or trickery. They are necessarily the result of the conditions of common life. There have been societies where they were perfectly justified, ones where they had reason to exist. Why should these reasons have been incapable of being understood by the man living in such societies, provided that — and this is doubtless an anachronism, but legitimate in the circumstances — we assume him to be sufficiently informed and enlightened? And how would he have not found practices rational that he judged well founded? For things to be otherwise, one would have had to be able to establish that these inequalities corresponded to no need, no social necessity. This is contrary to all likelihood, given their generality and persistence.

In the second place the two formulas, the two egalitarian conceptions that I mentioned a little while ago are so utterly contradictory that they form the basis for two opposing theories. One — to each according to his labour — is the favourite principle of orthodox economists; the other is that of moralists and ascetics. One cannot at the same time remove inequalities arising from worth and then stimulate them by rewards. Besides, I do not mean that we need to choose between these two formulas, sacrificing one to the other. Each has its place in moral reality. The fact remains that they tend to direct us on to divergent and even opposite paths.

Moreover, how is it possible to justify egalitarian ideas by purely logical considerations? The role of logic is to assist or force us to see things as they are. *Now, in fact, we are unequal.* We have not the same physical strength, the same intellectual power, or the same energy of willpower. The services that we render to society are of unequal importance. We are more easy, or less so, to replace in the functions that we fulfil, and we do them better, or less well, etc. In spite of this, morality demands that to a certain extent we should be treated as if we were equals. It attributes to us an equality that is not empirically justified. Thus some powerful cause must indeed intervene that causes us to view men in a different way than from the experience of our senses, that makes us see them from a vantage point where they appear equal to us, and consequently transfigures them. So long as the mode of this transfiguration has not been explained, I am afraid that the problem of egalitarian ideas remains entirely unresolved.

PARODI: Firstly, let me deal with the second objection that has been raised against me. I do indeed see that in certain extreme cases, or in plans for a complete reform of society, the two tendencies can be in conflict. But I maintain that in fact they are very often in harmony and work in the same direction. We seek to make social advantages proportional to merit, but to do this we are willingly led to restrict inherited or undeserved privileges, and therefore tend increasingly to place all men in situations of equality. But this can in turn better allow natural qualities of superiority to be revealed. Once again, can one decide if it is more immediately the first or the second tendency that inspires both progressive income tax and measures limiting inheritance, such as, for example, the abolition of the automatic bequeathal of property at a certain degree of kinship? Are not the arguments justifying such measures taken at the same time, and without discrimination, from both conceptions of equality? As for cases where one may really have to choose between the demands of distributive justice and the promptings of complete fraternal feeling, they appear to be extreme ones concerning the conscience, perhaps even questions of extent and opportuneness rather than ones revealing a radical, rational incompatibility. . . .

DURKHEIM: Parodi asks me how these two conceptions of equality are contradictory. But, according to the one, salaries and wages remain different depending on the relative importance of the tasks and services performed. It implies a rank order. The other, on the contrary, implies a levelling-out that is absolute. Once more, in practice these opposing tendencies are reconciled. But in that practical compromise I do not discern any manifestation of a logical need to remain in harmony.

Moreover, when I stated that the anti-egalitarian institutions of the past could be justified by their relationship to given social conditions, I meant solidly based justifications that derive their authority from the nature of things and not from blind tradition. Besides, the traditional justifications have often more value than is thought. They are symbolic and figurative, and need to be interpreted. But when beneath the symbol we learn how to uncover the reality that it mediates, we perceive that they are often very close to the facts and lead to a rational justification.

Finally, Parodi remarks that an institution in itself can be irrational, although firmly based in the social system. I cannot understand how an institution can be rational *in itself*. The rationality of a fact is a relative matter, like that fact itself. If an institution has its reason for existing in a given social system that itself has its reason for existing in the set of historical conditions on which it depends, which consequently cannot be other than it is at the time under consideration — how can that institution be irrational? If direct taxes were truly based upon the nature of our societies, we would have to admit that they were rational. But when one confines oneself to saying that it is wise to preserve them *for the time being* because it is preferable to replace them prudently and gradually, one does not thereby recognize that an irrational institution can be necessary and founded upon the nature of things. On the contrary, there was a moment in history when the feudal regime was tied in with the organization of medieval societies, these being, furthermore, all that could and were destined to exist in the age in question. At that moment the feudal regime was rational, in the same way as it was later to lose its rationality. Between these two stages there was an intermediate period when it was wise to retain it *provisionally*, whilst preparing it to be ready to evolve.

7

Patriotism and Militarism

THE STATE AND PATRIOTISM[1]

We should now set forth how the State, without pursuing a mystic aim of any kind, goes on expanding its functions. If indeed we work on the premise that the rights of the individual are not *ipso facto* his at birth; that they are not inscribed in the nature of things with such certainty as warrants the State in endorsing them and promulgating them; that, on the contrary, the rights have to be won from the opposing forces that deny them; that the State alone is qualified to play this part — then it cannot keep to the functions of supreme arbiter and of administrator of an entirely prohibitive justice, as the utilitarian or Kantian individualism would have it. No, the State must deploy energies equal to those for which it has to provide a counter-balance. It must even permeate all those secondary groups of family, trade and professional association, Church, regional areas and so on . . . which tend, as we have seen, to absorb the personality of their members. It must do this in order to prevent this absorption and free these individuals, and so as to remind these partial societies that they are not alone and that there is a right that stands above their own rights. The State must therefore enter into their lives, it must supervise and keep a check on the way they operate and to do this it must spread its roots in all directions. For this task, it cannot just withdraw into the tribunals, it must be present in all spheres of social life and make itself felt. Wherever these particular collective forces exist, there the power of the State must be, to neutralize them: for if they were left alone and to their own devices, they would draw the individual within their exclusive domination. Now, societies are becoming ever greater in scale and ever more complex: they are made up of circles of increasing diversity, and of manifold agencies, and these already possess in themselves a value to be reckoned. Therefore if it is to fulfil its functions, the State, too, must branch out and evolve to the same degree.

It would be easier to understand the need for this whole trend of expansion if we could form a better idea of the elements of these individual rights that the State secures by stages, overcoming the resistances of collective particularism. We may hold (with Spencer and Kant, to quote only the leaders of the school) that these rights derive from the very nature of the individual and only express the conditions necessary to him if he is to be himself. Then we are bound to conceive these rights as defined and determined once and for all, as well as that individual nature which they express and from which they derive. Take any human being: he is endowed with a certain mental and moral constitution; his rights are dependent on that constitution, being implicitly written into it, as it were. We could draw up an exhaustive and final list of them, with omissions no doubt, but there would be nothing indefinite about the list as it stood, and with adequate method, it could give a complete picture. If individual rights are to ensure a free functioning of the life of the individual, it only remains to settle what that life involves, to deduce the rights that must be conceded to the individual. For instance, according to Spencer, life in man presupposes a constant equilibrium between the vital energies and the exterior energies; this means that the process of repair must balance the expenditure of the energy or the wear and tear. Each one of us should therefore receive in exchange for his work a remuneration allowing him to repair the energies consumed by the work. That would be met if contracts were freely made and abided by, for the individual should never yield up what he has made or done in exchange for something of less value. Man, says Kant, is a moral being. His right derives from the moral nature he is endowed with and is thus determined by that very fact. This moral nature makes him inviolable;

anything that assails his inviolability is a violation of this right. That is how those who uphold what is called natural right (or the theory of individual right deriving from individual nature) come to represent it as being something universal; that is, as a code that can be laid down once and for all, valid for every period as for every country. And this negative character they try to give to this right makes it, apparently, more easily definable.

But the postulate on which this theory rests has an artificial over-simplification. What lies at the base of individual right is not the notion of the individual as he is, but the way in which society puts the right into practice, looks upon it and appraises it. What matters is not what the individual is but how much he counts and on the other hand, what he ought to be. The reason why he has more or fewer rights, certain rights and not others, is not that he is constituted in a particular way; it is because society attributes this or that importance to him and attaches a higher or a lower value to what concerns him. If all that affects the individual affects the society, the society will react against all that might diminish him. This would not only forbid the slightest offences against him, but even more, the society would hold itself bound to work towards increasing his stature and towards his development. If, on the other hand, the individual is held in only moderate regard, the society will be indifferent even to serious outrages on him and will tolerate them. According to ideas current at the time, grave offences will appear as venial or, on the contrary, it may be held that liberal, unfettered expression should not be too much encouraged. Those who believe in that theory of natural right think they can make a final distinction between what is and what is not a right. However, a closer study will show that in reality the dividing line they think they can draw is certainly not definite and depends entirely on the state of public opinion. Spencer remarks that the remuneration shall be equal to the value of the labour — that this must be and suffices. But how is this balance to be settled? This value is a matter of opinion. It is said that the contracting parties must decide this, provided that they decide freely. But again, what does this freedom consist of? Nothing has fluctuated so much in the course of time as the idea of freedom of contract. With the Romans, the contract came into force at the moment its text was declared and it was the phrasing of the text that governed the engagements entered into and not the intention behind the words. Later, the intention began to come into the reckoning and the contract made under material duress was no longer held to be regular. Some forms of moral pressure likewise began to be ruled out. What brought about this development? The answer is that people began to have a far loftier idea of the human person and the smallest attack on his freedom became more intolerable. Everything points to this development not having ended yet, and to our becoming even more severe in this matter. Kant declares that the human person should be autonomous. But an absolute autonomy is out of the question. The human person forms part of the physical and social *milieu*; he is bound up with it and his autonomy can only be relative. And then, what degree of autonomy is appropriate to him? It is obvious that the answer depends on the state of mind of the societies — that is, on the state of public opinion. There was a time when material servitude, imposed in certain conditions, seemed in no wise immoral; we have abolished it, but how many forms of moral servitude still survive? Can we say that a man who has nothing to live on governs himself, that he is master of his actions? Which kinds of subordination, then, are legitimate and which unlawful? There is no final answer to these problems.

The rights of the individual, then, are in a state of evolution: progress is always going on and it is not possible to set any bounds to its course. What yesterday seemed but a kind of luxury becomes overnight a right precisely defined. The task incumbent on the State, then, has no limits. It is not merely that it has to work out a definite ideal that sooner or later has to be attained, and that finally. But the field open to its moral activity is immeasurable. There is no reason why it should ever cease to be so or the work ever be considered as finished. Everything indicates that we are becoming more alive to what touches on the human personality. Even if we fail to foresee the coming changes along these lines and in this spirit, our lack of imagination does not warrant our shutting our eyes to them. Besides, there are already many changes that we can foresee will be necessary. These considerations explain more clearly the continuous advance of the

State and its justification, to some extent: they allow us to assume that far from being some kind of passing anomaly, this advance is bound to go on indefinitely in the future.

Meanwhile, it is now easier to see there was no exaggeration in saying that our moral individuality, far from being antagonistic to the State, has on the contrary been a product of it. It is the State that sets it free. And this gradual liberation does not simply serve to fend off the opposing forces that tend to absorb the individual: it also serves to provide the *milieu* in which the inidivual moves, so that he may develop his faculties in freedom. There is nothing negative in the part played by the State. Its tendency is to ensure the most complete individuation that the state of society will allow of. Far from its tyrannizing over the individual, it is the State that redeems the individual from the society. But whilst this aim is essentially positive, it has nothing transcendental about it for the individual consciousness, for it is an aim that is also essentially human. There is no difficulty in understanding its appeal, for ultimately it concerns ourselves. Individuals can become instruments of the State without any inconsistency, since the action of the State is towards giving them reality. We do not, even so, follow Kant and Spencer in making them into absolutes, as it were, almost self-sufficing, or into egotisms knowing only self-interest. For although this aim concerns them all, it cannot in the main be identified with the aim of any one of them in particular. It is not this or that individual the State seeks to develop, it is the individual *in genere*, who is not to be confused with any single one of us. And whilst we give the State our cooperation — and it could do nothing without it — we do not become the agents of a purpose alien to us; we do not give up the pursuit of an impersonal aim which belongs to a region above all our own private aims but which nevertheless has close ties with them. On the one hand, our concept of the State has nothing mystic about it, and yet, it is still in its essence individualistic.

The fundamental duty of the State is laid down in this very fact: it is to persevere in calling the individual to a moral way of life. I say fundamental duty, for civic morals can have no pole-star for guide except moral causes. If the cult of the human person is to be the only one destined to survive, as it seems, it must be observed by the State as by the individual equally. This cult, moreover, has all that is required to take the place of the religious cults of former times. It serves quite as well as they to bring about that communion of minds and wills which is a first condition of any social life. It is just as simple for men to draw together to work for the greatness of man as it is to work to the glory of Zeus or Jehovah or Athena. The whole difference of this religion, as it affects the individual, is that the god of its devotion is closer to his worshippers. But although not far removed, he does nevertheless still transcend them, and the role of the State in this respect is what it was formerly. It rests with it, shall we say, to organize the cult, to be the head of it and to ensure its regular working and development.

Shall we say that this is the sole duty incumbent on the State and that its whole activity should be directed into this channel? It might be so if every society lived in isolation, without having to fear any hostile acts. But we know that international competition has not yet ended and that even 'civilized' States still live to some extent on a war footing in their inter-relations. They threaten one another, and since the first duty of the State towards its members is to preserve intact the collective entity they make up, it must to that extent organize itself accordingly. It must be ready to defend itself, perhaps even to attack if it feels menaced. This whole form of organization presupposes a different kind of moral discipline from that implicit in the cult of the human being. It has an entirely different cast of direction. Its goal is a national collectivity and not the individual. It is a survival of the discipline of other days, since the former conditions of existence have not yet ceased to operate. There are, then, two diverging currents flowing through our moral life. It would be failing to recognize the existing state of affairs, if we wished to reduce this duality to unity here and now, if we wished to do away with all these institutions, all these practices inherited from the past, straight away, whilst the conditions that created them still survive. Just as we cannot make it a fact that individual personality shall not have reached the stage of evolution that it has, so we cannot make it a fact that international competition shall not have preserved a military form. Hence come these duties of an entirely different nature for the State. Nothing even warrants our assuming that some part of them will not always continue to exist. As a rule, the past never disappears entirely. Something of it always survives into the future. That said, it remains to add that, as we progress, so these duties (as explained) — once fundamental and essential, become secondary and anomalous: that is, always providing that nothing unusual occurs and there are no fortuitous setbacks. Once, the action of the State was directed entirely outwards: now, inevitably, it tends more and more to turn inwards. For it is through this whole structure of the State and through it alone, that society can succeed in achieving the aim it has to put foremost. And there is not likely to be any lack of substance to work on here. The planning of the social *milieu* so that the individual may realize himself more fully, and the management of the collective apparatus in a way that will bear less hard on the individual; an assured and amicable exchange of goods and services and the cooperation of all men of good will towards an ideal they share without any conflict: in these, surely, we have enough to keep public activity fully employed. No European country is free of internal problems and difficulties, and as we go on, so will these problems multiply. That is so, because, as social life becomes more complex, so does the working of its functions become more delicate. Further, since the more highly developed systems are precariously balanced and need greater care if they are to be kept going, societies will have a growing need to concentrate their energies on themselves to husband their strength, instead of expending them outwards in violent demonstrations.

This is where Spencer's arguments have some plausibility. He saw clearly that the receding of war and of the social forms or methods bound up with it was certain to affect the life of all societies very deeply. But it does not follow that this recession leaves no other sustenance for social life than economic interests and that there must inevitably be a choice between militarism and commercialism. If, to use his expression, the organs of depredation tend to disappear, this does not mean that the organs of a vegetative system should entirely take their place, nor that the social organs should one day be reduced to no more than a vast digestive apparatus. There is an inward activity that is neither economic nor commercial and this is moral activity. Those forces that turn from the outward to the inward are not simply used to produce as much as possible and to add to creature comfort, but to organize and raise the moral level of society, to uphold this moral structure and to see that it goes on developing. It is not merely a matter of increasing the exchanges of goods and services, but of seeing that they are done by rules that are more just; it is not simply that everyone should have access to rich supplies of food and drink. Rather, it is that each one should be treated as he deserves, each be freed from an unjust and humiliating tutelage, and that, in holding to his fellows and his group, a man should not sacrifice his individuality. And the agency on which this special responsibility lies is the State. So the State does not inevitably become either simply a spectator of social life (as the economists would have it), in which it intervenes only in a negative way, or (as the socialists would have it), simply a cog in the economic machine. It is above all, supremely the organ of moral discipline. It plays this part at the present time as it did formerly, although the discipline has changed. (Here we see the error of the socialists.)

The conclusion that we reach here gives an indication how one of the gravest conflicts of our day might be solved. By this I mean the conflict that has come about between equally high-minded kinds of sentiment — those we associate with a national ideal and the State that embodies it, and those we associate with the human ideal and mankind in general — in a word, between patriotism and world patriotism. This conflict was unknown to the ancient world, because in those days one cult alone was possible: this was the cult of the State, whose public religion was but the symbolic form of that State. For the worshippers there was therefore nothing to allow of choice or hesitation. They could conceive of nothing above the State, above its fame and greatness. But since then, things have changed. No matter how devoted men may be to their native land, they all today are aware that beyond the forces of national life there are others, in a higher region and not so transitory, for they are unrelated to conditions peculiar to any given political group and are not bound up with its fortunes.

There is something more universal and more enduring. It is true to say that those aims that are the most general and the most unchanging are also the most sublime. As we advance in evolution, we see the ideals men pursue breaking free of the local or ethnic conditions obtaining in a certain region of the world or a certain human group, and rising above all that is particular and so approaching the universal. We might say that the moral forces come to have a hierarchic order according to their degree of generality or diffusion.

Thus, everything justifies our belief that national aims do not lie at the summit of this hierarchy — it is human aims that are destined to be supreme.

On this basis, it has sometimes been held that patriotism could be regarded simply as a survival that would disappear before long. Here, however, we face another problem. In fact, man is a moral being only because he lives within established societies. There are no morals without discipline and authority, and the sole rational authority is the one that a society is endowed with in relation to its members. Morals do not look like obligations to us, that is, do not seem like morals to us — and therefore we can have no sense of duty — unless there exist about us and above us a power which gives them sanction. Not that the material sanction covers the whole of the duty, but it is the outward sign by which this is recognized, and manifest evidence that there is something above us to which we are subordinate. It is true that the believer is free to make an image of this power for himself in the shape of a superhuman being, inaccessible to reason or science. But for the theme under discussion, we need not debate the hypothesis or examine what is and what is not well founded about the symbol. The fact that shows us to what degree a social structure is necessary to morality is that any disorganization, any tendency to political anarchy, is accompanied by a rise in immorality. This is not solely because the criminal has a better chance of escaping punishment; it is that in general the sense of duty is weakened, because men no longer have a strong sense of there being anything above them to which they are subject. Now, patriotism is precisely the ideas and feelings as a whole which bind the individual to a certain State. If we suppose it to have weakened or to have ceased to exist, where is an individual to find this moral authority, whose curb is to this extent salutary? If there is no clearly defined society there with a consciousness of itself to remind him continually of his duties and to make him realize the need for rules, how should he be aware of all this? Let us take those who believe that morals themselves are inborn and exist *a priori* in the consciousness of each one, and who believe, too, that a man has only to look within his own breast to know what they consist of and needs only a little goodwill to understand that he should submit to them. To these, the State would indeed appear something entirely exterior to morals and therefore it seems that it might lose its dominion without there being any loss to morality. But since we know that morals are a product of the society, that they permeate the individual from without and that in some respects they do violence to his physical nature and his natural temperament, we can understand the better that morals are what the society is and that they have force only so far as the society is organized. At the present day, the State is the highest form of organized society that exists. Some forms of belief in a world State, or world patriotism do themselves get pretty close to an egotistic individualism. Their effect is to disparage the existing moral law, rather than to create others of higher merit. It is for this reason that so many minds resist these tendencies, though realizing that they have something logical and inevitable.

There might indeed be a solution of the problem in theory: this is to imagine humanity in its entirety organized as a society. Need we say that such an idea, whilst not altogether beyond realization, must be set in so distant a future that we can leave it out of our present reckoning. A confederation of European States, for instance, is advanced, but vainly, as a half-way course to achieving societies on a bigger scale than those we know today. This greater federation, again, would be like an individual State, having its own identity and its own interests and features. It would not be humanity.

There is, however, a means of reconciling the two ideas. That is, for the national to merge with the human ideal, for the individual States to become, each in their own way, the agencies by which this general idea is carried into effect. If each State had as its chief aim, not to expand, or to lengthen its borders, but to set its own house in order and to make the widest appeal to its members for a moral life on an ever-higher level, then all discrepancy between national and human morals would be excluded. If the State had no other purpose than making men of its citizens, in the widest sense of the term, then civic duties would be only a particular form of the general obligations of humanity. It is this course that evolution takes, as we have already seen. The more societies concentrate their energies inwards, on the interior life, the more they will be diverted from the disputes that bring a clash between cosmopolitism — or world patriotism, and patriotism; as they grow in size and get greater complexity, so will they concentrate more and more on themselves. Here we see how the advent of societies on an even bigger scale than those we know will constitute an advance in the future.

So that what breaks down the paradox is the tendency of patriotism to become, as it were, a fragment of world patriotism. It is a different concept of it that so often leads to conflict. True patriotism, it seems, is only exhibited in forms of collective action directed towards the world without; it seems to us as if we could only show loyalty to our own patriotic or national group at times when it is at strife with some other group. True, these external crises yield plenty of occasions for brilliantly devoted service.

But alongside this patriotism there is another kind, more given to silence but whose effective action is also more sustained; this patriotism is directed towards the interior affairs of the society and not its exterior expansion. It in no wise excludes any national pride: the collective personality and the individual personalities alike can have no existence without an awareness of themselves, of what they are, and this awareness has always something personal. As long as there are States, so there will be national pride, and nothing can be more warranted. But societies can have their pride, not in being the greatest or the wealthiest, but in being the most just, the best organized and in possessing the best moral constitution. To be sure, we have not yet reached the point when this kind of patriotism could prevail without dissent, if indeed such a time could ever come.

A DEBATE ON NATIONALISM AND PATRIOTISM (1905)[2]

PAUL DESJARDINS: To tackle the question methodically our first concern must be to agree together upon the meaning that we shall ascribe to the words we shall have to use. We have at our disposal terms whose meaning doubtless already precludes their unrestricted use. Usage has already endowed them with an approximate meaning, but we can give them an agreed exactness. On this preliminary question of nomenclature I have consulted historians on the terms 'region', 'country', 'population', 'people', 'State', 'nationality', 'nation', 'motherland', confusion about which would muddle this debate. I have also consulted a sociologist, M. Durkheim, who is present here and to whom I am pleased to give the floor.

DURKHEIM: What is important is not to distinguish between words, but to succeed in distinguishing the things covered by the words. Let us in a process of reflection confront different human groups, let us compare them, let us perceive which are those that resemble one another and come into the same category, and which are those that differ from one another. When this has been done, we shall ask what words may be used to designate the categories arrived at in this way, without doing undue violence to the everyday language. The most reliable procedure would be to leave on one side those words used in common parlance, substituting for them brand-new words, to which we would agree to ascribe a very clearly defined meaning. But this cannot always be done.

There is one grouping that may be called 'political society'. It is this one that, whilst it includes secondary groupings, is not itself included in any more extensive grouping. It is the highest and most individualized one. If we so desire, we can designate political society by the term 'the State', although that word is not without its disadvantages. In fact, it implies the existence of a central power, whereas there are political societies that lack any centrally organized power. But this reservation is not very important for the subject to be treated here. Thus the State is a grouping that does not depend upon any more extensive grouping.

On the other hand, there are large groups of men who do not constitute political societies and yet which nevertheless possess a unity. For example, Poland and Finland are not States, and yet express an historical reality; the same was true of Germany and Italy before their unification. Thus there are human groups that are united by a community of civilization without being united by a political bond. One may, for example, term 'nationalities' these groups, which are either former States that have not given up the idea of reconstituting themselves or are States in the process of becoming.

There are cases in which the two groups are absorbed into one, as in France, where the same group is both 'State' and 'nationality'. For that case, I suggest the word 'nation'.

There remains one word into whose meaning there enters a strong element of subjective impressions, the word 'fatherland' ['*patrie*']. Patriotism is a sentiment that joins the individual to the political society seen from a certain viewpoint. The 'fatherland' is the political society in so far as those who go to make it up feel themselves attached to it by a bond of sentiment. A political organization can exist without a corresponding patriotism: thus Finland belongs to the Russian State, but does a Russian patriotism exist among the Finns? The fatherland is the political society felt in a certain way; it is the political society seen from the affective angle.

These are the four principal groupings, and the most important.

PAUL DESJARDINS: We should like to know whether a geographer does not object to these definitions put forward by the sociologist who is the most attentive to questions of method. M. Vidal de la Blache, does this nomenclature correspond roughly to that which you follow?

VIDAL DE LA BLACHE: I am deterred by certain special cases: Switzerland, for example, is a nation, although one can observe in it differences in race, customs and languages. The same holds good for Belgium. Between the Flemish extremists [sic: 'flamingants'] and the Walloons, there are profound differences in language and customs; there was even a difference in their history up to 1830. The nation did not exist before then. Facts of a predominantly economic nature brought about its separation from Holland. Since then it has been cemented together by the effect of these same economic facts: I mean the colossal developments that have taken place in industry and the need for new outlets that has resulted from them. Thus I believe there is great importance to be ascribed to economic facts in the questions that we are dealing with.

DURKHEIM: I included economic facts in the term 'civilization'. Differences in civilization between the South of France, for example (to a certain extent a civilization of the Midi exists), and Northern France do not prove that the whole of France does not have a common civilization distinct from that of other countries.

VIDAL DE LA BLACHE: The real differences from the rest of France that are manifested in the South and the West (I am inclined to believe that in our case the West is the most distinct of all), have nothing in common with the differences that time has not resolved between the Flemish extremist of Antwerp and the Walloon of Liège. It is through economic questions that is to be explained the formation in Europe of certain small or large nationalities. Economic interests are an important element more than ever today in the formation of a nation.

DURKHEIM: I did not think of excluding it.

I shall myself raise an objection: according to the definitions I have suggested for State and nationality, it would be necessary to say that German nationality extends beyond the framework of the German State, and yet the German State is a nation.

ALBERT METIN: One might define nationality as 'a group of people that have common aspirations', instead of employing the term common *civilization*. This would be a way of reconciling Vidal de la Blache and Durkheim.

I would also like a distinction to be made between 'State' and 'government'. For Belgium at its origins there were two distinct political acts: firstly, political power was exerted by the King of

Holland, who maintained the union between the two States; a second political act created the Belgian State.

ARTHUR FONTAINE: What is the amount of autonomy that must be attributed to a group to make it a State?

DURKHEIM: There is no yardstick in such a matter. There are groups that do not form a part of other organized groups. . . .

ARTHUR FONTAINE: Austria and Hungary are separately organized from each other, save for their foreign relations.

DURKHEIM: That is an extreme case, such as one meets with in all these questions.

PAUL BUREAU: The word 'nationality' has two very different meanings, and Durkheim was perfectly justified in taking it in the way he did.

I would like to make one remark: I would dispute that 'the most individualized society' can be called a State. I believe that the family is much more organized and more individualized than the State.

DURKHEIM: I had not had in mind the family. I meant that the political society or State could encompass social groups without itself being encompassed by any group.

RAUH: Durkheim's classification, it seems to me, should be accepted in its entirety. However, I should like very much to make two corrections. First of all, there must clearly enter into the definition of the State the words 'organized power'.

In the second place, it seems to me that, according to Durkheim, the fatherland is the same as the State.

DURKHEIM: Not at all: it is a political society, but one felt in a certain fashion.

RAUH: Patriotism does not bind men solely to the political society, but also to *nationality*, as Durkheim has defined it — that is to say, to a certain civilization, or even to more concrete objects, the land, for example, or the tombs of one's ancestors, etc.

PECAUT: Perhaps one should define fatherland as a group of

men who wish or would like to form a State — since there can exist a patriotism that is common to populations that are politically separated.

DURKHEIM: In that case patriotism exists under special conditions. . . .

PAUL DESJARDINS: To restrict ourselves to what concerns us directly, in these ideas let us see which ones apply to France: France, according to Durkheim, is allegedly a nationality organized into a State, and therefore properly and fully a nation.

ARTHUR FONTAINE: It is rather a part of nationality organized into a nation. There are people of French nationality existing outside the French State.

PECAUT: It seems to me that France is a fatherland, a State. Is it a nation in the sense defined by M. Durkheim? I have no idea.

DURKHEIM: Do you not feel three different realities: 1 the Russian State; 2 Polish nationality; 3 the French nation?

ARTHUR FONTAINE: There are always exceptions, but this classification seems by and large necessarily to include all the phenomena.

VIDAL DE LA BLANCHE: French civilization, which you put forward in order to define France as a nation — is it distinguishable from Latin civilization as a whole?

DURKHEIM: Yes, because we alone carried out the French Revolution;[3] we alone have received a certain rationalist education, and then there is the fact that France became centralized earlier than the other nations.

PAUL BUREAU: I would suggest the substitution of the term 'people' for that of nationality.

RAUH: There is indeed some danger in applying two words deriving from the same etymology, such as *nationality* and *nation*, to things that are somewhat different.

PAUL DESJARDINS: We are not entirely free agents in our

choice of terms: age-long associations tie our hands; thus *nation* evokes the ideas of national defence, of national representation, of nationalism and even of internationalism; — and *nationality* reminds us of the famous *principle of nationalities*, by which the Germans and Italians before their unification, and Hungarians and Poles, backed up their claims from 1853 to 1859. This is what this term signifies in our choice.

DURKHEIM: Between 'nationality' and 'nation', if there is a relationship between the words, it is because there is a relationship of things. 'People' is something different; we need that word to designate those in a State that have no share in its government.

BRUNSCHVICG: We have no need of the word 'nation', because it signifies only a *success*, the coincidence of two elements, *nationality* and *State*; these words are the sole essential ones.

PAUL DESJARDINS: Finally we must tackle the definition of *motherland*. We must do so, it seems to me, by first defining patriotism. *Patriotism* in its turn — I mean modern patriotism — might be defined as 'an affective and moral bond whereby individuals subject themselves to the political society of which they are members, in so far as the latter is not subordinated to any organized group'. And the society itself to which they bind and subject themselves in this way is for them their fatherland.

LALANDE: Is it necessary to define the word patriotism at the outset? Unlike the terms previously discussed, it does not correspond to anything that is objective. It designates a sentiment that can be attached to groups of a very diverse nature. It is not possible to restrict it to one of those groups without prejudicing what must be the very object of our discussions.

DURKHEIM: I believe that we can define patriotism by its external characteristics.

LALANDE: I beg your pardon. We are trying to define realities beyond the words. But *patriotism* and *fatherland* do not designate realities, but symbols. To define patriotism we must first consider those sentiments that I shall term 'corporative', namely, those that bind the individual to a group of which he forms part.

Among these sentiments there are some that relate to a territorial grouping; and that territorial grouping to which we attribute the greatest importance we call *fatherland*. There is nothing set about it, apart from this judgement of appraisement. There is a local patriotism, a regional patriotism, a national patriotism. It might be defined as 'the corporative feeling experienced towards an organized group existing geographically and to which one attributes a higher value than to others'. But I do not think that would be of much use to us in our discussion.

DURKHEIM: We cannot classify all the possible groupings and the particular attachment of men to each one of these groupings.

THE STATE, MORALITY AND MILITARISM [4]

Ancient forms of civilization never completely disappear, but fade away gradually. Thus there is every reason for believing that war will always exist, but that it will occupy an ever diminishing place in the life of societies. Its natural adversary is the sentiment of human brotherhood, the fellow-feeling that man has for man in general, regardless of ethnic origins and nationality. Yet however great the progress this sentiment has made, it has still attained its full power only between peoples of the same civilization, and even there it remains prone to many temporary setbacks. The time is still distant when the pain felt by the savage will touch us as deeply as does that of civilized man, and national *amour propre* will frequently succeed in stifling the accents of human solidarity.

But if it is fitting that we should resign ourselves to warfare as an historical necessity, it is foolish to proffer an apologia for it, as certain statesmen have recently attempted to do. I would concede that even today it is not without its uses. What is more, I deem it scientific to postulate in principle that nothing real exists without some useful effect. The fact remains that war is clearly increasingly destined to give ground. Consequently it runs counter to historical evolution to seek artificially to preserve for it a moral value that it does not have, or is destined no longer to have. If it had its uses in former times, and if to a certain extent it remains of service, it is because it exercised men to practise what might be called a violent courage, namely a disdain for one's life and a taste for danger. But we have an increasing need for qualities of a completely different order. The scientist, the engineer, the doctor, the industrial entrepreneur — these also need endurance and energy, but a quieter form of endurance, a less strident form of energy that is calmer and likewise more sustained. Thus we must be trained in a different school. Consequently we cannot consider normal the way in which war continues to be glorified or the recrudescence of militarism we are witnessing at the present time.

That recrudescence, at least in so far as it concerns our own country, seems to me to arise from transitory circumstances. The memory of 1870, the desire to avenge the defeat, have had the effect of fostering in France devotion to the army, the necessary instrument of revenge, which is a veritable cult of superstition. We have been brought up in the idea that this should be our highest thought, and we have let that idea swamp us. The outcome has been that the army has ceased to be a profession like any other; it has become something untouchable and sacred. The mere act of submitting it to the critique of the reason produces the effect of committing an impiety. Have we not even gone so far as to declare it infallible? Doubtless in this fetischistic approach much is mere words, I know. I will even say that I fear so, for the tumultuous manifestations of this so-called nationalism prevent us from fostering, as we should, a more serious form of patriotism. Nevertheless the fact remains that the army has in this way acquired a prestige beyond all bounds, whose danger we are at last beginning to see.

The consequences of this situation are unfolding before our very eyes. A social group set apart, elevated above others, had needs come to isolate itself, considering loftily and without much sympathy the ideas, needs and aspirations of the society around it. From one viewpoint there is an inner contradiction for a people such as ours, whose historic role, whose reason for existence, has been to proclaim the right to unfettered enquiry, to declare the supremacy of the civil power. The contradiction lies in granting such preponderance to the military power, with the intellectual servitude that this comprises. Two such very opposing principles could not co-exist without one day coming into violent collision. It is this conflict that we are witnessing today. The sole remedy that I perceive for such an ill state of affairs is to change the direction of our public education system, so that the soul of the nation may be rid of this deplorable outlook. Undoubtedly we must be [strong] in order to be respected, but a great nation can be better occupied than in continually burnishing its weapons. It should have other preoccupations: there are other ideas, apart from this one, in which all Frenchmen can commune together, other common ends to be pursued. The cult of what is right, respect for the law, love of liberty, fitting attention to duties and responsibilities, whether they emanate from individuals or the collectivity, need for a more equitable kind of distributive justice — these are sentiments in no way military, and they cannot penetrate deeply enough into our consciousness. But experience has shown how weak are their roots. Let such an ideal be more actively yearned after, let us not be content to pay it lip service, let the mentors of youth cause it to penetrate more deeply into the very being of the people, and the army will lose the transcendental position it enjoys.

However, for the army to assent unresistingly to be in this way brought down to the common level, it must open itself more freely to that same spirit. For this to be brought about, the points of contact between the officer corps and civilian society need to be more manifold. We must put an end to the legend of the soldier ignorant of all that happens around him, a stranger to the passions and beliefs of his contemporaries. This is the sole way to end the moral divorce from which we are suffering.

DEBATE ON PATRIOTISM AND THE INTERNATIONALISM OF
THE SOCIAL CLASSES (1906)[5]

DURKHEIM: What strikes me about all that has been said up to now is how little economic facts appear to have contributed to the formation of internationalism. Two orders of facts have been pointed out: the moral homogeneity of the workers and then the facts of competition and industrial and commercial solidarity. The first phenomenon is one of the moral order, prepared for by the economic phenomena. As for the phenomena relating to industrial solidarity, they have always a dual aspect, as has been stated; they set up opposition as much as they draw closer together. Moreover, what shows clearly the limited effectiveness of economic phenomena is that their influence upon employers is very different from that upon workers. The workers are internationalists whereas the employers are not, although the latter are much more strongly linked to one another economically than are the former. When one contemplates the strength of capitalist interests one is even astonished at the passivity manifested by the employers to the threat of wars. On the contrary, the resistance to them is very strong among the workers. The effect of economic causes is thus entirely different according to the moral environments in which they are at work. It is the influence of the moral environment.

SEIGNOBOS: In reality, among capitalists there has indeed been a tendency to oppose war, but they have less energy than do the workers.

DURKHEIM: Most businessmen and industrialists are in favour of peace, but they do nothing to avoid war.

PAUL DESJARDINS: Thus, according to M. Durkheim, moral factors exercise a preponderant effect — if it is true that the same economic phenomena produce different reactions according to the environment, whether it is that of the workers or the employers. However, it might be said that if one reacts in one way and the other in the opposite way, this is still due to the economic conditions and the differences between the wealthy classes and the proletariat. . . .

PAUL BUREAU: The question raised here by M. Durkheim is very interesting and I wish that we could examine it attentively. I confess that I do not share Durkheim's opinion. M. Arthur Fontaine, with whom I have had the pleasure of exchanging a few ideas on the subject of this meeting, which he knew he was unable to attend, remarked to me that manual workers, even when they suffer in their own workshops from the competition of foreign workers, who come offering their labour for a lower salary, have no hostile feelings towards these foreigners: the strikes at Halluin a few years ago, and the recent strikes at Longwy, clearly demonstrate that, in spite of the suffering arising from competition, the feeling of solidarity and *fraternity* prevails, even among foreign workers.

SEIGNOBOS: They feel that they belong to the same corporation.

PAUL BUREAU: And it is very natural that the worker in regard to war should not have the same attitude as the employer; his interests are far from being involved to the same extent. The employer risks large capital sums that would be endangered by the conquest of the territory, but on the other hand, in the event of victory, can bring him fat profits. Look at the enormous dividends realized by German industrialists since 1871. Yet the condition of the German worker has improved little. It is therefore natural that the moral effect produced on the worker is different, since the economic conditions are different.

DURKHEIM: What indeed can the worker lose in a war?

SEVERAL VOICES: His life!

DURKHEIM: The employer too. It is not reasons of an economic nature that impel the worker to resist war. The employer, on the other hand, is actuated by economic motives, and his resistance is nil. When war broke out in 1870 we were sure of victory — I remember that very well. Yet not a single businessman wanted war. But the sole resistance that occurred was displayed by the workers. This is because to show resistance one must disdain what people may say. One must not be afraid to upset certain received ideas.

. . .

MADAME COMPAIN: I was present at the last anti-militarist trial, and I was able to realize that, both here and elsewhere, if workers no longer have any religious faith, they have another sentiment that has replaced it. The workers live in the future and work for it. They know that, if they may not profit from it for themselves, others will benefit from their efforts, and it is this thought that spurs them on.

DURKHEIM: The worker has no sense of the real future, he lives outside time, in the ideal world. If he had the misfortune to think overmuch about the future, his situation would be frightful.

What is this purely economic morality of which Rauh speaks? To explain a faith in internationalism it is not enough to say that one has ceased to believe in God. One must explain how the new morality has been formed.

RAUH: It is that explanation that I thought I had outlined by showing what were the causes of and what progress had been made in the patriotism of the worker. Man cannot do without morality. If he sees no more than the economic facts he will of necessity draw a morality out of those economic facts.

BELOT: Auguste Comte already expressed the idea that the proletariat was naturally Positivist, and that Positivist morality was destined to become the morality of the people.

DURKHEIM: Saint-Simon puts forward the theory that moral life and religion itself are part of economic facts, and that it is from these that religion and morality must be drawn. I understand this well, but within the system there is something else.

PREFACE AND INTRODUCTION TO
LETTRES A TOUS LES FRANCAIS (PARIS, 1916)

In July 1915 France followed with anxious gaze the retreat of the Russian army through Poland. One asked where this retreat of our Allies would stop and whether, their courage being paralysed through lack of munitions, the Russian forces were not on the verge of being broken for good. If this were the case, what would be the repercussions of so serious an occurrence upon the front in

France and on the pursuit of the war? Many did not conceal the anxiety these agonizing questions caused them.

We were among those who retained our confidence. It seemed plain to us that we and our Allies possessed a superiority in forces that was necessarily destined one day to prevail over those of our enemies, whose long preparation for war had brought them their early successes. We resolved to make known to the public the reasons for our assurance.

But we had first to spell out those reasons for ourselves. By addressing our fellow citizens in this way we had to bring them something more than our personal impressions, however well founded these might appear to us. We had to establish by the facts that the superiority of our forces was indeed real and that the Allies were working to exploit its full value. A serious preliminary study was indispensable. We have undertaken it.

We have not restricted ourselves to assembling and comparing information already published. We have turned to the various French authorities involved, who, so far as their preoccupation for the national interest allowed, have hastened to assist us. We have likewise consulted the embassies of our Allies, who have kindly responded to our appeal. In this way we have obtained *facts, figures and documents*. Each time we felt the need, we requested clarification. After this detailed work, which took up the second half of last year, having made sure that we were saying nothing that we could not in all conscience consider as proved, we have published the *Lettres à tous les Francais*.

These *Letters* are essentially a comparison between the resources of the two opposing coalitions. They prove that Germany, at the beginning of the war, needed to move quickly by every means and at all costs. But France having frustrated their attempt at speed by the victory on the Marne, time was vouchsafed the Allies to develop and organize their forces. Our *Letters* show how prodigious their effort has been, or rather is, for it still continues and will do so with intensity.

By presenting in this way the sum total of this effort we hope to have provided a solid basis for public opinion. In the state of continual emotion in which we live we are exposed to a nervous tension that is daily overstimulated by the news: we blow up the importance of this or that incident, smiling in the morning, downcast in the evening. But the outcome of such a long-lasting and wide-ranging war depends not on this or that ephemeral circumstance, but on permanent causes. It is these permanent causes that we have set out to ascertain.

Our *Letters* have appeared as separate leaflets, so that they could be more easily distributed as widely as possible. Three million copies of each have been given out. We are grateful to men of all faiths and parties that have concerned themselves with their distribution. In particular we thank the primary school teachers, both men and women, who have been the best helpers in our work of propaganda. But we must also thank all those among our readers who have encouraged and sustained us: hundreds of letters have come to us in this way; we have found they expressed some very laudable sentiments. . . .

It is a commonplace that the present war resembles none that has occurred in the past. But if this phrase is on all lips its entire significance is not wholly perceived. The new conditions of war do not require only profound changes in tactics and strategy. They impose upon us all, and in particular upon the non-combatants, new duties of which it is important that we become aware.

I

Victory, a labour of patience

Up to now, in all known wars the armies that faced each other represented only a small proportion of the belligerent nations. Even when a coalition was formed, such as that which put an end to the hegemony of Napoleon, the total number of troops involved did not exceed more than a few hundred thousand men. It was by no means impossible for armies of such a size to be engulfed, or scattered and destroyed. Thus a purely military event could occur, and sometimes very rapidly, that put an end to the war. Under these conditions, war, although arising out of politics, became an exclusively military matter as soon as the signal for it had been given. The generals and soldiers alone bore responsibility for it. As for the civilians, they took part in it in their hearts, since all their interests, moral and material, were at stake — but they did not play an active part. They suffered under it or profited from it, but they were not actors in it.

Things are very different in the present war.

This time two coalitions of unparalleled size are at grips with each other, for with the exception only of America, almost all the great States of the civilized world are involved. On the other hand, the armies in question are not professional armies, in which only a limited number of citizens would be affected, but each army is equated with the nation whose mission it is to defend. It includes all the adult population up to about the age of 50; it is the nation in arms. We may estimate at some 15 millions the number of combattants to be found in each of the two camps; and these armies are operating over huge surfaces almost equal to the area of Europe.

It seems singularly difficult, if not impossible, for such considerable masses of human beings, moving over such vast areas, to be surrounded, dispersed and destroyed. Armies of such magnitude can undergo partial setbacks of varying importance; they can be forced to retreat, to give ground. But an army that retreats is not an army that has been wiped out. If annihilation on this scale had been possible we would have seen it happen at the beginning of the war, when Germany, strong in the superiority that its long preparation had given it, hurled itself upon Belgium and France. The French army withdrew but kept its internal unity and organization. Thus the retreat lasted only a short while and a few weeks later fortune changed sides. There occurred the battle of the Marne.

Thus we fail to see how a purely military success could in itself be decisive enough to put an end to the war in the near future. We must undoubtedly guard against stating to be impossible for all time something that at present appears contrary to all likelihood. Circumstances may perhaps arise which, at a stroke, may precipitate the course of events. But this reservation having been made, we may say that the decision will, it seems, result not from some brilliant stroke, but from a slow continuous action that requires much time to be able to produce results. Hence, since a sharp blow cannot destroy definitively either of the two systems of forces that are in conflict, only the passing of time can weaken one side enough for the equilibrium to be upset and the balance swing irrevocably in one direction. The conqueror will be he who can best resist the test of time, the one who can hold out longest. Victory can only be a long drawn-out, patient task.

II

The duty of civilians

This means that the prime condition for victory is an unshakeable will, ever remaining steadfast, in order to continue the struggle for as long as is necessary. If we wish to conquer we must remain sufficiently in command of our nerves not to let ourselves recoil from the length of the ordeal, discouraged by temporary reverses, or lulled by partial successes. There must be neither impatience, nor a blind and idle confidence, nor depression. Our energies must always be directed towards the goal, without contrary emotions causing them to slacken. Thus the moral condition of our peoples is called upon the play a role of the utmost importance in the war.

Here there appear new and serious duties that are laid upon civilians.

A people's willpower is made up of the willpower of each individual. It is the affair of all, in which it is up to everybody to cooperate. For the nation to remain patient, calm and unshakeable in its resolution, we must all sustain one another, all carry one another along, all strengthen one another continually by word and example in that patience and firmness. Thus, giving and receiving in turn, each of us is stronger and more resolute because he shares in the strength and resolution of us all.

Thus civilians cooperate in the victory, since they contribute to creating the moral state upon which victory depends. We, the ncn-combattants, have also our battles to undergo. We should struggle against ourselves, against our nerves, against those causes of all kinds that threaten our inner equanimity and that of our country. And we must also fight against the same weaknesses in others. We must strive to prevent any enfeebling impressions from making headway among us, and to awaken and reinforce the opposite impressions within ourselves as within our fellows. We do not belong to ourselves, as we do in peacetime: we are accountable for the sentiments that we experience and, even more so, for the words we utter. For if, in the heat of conversation, we pronounce a single word of discouragement, we diminish the courage of those around us. It is as if we were draining off from the country a little of its strength to resist.

This will to struggle must not, moreover, be expressed solely in the form of a patient passivity, of endurance in bearing the sufferings and anguish of war. It must act, and there is no fear that the material for action is lacking.

We know how much victory depends not only upon the number of soldiers, but on the number of machines, guns, machine guns, and the quantity of munitions: of these there cannot be too many. Thus all those who can contribute to increasing their production must give themselves to that task without counting the cost, just as our soldiers are giving their blood without counting the cost.

To cope with the war expenditure, money is needed. We shall find it, provided that we restrict our own expenditure. Nowadays to economize becomes a strict duty towards our country, and we cannot remind one another of this often enough.

The army has absorbed millions of workers of all kinds whose absence could disturb national life. Those who remain must try to replace those that are elsewhere, whilst still carrying out their regular functions. They must take on additional tasks.

In short, we are all bound to participate actively in the war, each in his own way; such active participation, besides being useful in itself, helps in strengthening our resolve to hold on. For faith is only sustained by action.

III

War news and public opinion

But in order to act energetically we must believe in the successful outcome of our action. Doubt casts down and paralyses; confidence gives strength. Victory is only possible when one hopes for victory. What are the reasons that give us hope?

We seek such reasons above all in the daily events of the war, which we never tire of analyzing and commenting upon. Thus we are eager for news; we search it out in every possible way; we rush for the newspapers, open and read them anxiously with great avidity; we question one another; we put questions on all sides as to what is known, what is being said, hoped for or feared and, depending on what we learn, our level of morale fluctuates.

We believe that there is no moral hygiene less appropriate to the situation, or less conducive to producing the desired effect.

How indeed can we retain that self-possession that a long war of necessity requires, if our moral state depends to such an extent upon day-to-day events. Undoubtedly, despite the native nervous excitability that has occasionally been attributed to us, our country has a kind of instinctive wisdom that has allowed it to maintain its equanimity through all the crises it has undergone. One cannot pay too great a tribute to the manner in which it has been able to exercise self-control in every kind of circumstance, both during the hours of anguish and on the day when it saw deliverance dawn. But we must think of the future. The longer the war lasts, the more necessary it becomes to adopt ways that allow us to husband our strength, and also our moral strength. But the habit we have just mentioned can only weaken that strength through this state of continual excitement that it risks awakening and prolonging in us.

Naturally this does not mean that military events should or could leave us indifferent. It is human and legitimate to rejoice when they go in our favour, and to be saddened when the reverse occurs. Even when, casting our gaze behind us, we attempt to represent to ourselves what we have done in the past, when we think that for 16 months we have held our own against the most formidable military might that has ever existed, when we recall that we have rolled back the German army at a time when already it had all its forces marshalled, whilst our preparations and those of our Allies were far from complete, we have a right to feel some reassurance and pride. But it is dangerous to abandon oneself unresistingly and unreservedly to that sentiment, just as on a day of reverses it is to the opposite sentiment.

If we wish to be above such fluctuations we must view things from a different vantage point.

IV

Our aim

Instead of letting ourselves be hypnotized by the necessarily changing spectacle of military events, we must seek to fathom the deep, lasting and permanent causes that determine in advance the final outcome. Since the war we are waging is a protracted one, since victory goes to the one that can hold out longest, we should know which of the two belligerent groups is more capable of a prolonged resistance, one less threatened by the abrasion of time. This is precisely what we propose to investigate in the series of short studies we are launching today.

By proofs whose worth our readers will be able to appraise we shall establish that we — our Allies and ourselves — are in a better condition than our enemies to sustain a long drawn-out war, for our forces are still destined to grow, whilst Germany and Austria are close to exhausting their effort. Far from the prospect of a protracted war needing to worry us, we find in this substantial reasons for confidence. And this confidence is appropriate in sustaining our patience. How should we not be patient, knowing that patience is destined to give us victory? Let us last out and we shall conquer — on condition, however, that we do not stand with arms folded, declaring in the words of a slogan too often used, 'Time is on our side'. Time is on nobody's side. It is we who must work and act with all the energy with which we are capable.

Thus is explained the motto we have adopted: *Patience, Effort, Confidence.*

In itself there is certainly nothing new in this theme. But it seemed useful to us to expound upon it, stripping it of all irrelevant considerations and presenting, in a kind of picture, the principal facts that justify it. Once this picture has been built up, it will be able to serve as a steadying counterweight to the variable emotions that the vicissitudes of war arouse in us. On the difficult days we shall be able to refer back to it; in it will be found constant reasons for hope. At all times it will remind us of the need for energetic, persistent effort.

THE STATE, MILITARISM, WAR[6]

It is said to be inconceivable that Germany, which only yesterday formed part of the great family of civilized peoples, even playing among them a role of prime importance, could have belied to such an extent the principles of human civilization. It is not possible that the men whom we knew, whom we esteemed, who belonged irrevocably to the same moral community as ourselves, could have turned into those barbarous, aggressive and unscrupulous beings that are denounced to the indignation of the public. It is believed that our belligerent passion is leading us astray, preventing us from seeing things as they are.

Yet these acts that are so disconcerting, and for this reason one would wish to repudiate, have precisely their origin in that complex of ideas and feelings that we propose to study. They flow from them as the consequence of its premises. There is here a whole intellectual and moral system that, constituted as it was with a view to warfare, remained in peacetime in the background of consciousness. Its existence was known, and there was some suspicion of its danger, but only during the war has it become possible to evaluate the extent of its influence from the size of its

operation. It is that system that is summed up in the celebrated
maxim ['Germany Above All Things'].

That mentality will be studied using Treitschke. To describe it
there will be no need to seek here and there its constituent
elements, in order to fit them together, linking them more or less
artificially. There is one German writer who has for his own
purposes expounded that system in complete and clear consciousness of the principles upon which it rests and the consequences it
implies: this is Heinrich von Treitschke, in his works as a whole,
but more especially in his *Politik*.[7] Therefore we cannot do better
than to take him as our guide: we shall follow his exposition in
our own exposition. Withdrawing into the background, we shall
even insist on letting him speak. In this way we shall not incur the
risk of deforming German thinking by interpretations of a
tendentious and emotive nature.

If we select Treitschke as the main object for our analysis, it is
not because of the value attributable by us to him as a scholar or
philosopher. Quite the opposite: if he is of interest to us it is
because his thinking is less that of an individual than of a
collectivity. Treitschke is not an original thinker who might have
worked out in the silence of his own study his own personal
system. But he is a personality who is eminently representative,
and it is in this capacity that he can instruct us. Very caught up in
the life of his times, he expresses the mentality of his environment. . . .

I

The State above international laws

The system consists almost entirely in a certain way of conceiving
the State, its nature and role. May one perhaps find that such an
idea is too abstract to have a profound effect upon people's
minds? But it will be seen that it is abstract only in appearance,
and conceals in reality a sentiment that is very much alive.

It is generally agreed that sovereignty may be viewed as the attribute characteristic of the State. The State is sovereign in the sense that it is the source of all the juridical powers to which its citizens are subject. Also, it does not acknowledge any power of the same order to be superior to itself, or on which it depends. All laws proceed from it, but there is no authority competent to overrule it. However, the sovereignty that is thus normally ascribed to it is never anything but relative. It is well known that in fact the State depends upon a multiplicity of moral forces that, although they may not have a strictly juridical form and organization, remain real and effective. The State depends upon the treaties it has signed, the undertakings it has freely entered into, the moral ideas that the State's function is to see respected, and that consequently itself must respect. It depends upon the public opinion of its subjects and that of foreign peoples, which it is forced to take account of.

Exaggerate that independence, on the contrary, free it from all bounds and reservations, carry it to the utmost limit, and you will have some idea of what Treitschke conceives the State to be.[8] For him the State is αὐτάρχής in the sense that the Greek philosophers gave to the word: it must be utterly sufficient unto itself. It has need of nothing other than itself, and should not have, in order to exist and be sustained. It is an absolute. Fashioned solely to command, its will must never obey anything other than itself. 'Above me,' Gustavus Adolphus was wont to say, 'I acknowledge no one save God and the sword of the conqueror.' This proud formula, states Treitschke, applies identically to the State.[9] Even the supremacy of God is scarcely retained for more than convention's sake. In short, 'it is of the very essence of the State to admit no force that is above itself.'[10]

Any kind of superiority is intolerable to it, even if only apparent. It cannot accept that an opposing will should set itself up in the face of its own, for to attempt to exert any pressure upon it is to deny its sovereignty. It cannot appear to cede to a kind of external constraint without weakening and diminishing itself. Expressed in these terms, a concrete example will enable us better to understand the meaning of this and its extent. It will be recalled how the Emperor William II, during the Moroccan affair, sent one of his gunboats to Agadir. It was a menacing way of reminding

France that Germany did not intend to stand aside from the Moroccan question. If France at that moment, in order to respond to this threat, had sent into the same port one of its ships alongside the *Panther*, this simple affirmation of its rights would have been construed by Germany as a challenge, and war would most likely have broken out. This is because the State is an extremely sensitive entity, very quick to take offence. It cannot be too jealous of its prestige. However sacred in our eyes the human personality may be, we do not accept that a man should avenge by bloodshed a mere failure to comply with the normal rules of good behaviour. A State, on the other hand, must consider the least slight to its self-esteem as a grave insult. 'To reproach the State for having too acute a sense of honour', declares Treitschke,

> is to mistake the nature of the moral laws of politics. A State should have the sentiment of honour developed to the utmost if it wishes to remain true to its essential nature. The State is not a violet that blooms only when hidden; its power must stand proudly in the full light of day; it must not let that power be disputed, even symbolically. If the flag has been insulted its duty is to demand satisfaction and, if this is not forthcoming, *to declare war, however trivial the grounds may appear to be, for it must insist to the utmost on due respect being paid it, in accordance with the position that it occupies in the community of nations.'*[11]

The sole limitations possible on the sovereignty of the State are those that itself consents to when it commits itself to contractual treaties with other States. Then, at least, one might believe that it would be bound by the undertakings that it has made. It would seem that from that point on, the State has to reckon with something other than itself: is it not dependent upon the treaty it has concluded? Yet in fact this dependence is only apparent. The ties it has contracted in this way are the expression of its will. For this reason therefore they remain subordinate to that will. They have binding power only to the extent that it continues to wish them to do so. The contracts from which these obligations derive were intended to deal with a certain situation; it was because of that situation that the State had accepted them. If a change occurs, it is released from them. And as it is the State that decides

in a sovereign capacity and without any checks upon it whether
the situation has or has not remained the same, the validity of the
contracts to which it has subscribed depends solely on how at any
given time it assesses the circumstances and its own interests. In
law it can denounce or cancel them, i.e. it can break them when
and how it pleases. . . .

V

The morbid nature of this mentality

Thus there really does exist a system of ideas that skilful hands
have organized within the German mind, and which accounts for
those acts of which we would like to believe Germany incapable.
We have not reconstructed this system artificially by some indirect
process; it revealed itself spontaneously to our analysis. The
practical consequences have not been deduced by us through any
dialectic. They have been enunciated as being legitimate and
natural by the very ones who have most contributed to building
up that system. So we can see in what way and how they are
linked to a certain form of the German mentality, and to their
own principle. Far from there being any reason for astonishment
that they have occurred, they could easily have been foreseen
before the event, just as the effect can be foreseen from its cause.

　　Furthermore, we do not mean to maintain that Germans as
individuals are infected with a sort of constitutionally moral
perversion that corresponds to the actions that are imputed to
them. Treitschke was a rough-natured person, but passionate and
disinterested, a highly noble character, 'full of indulgence towards
men.'[12] The soldiers that have committed the atrocities that
arouse our indignation, the leaders that ordered them, the
ministers that have dishonoured their country by refusing to
honour its signature are likely, at least for the most part, to be
honourable men who carry out meticulously their daily duties.
But the mental system just studied is not made for private,
everyday living. It has in view public life, and particularly a state
of war, for it is at that time that public life is at its highest pitch.

Thus immediately war is declared, the system takes hold of the German consciousness, driving out those ideas and sentiments that are opposed to it, exercising a mastery over every will. Thenceforth the individual sees things in a peculiar light and becomes capable of actions that in peacetime he would severely condemn.

What are the characteristics of this mentality?

It has sometimes been treated as materialist. The expression is neither exact nor appropriate. On the contrary, for Treitschke and Bernhardi, as for all theorists of PanGermanism, materialism is the enemy that cannot be fought against enough. In their eyes, economic life is only the vulgar, mean form of national life, and a people that sets up wealth as the ultimate goal for its efforts is condemned to decadence. According to them, peace becomes a moral danger if it is prolonged, because it develops a liking for the comfortable life, for soft and easy living. It is because it flatters our less noble instincts. If, on the other hand, they make an apologia for war, it is because it is a school of self-denial and sacrifice. Far from their manifesting any indulgence for the appetites of the senses, one can feel sweeping through their doctrine a breeze of ascetic and mystical idealism. The goal to which they require men to subordinate themselves goes infinitely beyond the sphere of material interest.

Yet this idealism has about it something that is abnormal and harmful, which makes it a danger for the whole of humanity.

In fact there is only one means for the State to realize that total autonomy that is, so it is alleged, its essence, and so to free itself completely from dependence on other States: this is to make the latter dependent on it. If it does not rule over them, it runs the risk of being ruled by them. So that, following the doctrine of Treitschke, there may be no power mightier than its own, its power must be mightier than all others. The absolute independence to which it aspires can therefore only be guaranteed by its own supremacy. Doubtless Treitschke esteems it neither possible nor desirable for one and the same State to absorb within itself all the peoples of the earth. A world State, in the strict sense of the term, seems to him to be a monstrosity, for human civilization is too rich to be realized in its entirety by one single nation.[13] Yet it is no less evident that from this viewpoint a universal hegemony represents the ideal limit towards which a State should strive. It can tolerate no equals outside itself, or at least it must seek to reduce their number. In its view equals are rivals that it must needs outstrip in order not to be outstripped by them. In its headlong rush for power it can only stop when it has reached a level of might that cannot be equalled. If, in fact, this point can never be attained, its duty is to draw continually closer to it. This is the very principle of PanGermanism.

It was generally believed that the origin of this political doctrine lay in the exaggerated esteem Germany has for itself, its worth and its civilization. It is said that if it has come to acknowledge within itself a sort of inborn right to dominate the world, it is because, by virtue of some kind of illusion, it has turned itself into an idol in front of which it has invited the world to prostrate itself. Yet we have just seen that Treitschke has led us to the very portals of PanGermanism without evoking this apotheosis.[14] Thus we can ask ourselves if it is not an effect rather than a cause, an explanation found after the event, of some more primitive, deeper fact.[15] What is fundamental is the need to assert itself, to feel that there is nothing above it, an impatience of all that represents a limit or dependence — in short, the will to power. To explain to itself the thrusting energy that it feels within, which imperiously casts aside every obstacle and every constraint, Germany has constructed a myth that has continued increasingly to develop, growing ever more complicated and becoming more systematized. To justify its need for sovereignty, it has naturally attributed to itself every kind of superiority. Then, to make this universal superiority intelligible, it has sought its causes in race, history and legend. In this way was born that PanGerman mythology, diverse in form, sometimes poetic, sometimes scholarly, which makes out Germany to be the highest earthly embodiment of divine power. Yet these conceptions, sometimes passionately held, have not been self-constituted — we do not know the whys and wherefores of them. They merely interpret a fact of a vital kind. This is why we could say that, in spite of its abstract appearance, the notion of the State, which is at the basis of Treitschke's doctrine, conceals a concrete, living feeling: at the heart of it is a certain attitude of the will. Undoubtedly the myth, as it took shape, came to confirm and reinforce the tendency that it had stimulated, but if we seek to understand it, we must not stop at the literal meaning of the formulas that express it. We must penetrate to the very condition that is its cause.

This condition consists in a morbid inflation of the will, in a sort of mania of desire. The normal and healthy will, however energetic it may be, knows how to accept those necessary states of dependence that are inherent in the nature of things. Man is part of a physical environment that sustains him, but also limits him, and upon which he depends. Accordingly, he submits himself to the laws of that environment. Not being able to make them other than what they are, he obeys them, even when he makes them serve his own purposes. This is because to free himself completely from these limitations and constraints he would have to create a vacuum around himself, which means to place himself beyond the conditions of life itself. Yet equally there are moral forces that exert themselves on peoples and individuals, although in a different respect and in a different way. There is no State powerful enough to be able to govern for ever despite its subjects and to force them purely by external coercion to bend to its will. No State exists that is not engulfed in the larger environment constituted by the totality of all other States, i.e. that does not form part of the great community of mankind, and is not subject to some constraints. There is a universal consciousness and a world opinion from whose sway we can no more remove ourselves than we can from the sway of physical laws, for they are forces that, when they are disturbed, react against those that offend against them. A State cannot be sustained when it has humanity against it.

Now what is found to be the basis of the mentality we have just studied is precisely a kind of effort to raise oneself up 'above all human forces' in order to dominate them, to exert over them a full and absolute sovereignty. In our analysis it was with this word 'sovereignty' that we began. In concluding, we must return to it, for this sums up the ideal that is held out. That ideal, essentially made up of domination, is one that the individual is too weak to attain, but the State can and should reach it by organization, holding tightly the cluster of forces made up of individuals and obliging them all to concentrate on this one aim. The State — this is the sole concrete, historical form that the superman whose prophet and harbinger is Nietzsche can assume. It is so as to become that superman that the German State should apply all its powers. The German State must be 'above all things'. Superior to all private wills, both collective and individual, superior to the laws of morality itself, knowing no law save that which it imparts to itself, it will be able to triumph over all resistance and impose its will by constraint where it will not be spontaneously accepted. We shall even see it stir up the universe against it, making a sport of its defiance, in order to assert its power more strikingly.[16] The outrageousness of its ambitions alone would suffice to demonstrate their pathological nature. Moreover, is it not this self-same characteristic of morbid enormity that is to be found even down to the very detail of the material methods that German strategy and tactics are employing before our very eyes? Those plans to carry out an invasion of England by air, those dreams of guns whose missiles would be almost exempt from the laws of gravity — all this makes us think of the novels of Jules Verne or H. G. Wells. We might imagine that we are being transported into an unreal environment where nothing any longer can resist the will of man.

Thus we are faced with a clear-cut case of social pathology. Historians and sociologists will later have to investigate its causes. Today it is enough for us to demonstrate its existence. That demonstration can only confirm France and its allies in their legitimate confidence, for there is no greater strength than to have on one's side what is the very nature of things. One cannot do violence to it with impunity. Doubtless there are great psychoses in the course of which it may happen that the strength of the sick person is, as it were, over-stimulated; his power to work and power of production are increased; he does things that he would be incapable of in the normal state. He also knows no bounds to his power. Yet this hyperactivity is never more than temporary; it is worn down by its own excesses and nature does not delay in taking its revenge. We are witnessing some such spectacle with

Germany. That sickly tension of a will that is trying to free itself from the effects of natural forces has caused it to accomplish great things. Thus it has been able to mount the monstrous war machine that it has launched upon the world with the intention of subduing it. But the world cannot be subdued. When the will refuses to recognize the limits and the moderation from which nothing human can be free, inevitably it lets itself be swept along by excesses that exhaust it, one day or another coming up against superior forces that shatter it. Indeed, already the headlong thrust of the monster has been halted. If all those peoples that Germany disturbs or whose existence it threatens — and they are legion — succeed in joining against it, it will then be in no condition to stand against them and the world will be freed. Chance combinations of interests, persons or circumstances can delay that day of liberation, yet sooner or later it will dawn. Germany cannot fulfil the desiny that it has charted for itself without preventing humanity from living in freedom, and life does not allow itself to be perpetually enchained. It can certainly be contained and paralysed for a time by some mechanical action, but it always ends by continuing on its course, casting up on its banks those obstacles that impeded it from moving freely.

Notes

INTRODUCTION

1. This Introduction draws heavily upon my article, 'Durkheim's political sociology', originally published in *The Sociological Review*, vol. 20, 1972, pp. 477−519. I am grateful to the editor for permission to include the relevant sections.
2. Durkheim, *Professional Ethics and Civic Morals*, London: Routledge, 1957, pp. 47−8. First published as *Leçons de sociologie*, Paris: Presses universitaires de France, 1950.
3. Durkheim, *The Division of Labour in Society*, London: Macmillan, 1984, p. 226. First published as *De la division du travail social*, Paris: Alcan, 1893.
4. Durkheim, *Montesquieu and Rousseau*, Ann Arbor: University of Michigan Press, 1960, p. 33. First published as *Montesquieu et Rousseau*, Paris: Rivière, 1953.
5. Durkheim, 'Deux lois de l'évolution pénale', *Année sociologique*, vol. 4, 1899−1900, pp. 65−95.
6. Ibid., p. 65.
7. Ibid., p. 67−8.
8. Ibid., p. 69.
9. Ibid., pp. 88, 93.
10. For a divergent view, see Bernard Lacroix: *Durkheim et la politique*. Montreal: Presses de l'Université de Montréal, 1981; cf. also J-C Filloux: *Durkheim et le socialisme*, Paris: Droz, 1977.
11. Durkheim, *Professional Ethics and Civic Morals*, pp. 82−3.
12. Ibid., p. 87.
13. Ibid., p. 89.
14. Ibid., pp. 96, 106.

15. Ibid., p. 106.
16. Ibid., p. 51.
17. Ibid., p. 56.
18. See, for example, John Horton, 'The De-humanisation of Anomie and Alienation', *British Journal of Sociology*, vol. 15, 1964, pp. 283–300; and Irving M. Zeitlin, *Ideology and the Development of Sociological Theory*, New Jersey: Prentice-Hall, 1968, pp. 241ff. Zeitlin speaks of 'a conservative and authoritarian ideology that dominated [Durkheim's] entire sociological system' (p. 241). Cf. Aron who says, 'From the outset Durkheim posits man motivated and dominated by his natural egoism — Hobbes's man with unlimited desires and consequently a need for discipline': Raymond Aron, *Main Currents in Sociological Thought*, London and New York: Penguin, 1968, vol. 2, p. 86.
20. Durkheim, *The Rules of Sociological Method*, London: Macmillan, 1982, p. 121. First published as *Règles de la méthode sociologique*, Paris: Alcan, 1895.
21. Durkheim, *Suicide*, London: Routledge, 1951, p. 360. There are major unresolved difficulties in Durkheim's writings on this point, however, analysed in my 'The "individual" in the writings of Emile Durkheim', in *Studies in Social and Political Theory*, London: Hutchinson, 1977, pp. 273–91.
22. 'The Dualism of Human Nature and its Social Conditions', in K. H. Wolff: *Emile Durkheim*, New York: Harper, 1960.
23. Melvin Richter, 'Durkheim's politics and political theory', in Wolff: *Durkheim*.
24. See my *Capitalism and Modern Social Theory*, Cambridge and New York: Cambridge University Press, 1971, chapter 14. Cobban remarks: 'A revolution had laid the foundations of an intensely conservative society, nor is this difficult to understand. The classes which consolidated their victory in the Revolution were the peasant proprietors in the country and the men of property in the towns, neither with any vision beyond the preservation of their own economic interest, conceived in the narrowest and most restrictive sense'. Alfred Cobban, *A History of Modern France*, Harmondsworth: Penguin, 1968, vol. 2, p. 219.
25. Talcott Parsons, *The Structure of Social Action*: Glencoe, Free Press, 1949, p. 307 and *passim*.
26. See the important analysis given in chapter 14 of Dieter Lindenlaub: *Richtungskämpfe im Verein für Sozialpolitik*, Wiesbaden: 1967, pp. 272–384; also my *Politics and Sociology in the Thought of*

Max Weber, London: Macmillan, 1972. As Friedrich Neumann remarked in 1911: 'Ungefähr so wie der Franzose sein Thema hat: was ist die grosse Revolution, so haben wir durch unser Nationalschicksal für lange Zeit unser Thema bekommen: was ist der Kapitalismus?'. Quoted in Lindenlaub, p. 280.

27. Durkheim, *The Division of Labour in Society*, p. 228.
28. Durkheim, L'Individualisme et les intellectuels', *Revue bleue,* vol. 10, 1898, pp. 7−13. A translation appears in Steven Lukes, 'Durkheim's "Individualism and the Intellectuals"', *Political Studies*, vol. 17, 1969, pp. 14−30.
29. In saying this, of course, I do not wish to hold that Saint-Simon and Comte were the only important intellectual influences exerting an important positive influence over Durkheim: other, more immediate sources were Renouvier, Fustel de Coulanges, and Boutroux.
30. Cf. Alvin W. Gouldner: Introduction to Durkheim's *Socialism*, London: Routledge, 1952, and New York: Collier, 1958, pp. 13−18.
31. Cf., on this point, Durkheim's interpretation of the final phase of Saint-Simon's career, as manifest in the latter's *Nouveau christianisme*, in ibid., pp. 229ff.
32. See Lukes, '"Individualism"', pp. 15−19.
33. Durkheim, 'L'Individualisme et les intellectuels', p. 7.
34. Ibid., p. 8.
35. Ibid., pp. 11, 13.
36. Richter, 'Durkheim's politics', pp. 172ff.
37. See, for example, Simon Deploige, *Le Conflit de la morale et de la sociologie,* Louvain: 1911. Durkheim reviewed the book in the *Année sociologique*, vol. 12, 1909−12. For an earlier exchange of letters between Deploige and Durkheim, see the *Revue néoscolastique*, vol. 14, 1907, pp. 606-21.
38. See, above all, Durkheim, *L'Evolution pédagogique en France*, Paris, 1969 (first published, in two volumes, in 1938).
39. Georges Davy, 'Emile Durkheim', *Revue de metaphysique et de morale*, vol. 26, 1919, p. 189.
40. Cf. J. E. S. Hayward, 'Solidarist Syndicalism: Durkheim and Duguit', *Sociological Review*, vol. 8, 1960, parts 1 and 2, pp. 17−36 and 185−202.
41. Marcel Mauss, Introduction to the French edition of Durkheim's *Socialism*, p. 32.
42. Durkheim, *Moral Education*, Glencoe: Free Press, 1961, p. 137.

43. Cf. K. Marx, 'The Civil War in France', in *Selected Works*, Moscow: Foreign Languages Publishing House, 1958, vol. 1, p. 542.
44. Durkheim, Review of Antonio Labriola's *Essais sur la conception matérialiste de l'histoire, Revue philosophique*, vol. 44, 1897, pp. 649, 651.
45. Ibid., pp. 648–9.
46. See Lindenlaub, "Richtungskämpfe".
47. Sorel played an important part in this; for his evaluation of Durkheim, see 'Les théories de M. Durkheim', *Le Devenir Social*, vol. 1, 1895, pp. 1–26, 148–80.
48. Mauss, Introduction to *Socialism*, p. 34.
49. Durkheim, *Socialism*, p. 283.
50. Ibid., p. 284.
51. 'Socialism is to the facts which produce it what the groans of a sick man are to the illness with which he is afflicted, to the needs that torment him. But what would one say of a doctor who accepted the replies or desires of his patient as scientific truths?' Ibid., p. 41.
52. Ibid., p. 285.
53. Ibid., p. 40.
54. Ibid., p. 90. For further discussion of Durkheim's evaluation of Marx, see my *Capitalism and Modern Social Theory*, chapter 13.
55. Durkheim, *Socialism*, pp. 39–79.
56. Ibid., pp. 70–1.
57. Ibid., p. 71.
58. See Hayward, 'Solidarist Syndicalism'.
59. Durkheim, 'La Science positive de la morale en Allemagne', *Revue philosophique*, vol. 24, 1887, part 1, p. 38.
60. Ibid., pp. 98, 99.
61. Ibid., pp. 102–3.
62. Durkheim, *The Division of Labour in Society*, pp. 280–2; also pp. 405–6.
63. Durkheim, *Professional Ethics and Civic Morals*, p. 75.
64. See Durkheim and E. Denis, *Qui a voulu la guerre?*, Paris: Colin, 1915; and Durkheim, *'L'Allemagne au-dessus de tout'*, Paris: Colin, 1915.
65. Durkheim, *'L'Allemagne au-dessus de tout'*, p. 7.
66. Ibid., p. 5.
67. Ibid., p. 22.
68. Ibid., p. 7.
69. Ibid., p. 45.
70. Cf. Richter, 'Durkheim's politics', pp. 201–2.

71. See especially Robert Nisbet, 'Conservatism and Sociology', *American Journal of Sociology*, vol. 58, 1952, pp. 165–75, and *The Sociological Tradition*, London: Heinemann, New York: Basic Books, 1967; and Lewis A. Coser, 'Durkheim's Conservatism and its Implications for his Sociological Theory', in Wolff, *Durkheim*, pp. 211–32.

72. Coser, 'Durkheim's Conservatism', p. 212.

73. Ibid., pp. 211–12. Cf. Parsons: '(Durkheim) was almost wholly concerned with what Comte would have called "social statics".' (*Structure of Social Action*, p. 307.)

74. Coser, 'Durkheim's Conservatism', p. 212.

75. Durkheim, *The Division of Labour in Society*, p. 337.

76. Durkheim, *Montesquieu and Rousseau*, p. 59.

77. Durkheim, *The Rules of Sociological Method*, p. 47.

78. Durkheim, Review of Deploige, p. 327.

79. Durkheim, *The Division of Labour in Society*, p. 29.

80. Cf. my '"Power" in the Recent Writings of Talcott Parsons', *Sociology*, vol. 2, 1968, pp. 333–46.

81. Cf. Aron, *Main Currents*, pp. 82ff.

82. Durkheim, *Professional Ethics and Civic Morals*, pp. 50–1.

83. Ibid., p. 78.

84. For background material on Weber's conception of the State, see my *Politics and Sociology in the Thought of Max Weber*.

85. Parsons, *Structure of Social Action*, p. 341; but cf. Richter, 'Durkheim's Politics', p. 208.

86. The publication of Marx's early writings has, however, made it apparent that this thesis of Durkheim's is erroneous, at least as applied to Marx. Marx was primarily concerned with the alienative dominance of economic relationships under capitalism: the regulation of the market was to Marx a means, not an end. See my *Capitalism and Modern Social Theory*, chapter 15.

87. Durkheim, *Professional Ethics and Civic Morals*, p. 213.

88. 'A limitation to the right of disposal is in no way an attack on the individual concept of property – on the contrary. For individual property is property that begins and ends with the individual.' Ibid., pp. 216–17.

89. Durkheim, *The Division of Labour in Society*, pp. 374, 377.

1 THE CONCEPT OF THE STATE

1. 'The Concept of the State' is translated in part by Cornelia Brookfield and in part by W. D. Halls. The first section is from Durkheim, *Professional Ethics and Civic Morals*, pp. 42–54.
2. Montesquieu, *De l'esprit des lois*, book II, chapter IV.
3. From the *Revue Philosophique*, 148 (1958). This is a posthumous publication of a course dating from the turn of the century, according to M. Raymond Lenoir, the presenter of the manuscript, who wrote the following introductory note:

> In 1915, as a result of a wartime reform, a delegation for the teaching of philosophy at the lycée of Laval prompted Emile Durkheim to hand over to us a set of double sheets of school paper, with a red ruled margin, comprising a course in ethics written in violet ink, and, inside a cover bearing the title 'The teaching of ethics', lesson plans in violet ink, and also sometimes written in violet ink, sometimes in the black ink used in Bordeaux, a set of pages written at different times, but which logically constituted a unity. Ethical method, civic ethics, the right and duty of voting, the State, democracy, justice and charity – these are all complete writings. The speed of the writing and the use of abbreviations that were personal to the writer make the deciphering of the manuscript particularly difficult. The sureness and continuity of ideas that are based, from the very first decade of his university career, on a comparative study of facts; the complete indifference manifested towards doctrines, systems and dialectics; a latent Saint-Simonism – these all testify to the reciprocal effect exerted by ideas and knowledge for many years, in which teachers, students, pupils and children shared a common ideal of peace and justice.[a]
>
> Paris, 10 November 1958   Raymond Lenoir

[a] The text of 'The State' very likely dates from a time between 1900 and 1905.

Reading of the manuscript has been rendered difficult because of the speed at which it was written and the use of personal abbreviations.

Where a word that is unreadable could be omitted without the understanding of the text being affected, dots are placed. . . .

Where, thanks to the context, a word that is unreadable could be

replaced by a word that is most likely equivalent, the latter has been inserted in square brackets [ ].
4. From Durkheim, *Professional Ethics and Civic Morals*, pp. 76 – 84.
5. Montesquieu, *De l'esprit des lois*, book II, chapter II.
6. Ibid., chapter I.
7. From *L'Année sociologique*, vol. 4, 1902.
8. *L'Année sociologique*, vol. 4.
9. From *L'Année sociologique*, vol. 2, 1897 – 8.

2   DEMOCRACY AND POLITICAL REPRESENTATION

1. 'Democracy and Political Representation' is translated by Anthony Giddens. It first appeared in Giddens (ed.), *E. Durkheim. Selected Writings*, Cambridge: Cambridge University Press, 1972. The first section is from Durkheim, *De la division du travail social*, pp. xxxiv – xxxv, 360 – 2, vi – viii and xxvii – xxx.
2. From Durkheim, 'L'individualisme et les intellectuels', pp. 7 – 8 and 12 – 13.
3. From the *Revue philosophique*, vol. 27, 1889.
4. From the *Revue philosophique*, vol. 19, 1885.

3   THE CONCEPT AND NATURE OF SOCIALISM

1. 'The Concept and Nature of Socialism' is translated by W. D. Halls. The first section is from Durkheim, 'The Definition of Socialism', part I, *Revue de métaphysique et de morale*, vol. 28, 1921, pp. 479 – 95.
2. From Durkheim, 'Note on the definition of socialism', *Revue philosophique*, vol. 36, 1893, pp. 506 – 12.
3. G. Belot, 'Enquête d'une morale positive', *Revue de métaphysique et de morale*, vol. 13, 1905 – 6.
4. Durkheim notes: 'Moreover, the author seems to have abandoned this by the conclusion of the article.'
5. Durkheim notes: 'What is more, we cannot see how we can affirm to be erroneous and abnormal one kind of socialism or another before we have constituted the normal type. We must know what it is in fact, before investigating what it should or should not be.'
6. Belot, p. 564.

7. Durkheim, *De la division du travail social, passim,* and particularly pp. 230–9.
8. Durkheim notes: 'This is why we should not make socialism consist of "common action". This is rather a definition of communism.'

4 SOCIALISM AND MARXISM: CRITICAL COMMENTARIES

1. 'Socialism and Marxism: Critical Commentaries' is translated by W. D. Halls. The first section is from Durkheim, Review of Richard: *Socialisme et science sociale,* in the *Revue philosophique,* vol. 48, 1899, pp. 200–5.
2. From Durkheim, Review of Labriola, pp. 645–51.
3. See Karl Marx and Frederick Engels: *Selected Works in One Volume,* London: Lawrence and Wishart, 1981, pp. 35–63.
4. Durkheim notes: 'Although orthodox "economism" has also its own materialism.'
5. From the *Revue philosophique,* 1899, pp. 433–9.
6. Extract from the *Libres entretiens* of the *Union pour la vérité,* series 4.

5 POLITICAL OBLIGATION, MORAL DUTY AND PUNISHMENT

1. 'Political Obligation, Moral Duty and Punishment' is translated by W. D. Halls. The first section is from Durkheim, *Sociologie et philosophie,* Paris: Alcan, 1924, pp. 49–54.
2. From Durkheim, *Montesquieu et Rousseau,* pp. 194–8.
3. From Durkheim, *Les Formes élémentaires de la vie religieuse.* First published Paris: Alcan, 1912. Published in English as *The Elementary Forms of the Religious Life,* Glencoe: Free Press, 1960.
4. From Durkheim, 'Deux lois de l'évolution pénale', *L'Année sociologique,* vol. 3, 1900, pp. 65–68.
5. Durkheim, *Rules of Sociological Method,* chapter IV.
6. From *L'Année sociologique,* vol. 8, 1905, in collaboration with Paul Fauconnet.
7. From *L'Année sociologique,* vol. 1, 1898.

6   THE STATE AND EDUCATION

1. 'The State and Education' is translated by W. D. Halls. The first section is from Durkheim, *L'Evolution pédagogique en France*, pp. 383 – 5.
2. From Durkheim, *Education et sociologie*, Paris: Alcan, 1922, pp. 59 – 63.
3. Ibid., pp. 69 – 73.
4. From the *Bulletin de la Société française de philosophie*, 10, 1910.

7   PATRIOTISM AND MILITARISM

1. The first section of 'Patriotism and Militarism' is translated by Cornelia Brookfield. It is from Durkheim, *Professional Ethics and Civic Morals*, pp. 65 – 75. The remaining sections are translated by W. D. Halls.
2. From the *Libres entretiens* of the *Union pour la vérité*, series 1.
3. The *Union* notes: 'An Alsatian present at the debate writes to us that at this point he would have liked to have intervened, if he had dared, to testify that the persisting attachment of Alsatians to France in fact derives for the most part from the consciousness they have still maintained that together they carried out the French Revolution. This word by Durkheim evokes a response from the direction of Strasburg.'
4. From *L'Humanité nouvelle*, May 1899. A reply to the 'Enquête sur la guerre et le militarisme'.
5. From the *Libres entretiens* of *L'Union pour la vérité*, series 2.
6. From Durkheim, *Etudes et documents sur la guerre*, Paris: Colin, 1915, pp. 3 – 9, 41 – 7.
7. This book consists of a course that Treitschke delivered every year during the winter semester at Berlin. Quotations are taken from the second edition (Leipzig, 1890).
8. Treitschke, *Politik*, vol. I, p. 41.
9. Ibid., p. 37.
10. 'Das Wesen des Staates besteht darin, dass er keine höhere Gewalt über sich dulden kann.' (Ibid.)
11. 'Mag der Anlass noch so kleinlich erscheinen', ibid., vol. II, p. 559.

12. A. Guilland, *L'Allemagne nouvelle et ses historiens,* Paris, 1899, p. 255.
13. Treitschke, *Politik,* vol. I, p. 20.
14. Durkheim notes: 'Undoubtedly Treitschke does not fail to celebrate occasionally the incomparable merits of Germany. But his language is free from any mysticism; he glorifies Germany as any enthusiastic patriot glorifies his country. Never does he claim for it a hegemony springing from Providence. But Bernhardi had only to develop the principles of his master to arrive at classic PanGermanism. (Cf. F. Bernhardi, *Der nächste Krieg,* Berlin, 1899, chapters III and IV.)'
15. Durkheim notes: 'The belief in the superiority of German culture moreover explains very little. For a people can consider itself morally and intellectually superior to others without experiencing any need to dominate them. Germany might believe itself to be godlike in essence without seeking to conquer the world. Megalomania does not necessarily entail a taste for hegemony, but serves to consolidate it after the event.'
16. Durkheim notes: 'Written on the very day when the torpedoing of the Lusitania became known.'

Index